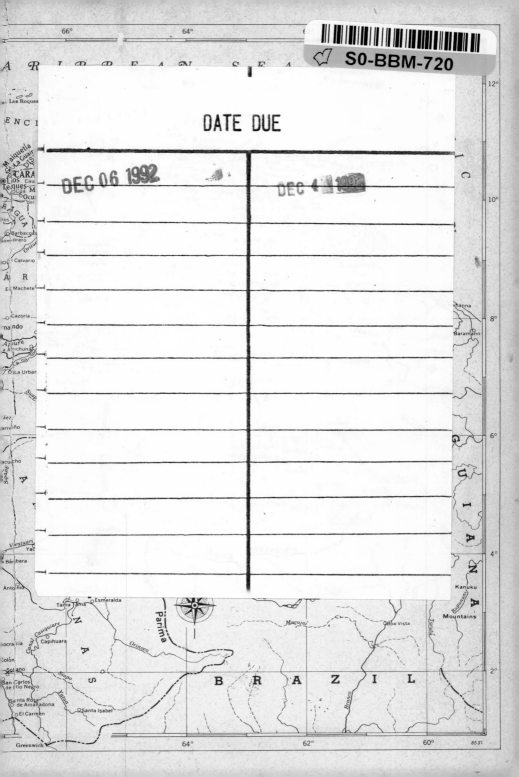

VENEZUELA THROUGH ITS HISTORY

Santa Rosa del Agua in the state of Zulia in northwestern Venezuela.

Venezuela Through Its History

WILLIAM D. (and AMY L.) MARSLAND

THOMAS Y. CROWELL COMPANY
New York

*Manufactured in the United States of America by the
Vail-Ballou Press, Inc., Binghamton, New York*

To our Venezuelan daughter,
ALICIA ANDREA

ACKNOWLEDGMENTS

WE WISH TO acknowledge our gratitude to the Instituto Cultural Venezolano-Britannico and the Centro Venezolano Americano, for indefinite loans of research books from their shelves, and Señorita Luisa Martinez López-Mendez for the use of her private library. We are indebted to Dr. Enrique Planchart, Director of the Biblioteca Nacional, for suggesting source material, and Dr. Arturo Uslar Pietri for reading the manuscript and pointing out many errors and oversights.

THE AUTHORS

Caracas, August 1952

CONTENTS

Chapter I

TRIBES AND TRIVIA

VENEZUELA IS ONE of those countries whose early history may be defined in terms of the present. Its "past"—the way of life its people followed for centuries before any European saw its jungled strand—still exists.

In the fall of 1951, for example, a week before Russia exploded its second experimental atom bomb, a commission of Venezuelan National Guardsmen, sent out to investigate smuggling along the Colombian border, was crossing a river in a launch when a barrage of arrows zinged out of the forest and across the water. Two men grunted and lurched forward, victims of Indian marksmanship. To make the whole situation completely incongruous, the wounded guardsmen were evacuated from the area in an airplane.

The Indian ambush was not an isolated incident. A Caracas newspaper, reporting the assault, said, "Indians have killed scores of persons at this same spot. Efforts to combat them have not been successful as the Indians are so good at hiding themselves that the soldiers never know they are there until the arrows begin flying." Not many weeks before the attack on the guardsmen, Indians subjected an oil camp to a night-long rain of arrows as part of their incessant war against interlopers—a war that began in Venezuela when the first settlers were challenged by the aborigines.

1

The Indians who staged the attacks are remnants of the powerful Carib and Arawakan tribes. Though the descendants of most Carib and Arawakan warriors now form part of Venezuela's huge mestizo population, distant relatives still fight to preserve the simple way of life they enjoyed before Columbus intruded.

No one knows exactly when man arrived in Venezuela. Nor are authorities completely agreed upon how he got there. What definite data exist seem to indicate that the aboriginal American came from Asia via the Bering Strait and to South America by the Isthmus of Panama. There are some anthropologists, however, who claim the emigration route to South America was along the Antillean chain from Florida.

Regardless of how the first immigrant to America arrived, we know that he did not bring very much with him. He had just graduated from the Stone Age during which he fashioned a spear, learned how to make crude pottery and became a fire maker. Metalwork was a mystery to him, and aside from beating soft gold and silver into different forms, which some early Americans learned to do, he never solved it. The epoch-making inventions of the wheel and written language were unknown until the Conquest, if one excepts the pictograph scripts of some Central American cultures. Even the Incas, whose advanced political organization and technical knowledge made them masters of the Andes, could not write, much less the tribes which inhabited what is today Venezuela.

This Venezuela which the Indian inherited was and is an area of sharp geographical and climatic contrasts, a condition created by the Venezuelan Andes. The South American Andes split and form a Y in Colombia. One arm of the mountain range veers northeast to become the volcanic backbone of Central America and the Rockies in North America, while the eastern arm crosses Venezuela roughly from southwest to northeast. It is this great spine of mountains, some of whose snow-capped summits jut more than 16,000 feet into the sky, which gives Venezuela its geographical and climatic contrasts.

A rough rule to follow in translating our horizontal climatic concepts to vertical ones is: 1,000 feet of altitude equals 1,000 miles of latitude. Thus Venezuela, which lies entirely in the tropics, offers equatorial and polar climates within a hundred miles of each other.

Venezuela has frosty peaks, tundra-like wastes, barren mountains, deserts, jungles, prairies, semitropical valleys, fertile hills, and variations of these extremes. The cold heights of the Andes enclose fertile valleys. The valleys of the foothills are pleasant and healthful, too. Dense jungle forests border the Maracaibo Basin and give way to dry, inhospitable scrub country northwest and northeast of the lake. East of the mountains stretch the llanos—the "Great Plains" of Venezuela—a trackless prairie in the dry season and an ocean in the wet. Jungles border the llanos, fringe the mighty Orinoco, and lose themselves in the little-known Guayana Highlands.

The firstcomers to this varied land were probably nomads—roving bands who lived by hunting and fishing, as most North American Indians did when that country was discovered. Though all the Indian racial stock that migrated to South America presumably came in successive waves from Middle America via Panama, the cultural influences that changed the nomads into farmers probably moved from south to north. The nomadic Indians who continued south, instead of veering east as Venezuela's first settlers did, developed higher cultural patterns after many generations.

This advanced culture incubated in the general area of the Andes where the Inca civilization eventually arose. Venezuelan culture showed scant Inca influence. In Venezuela most tribes were affected by the kind of cultural development out of which Inca society sprang rather than by direct contact with Inca society itself. In other words, the two cultures were probably descendants of the same ancestor.

The impact of this southern culture upon Venezuelan Indian life diffused the area's nomadic pattern, but it did not wipe it out. In the year 1500 some Venezuelan Indians were farmers, others still nomads. The nomads either hadn't heard of the Andean culture or couldn't adopt it because their land was untillable. In short, at the time of the Conquest, Venezuela had everything from cannibals to fruit farmers.

The most advanced culture in Venezuela was that of the Timote Indians, who lived in the Venezuelan Andes near present day Mérida. Their villages had a temple in the center and stone-walled houses grouped in orderly rows around it. The temple housed crude idols of wood, clay, or stone. The Timotes worshiped a supreme being who lived on the mountains and in the lakes. To please him, priests offered deer bones and balls of cotton thread to the idols. Only the priests were allowed to enter the temple. Anyone else who trod on holy ground was supposed to be swallowed up by the earth. The Timotes did not practice human sacrifice, although one related tribe used to placate a water god by throwing children into lakes.

The Timotes were intensive farmers. They planted their crops on terraced mountain slopes and channeled water to them through primitive irrigation ditches. In these permanent fields grew fruit trees, cotton, tobacco, yams, maize, beans, and sweet manioc. Their irrigation system represents a unique achievement in Venezuelan Indian culture.

We know nothing about the social customs of the Timotes. The Zorca Indians, whose culture approximated that of the Timotes in advancement, betrothed children at birth. The boy then lived in the house of the girl's parents and slept with her until he was prepared to do something about it, at which time they were married. Perhaps owing to the complete absence of personal choice in this arrangement, a Zorca woman who committed adultery was treated leniently if caught. On the other hand, her lover fared badly. The adulterous wife stayed with her husband without being punished if her nearest kin killed the man who seduced her. If they didn't, the girl returned home to her family in disgrace.

Timotean culture was one of the Conquest victims, but descendants of this tribe still till Andean soil, cherishing shreds of the old folkways. To this day, Ches, the god the ancient Timotes worshiped, receives offerings of deer bone and cotton thread from nominal Catholics, who can tell when he is displeased. They worship him secretly and beg his indulgence when he sends winds howling through the highlands and wraps the mountain heights with cloud and mist.

The Chaké, the unfriendly tribe who wounded the two National Guardsmen, have resisted all advances—cultural or otherwise. Except that today they tip their arrows and spears with metal, their way of life in the Maracaibo Basin has changed very little in post-Columbian times. It is possible, however, that the Chaké possessed a higher culture before the Conquest, when they retreated from the mountains and took to the jungle fastnesses.

The Chaké pursue their simple way of life in the general area from the Catatumbo River to the Rio Negro in the Maracaibo Lake Basin. A seminomadic and semiagricultural people, they spend the rainy season in wooded highlands and filter down to the river-fed plains following game during the dry. They are part of a vast Indian community—the remnants of the proud braves whose dominion once stretched from Lake Maracaibo to both extremes of the Andean cordillera—which we call Motilone. The term Motilone, meaning "cut hair," once denoted a tribe of Indians who did wear their hair short, but it has come to signify any wild Indian and more particularly those of the Lake Maracaibo Basin.

The Chaké hack clearings out of jungle brush large enough to hold a communal dwelling and its crops. They cultivate sweet potatoes, yams, sweet manioc, maize, and bananas. Chaké men clear the fields and plant crops while the women do the harvesting. They are good hunters and build blinds on the ground and in trees from which to shoot game and birds, as well as an occasional white man. Contrary to popular belief, they do not use poisoned arrows.

Consistent with their seminomadic culture, the Chaké have a loose and ill-defined social order. Society is classless, and although tribes often have chiefs, the man selected exercises little power, serving simply as a village headman.

Chaké religion remains a mystery. The Indians celebrate a harvest festival during which they drink chicha, a potent mead made from maize, and beat each other with sticks, but nobody knows whether this ritual has any religious significance or not. When a person dies, the mourners allow his body to decompose before they celebrate his funeral with dancing, drinking and flute playing. His remains are hung in a bag from the roof of a special hut for two or three more years before burial in a cave.

The Guajiro Indians who live on the Guajira Peninsula, northwest of Maracaibo, are Venezuela's richest aborigines. When Spanish settlers introduced cattle to Venezuela, the Guajiros became herdsmen. They have raised stock ever since, leading a pastoral, nomadic existence governed by the availability of water. How they lived prior to the sixteenth century no one seems to know.

The Guajiro regards farming as inferior to a migratory way of life, and even though sections of the peninsula offer opportunities for intensive cultivation, only poorer caste Guajiro Indians farm. Most Guajiros plant nothing more than a little maize from which they make intoxicating chicha beer.

The Guajiro considers his cattle as wealth and is reluctant to kill them for food. Instead he trades the animals for textiles and corn, while sheep, goats, and milk products provide the substance of his diet. Because he is a nomad, the Guajiro builds flimsy, rude lean-tos which can be carted about or left behind when he moves.

Guajiro society is subdivided into matrilineal tribal units, composed of near and distant relatives, each occupying a part of the peninsula. These are called sibs. Each sib has an hereditary chief, usually the wealthiest member of the tribal entity, whose powers are limited to the settlement of minor disputes. Any major grievance is settled privately by the disputants according to a rigid code. For instance, a thief injured while trespassing on the property of the person he planned to rob may demand payment from the intended victim. A person hurt while drunk can sue the person who sold him the liquor. A man who lends an animal is liable should it injure the borrower. The indemnities vary with the seriousness of the crime. For homicide the dead man's family collects two hundred or more cattle; otherwise a member of the murderer's sib, of the same rank as the victim, must forfeit his life. Since the Guajiros believe in group responsibility, any sib member may be held responsible for the sins of a fellow member. This concept has led to frequent misunderstandings with whites, who, the Guajiro thinks, all belong to the same sib. If cheated or harmed by an outsider, he settles the account by shooting the next white man who happens along.

Hereditary status is important in Guajiro society. A man born poor cannot achieve high social position despite the fact that he may achieve great wealth. Theoretically, the sib and not the individual owns the cattle, but in practice, the animals are privately owned, making some Guajiros very rich. Men have been known to pay thousands of cattle, worth as much as $10,000, for a bride.

Although the Guajiros have been the subjects of intense missionary work by Capuchin fathers, their way of life has changed only slightly. Of course, such possessions as guns, textiles, and utensils are of foreign origin. The Guajiros have also adopted Christian baptismal rites and Spanish names, but only because these innovations dovetail with features of their own culture. As it is considered a crime, almost as serious as murder, to mention a Guajiro's true name, the tribe finds Spanish names a convenience and gives a child both a real name and a pseudonym in Spanish.

One of the many tribes which inhabited the area east of Lake Maracaibo was the Quiriquire—a people who practically vanished with the Conquest.

A courageous tribe, the Quiriquire hastened their own obliteration by fiercely resisting the Spanish. They were superior boatmen and dominated Lake Maracaibo and nearby coastal waters until Spanish men-of-war began patrolling the area. Even then the fearless Quiriquire used to engage Spanish galleons, advancing across the water in their four-man dugout canoes to battle Spanish cannon balls with clubs and arrows. The conquistadors wiped them out by the thousands in the first years of the Conquest and the few who remained were enslaved.

The Spanish treated the Quiriquire as cannibals and burned a "C" into their flesh with hot irons before selling them to slave dealers. However, there is no record of the Quiriquire practicing cannibalism. The Caquetío tribe, which lived in the same general area, were cannibalistic to the extent that they used to grind up the bones of their dead and consume the dust in a drink. The Caquetío also made human sacrifices to a sun god. They bought a ten-year-old girl from her mother, decapitated her with a stone knife and offered her blood to the sun.

Like the ancient Swiss, the Quiriquire were lake dwellers. They built their houses on piles, amid forests of aquatic plants, for protection against their enemies. The structures were reached by channels and canals hidden in the rushes, and it was this custom that gave Venezuela its name. The Spaniards were reminded, not a little ironically, of one of Europe's most civilized cities. They called the area "Little Venice"—Venezuela.

The Quiriquire may have colored Venezuelan history by giving the country its name, but the Achagua group, who occupied the territory now comprising the states of Bolívar, Guárico, and Barinas, helped feed a fantasy that led to the wildest hegira in the history of the human race—the search for El Dorado. The vision of Manoa, the hidden lake city whose gleaming gold turrets rivaled the brilliance of the sun, drew men from the courts, counting houses, and jails of Europe and lured them through steaming jungles and over jagged crags to death and disappointment. It was El Dorado, the dream of gold and jewels, that abetted the jet-propelled exploration and settlement of Central and South America. The pregnant minds of Europe, who gave birth to such notions as the possibility of reaching the east by sailing west, could have conceived the fable of El Dorado without any help from savage aborigines; but the fact that Indians like the Achagua believed the myth convinced even unimaginative Europeans that Manoa was just on the other side of the next mountain ridge or right beyond a tangled wall of jungle vines and trees.

The Achagua, like the ancient Jews and some modern Christians, thought that at some time in the past a flood had drowned all living things. The waters covered the earth, forming "catena manoa"—a "large lake," they said, and everyone perished except a few Indians who took refuge at the top of a mountain. The Achagua believed that just beyond their territory existed a lake with a gilded city in the center of it, but unlike the commercial European, the Achagua had no use for gold and never bothered to look for "Manoa"—the fabulous domain of King Paititi, whom the Spaniards called El Dorado.

The Achagua seemed content with their lot and planted their crops of maize, beans, sweet potatoes, sweet manioc, and yams with no more thought about El Dorado than to perpetuate the legend by telling their children about it. They lived in villages strongly resembling communities of North American Indians in the eastern part of what is now the United States. Each settlement was enclosed by a palisade of poles and earth inside which there

were circular communal houses—sometimes accommodating as
many as five hundred—and a club building for the men. Their
social order was subdivided into patrilineal sibs, which had many
members since each man tried to have three or four wives. Tribal
chiefs had harems of young girls.

The men's clubhouse held a special place in Achagua culture.
As the women tilled the fields, the men gathered in their club
every afternoon to lounge and talk. Occasionally they broke the
monotony with drunken festivals. The club was also used as the
center for puberty rites, which involved intoxicating the twelve-
year-old male subject to the point of insensibility and scarifying
his body and arms.

The Achagua practiced infanticide, killing the first-born daughter, perhaps to ensure that the oldest child, who inherited the
father's privileges, would be a son. The Sáliva, a nearby tribe,
killed the first-born of twins, believing that the husband could
only have sired one, while the other must be the child of another
man.

The Achagua built their villages with high gates from which
to throw stones and shoot at attackers. Their principal weapon
was the bow and arrow. The arrow was tipped with curare, which
they sometimes bought from the Caberre Indians, the area's principal manufacturers of the poison. The Caberre made curare from
a swamp root. According to one chronicler, it was mashed and
cooked by old women, who worked in relays. When one keeled
over from the fumes, a second crone was put to the task. When
she died, it indicated that the curare was ready.

Achagua shamans served as witches as well as medicine men.
The Indians used the shaman's magic to dispose of enemies far
away. If the enemy were close at hand, the Achagua dispatched
him personally by dropping a poison made of snakeskin into a
drink. The victim vomited blood until he died.

The Achagua worshiped various gods and revered lakes. They
did not have idols, but represented deities with masks and costumes during dance festivals. This kind of observance has been
preserved in Venezuela to the present time though changed and
modified by a Roman Catholic framework. In the little town of

San Francisco de Yare, south of Caracas, the villagers dress in red costumes and devil masks every Corpus Christi Day and dance to demonstrate the power of the cross over evil.

Neighbors to the Achagua in the Venezuelan llanos were the Otomac Indians, but how they got there is a mystery. Anthropologists say their culture bears no resemblance to any other South American tribe. Their nearest cultural relations are in Central America. Besides this, they are unusual because they seem to have had more fun and less sleep than any other tribe in Venezuela.

These Indians began every day in sorrow, but ended it with a festival that lasted until midnight. Before dawn the Otomac observed a lament for the dead which continued until the sun rose. Then, the chiefs assigned the daily tasks. Parties were sent to work in the fields or to hunt and fish. The rest of the Otomac stayed in the village and played ball. After the workers left and the women started their chores, the ball players divided into teams of twelve and began a soccer-like game, hitting a large rubber ball with their shoulders. At noon, the women joined the contest, which lasted until the men sent out in the morning returned. With their appearance, produce and game were distributed to the villagers according to the number of mouths they had to feed. Afterward the Otomac enjoyed a feast, the only meal of the day, followed by bathing in the river and the nightly dance. After a few hours' sleep the daily ritual began again.

The Otomac were economical farmers. Each field was planted with maize while other crops were sown between the rows. They cultivated clearings and took advantage of fertile areas inundated annually by rivers. A signal feature of their culture was the fact that the men, rather than the women, did all the farmwork.

Otomac family life was characterized by marriages between old men and young girls and between widows and youths, toward the end that at least one spouse would always be expert in the secrets of married life. When he grew old, an Otomac dug his own grave and after his death was buried in it with weapons and food. A year later the tribe dug up his skull and carried it to a hill where it was deposited in a cave. On the hill stood many rocks, which, the Otomac believed, were their petrified forefathers; they called the largest one "grandmother" and a huge rock on a nearby hill "grandfather." They said the boulders founded their tribe, and as far as baffled anthropologists are concerned, they may have been right.

The Guahibo Indians, whose habitat was also the llanos, were Venezuela's most primitive tribe. Even today the Guahibo are nomadic food gatherers. Ethnologists view them as an important link in piecing together the nomadic culture pattern which at one time must have stretched unbroken from Bering Strait to Patagonia.

The Guahibo subsisted solely on the wild animals they killed and the roots and vegetable matter they gathered. They were the "gypsies" of the Venezuelan llanos, trading surplus game and captured slaves for products of their sedentary neighbors and stealing what they could from the agricultural tribes. Since they never spent more than two or three nights in one spot, they had no houses. They slept in hammocks or on the ground. They lacked social organization and what political structure they had, revolved around a small band of seven or eight families headed by a chief. Many bands moved in a tribal unit for the added advantage greater numbers gave them in battle.

Quite naturally, their methods of moving from place to place were well organized. The Guahibo moved in a single file through the six-foot-high grasses of the llanos in a line, composed of six distinct groups, stretching for miles. The unmarried youths formed the vanguard, prepared for any emergency and charged with the task of breaking a path. This was not an easy assignment. The lead man had to be replaced periodically by a substitute and would fall back to the end of the line, his legs bleeding from cuts caused by the tough grass. The second section was composed of married men, carrying weapons and some of the children not old enough to walk, while the old and physically disabled followed in the third division. Married women, loaded down with babies and utensils, came next with the children old enough to walk. The fifth section was formed by the strongest men carrying the sick in baskets on their backs. Last came warriors.

Guahibo life was rudimentary in the extreme. Women who gave birth while traveling washed themselves and the child in the next stream and then went on. The dead were buried where they fell or left behind unburied. People running a temperature were packed neck-high in clay or water, a treatment so effective it frequently killed them. Snake bites were cured by instant amputation of the bitten hand or foot.

Along the coast of the Caribbean from Caracas to the Orinoco flourished Carib cultures, almost as advanced as that of the Timotes.

The Caracas, the most westerly of these tribes, were a warlike group. They developed a strong, closely-knit social order behind the natural mountain bulwark that separated their palisaded villages from the sea and the Spaniards. They combined hunting and fishing with agriculture to form the basis of their economy and grew such crops as cotton, tobacco, sweet manioc, and maize, supplementing their diet with both wild and cultivated fruits. The Caracas, one of the few tribes in Venezuela to have domesticated wildlife, kept bees, and had mastered a technique for drying food, which they stored as a war reserve.

The essential feature of Caracas tribal life was its political organization. The Caracas had a graded military class with ranks indicated by tattooing. Caracas subtribes each had a cacique and in time of war they often formed a confederation under a single leader. This kind of confederation gave the Spaniards their most formidable opposition in the conquest of Venezuela and produced Venezuela's first national hero.

Guaicaipuro, chief of the Teques, organized a confederation of tribes to resist incursions of the Spanish. Banding together the Caracas, the Teques, and related tribes, Guaicaipuro produced a fighting force of 10,000 braves and massacred the first expeditions sent to conquer his land. He terrorized the first two settlements in the Caracas area to such an extent that Nuestra Señora de Caraballeda on the Caribbean two miles east of present-day La Guaira, and San Francisco, further inland, were both abandoned soon after their founding in 1562. His confederation kept the Spaniards from the richest lands in Venezuela for several years. By a sneak attack, the invaders eventually destroyed him. They fell upon his camp at night. Guaicaipuro with his wife and twenty-two warriors fought shoulder to shoulder until they were skewered on

Spanish swords. His life and resistance to enslavement have made him a symbol of Venezuelan liberty.

East of the Caracas tribes dwelled other Carib Indians like the Chaima, Palenque, and Tumuza, whose ways of life became more and more striking in social stratification and in development of comfortable patterns of living and eating, the closer they lived to the mouth of the Orinoco. They had villages, sometimes with as many as two hundred houses, near well-watered and semi-permanent fields.

Chiefs in this area were generally hereditary, but sometimes tribes elected them to their posts. They had great authority and were surrounded by ceremony. In one tribe common people could not enter the chief's tent. He made decrees from a special mound, was carried around in a litter and possessed a harem guarded by eunuchs. The shaman also commanded great respect although the man who held the office often did not live long enough to enjoy it: the Orinoco tribes decreed that if his patient died, the shaman should be killed.

Along the coast the Caribs were only slightly more cannibalistic than their mountain relatives, among whom only the Maracapana seemed to practice the custom. The Maracapana used to cut off the arms and legs of a captured chief and when he died, they opened his stomach and ate his intestines. Carib Indians living on the islands of the sea which bears their name, had such a pronounced predilection for roast Arawak that they are responsible for the word "cannibal." Cannibalism along the coast of Venezuela, however, was restricted to a few tribes who ate slain enemies.

It was in this area, along the eastern coast of Venezuela, that Christopher Columbus first touched the mainland and precipitated the wholesale slaughter and enslavement of Venezuelan aborigines which was to mark the foundation of a colony. In this struggle for survival on the one side and for dominion on the other, the more advanced tribes suffered to the point of extermination, while the backward and nomadic peoples who could retreat into those jungles and plains which the Spaniard did not want were to preserve their independence even to the present day.

Most of the sedentary cultures developed in areas where colonial life was to thrive and for the same reasons—both economies were founded upon agriculture. The Spaniards needed the land to basement the fabric of a colonial structure. The Indian farmers had to have it because they could not transplant their culture to the arid soil of the llanos or to tepid jungle swamps. Their roots reached deep into the ground. They had no choice. They remained and fought. But the Stone Age Indian was a sapling before the ax of European aggression; he was quickly felled, and the Spaniard used him to build the New World.

In a larger sense, however, one wonders if the Spaniard actually conquered the Indian. After four centuries it seems as precise to say it was the Indian who conquered the Spaniard. The impact of the two races on each other produced a mestizo nation which has assimilated many Spanish ways, but remains more different from Spain than the United States is from England. Carib and Arawak blood flows through Venezuelans who today govern their country's institutions, till its fields, and tap its natural resources. Descendants of the Otomac rode with Páez across the Venezuelan llanos, forging the trail of independence. Guaicaipuro had his proxies on the fields of Carabobo when Venezuelans secured their liberty.

Venezuelan history began with the marriage of Indian and Spanish cultures. The wedding day was August 1, 1498—the day Christopher Columbus sailed into the Gulf of Paria.

Chapter II

EDEN

THE PEOPLE WHO lived during the fifteenth century did not know very much about each other. Their world was a jail so well insulated that the occupants of one cell scarcely dreamed there were any other prisoners.

Europe had heard of Asia, to be sure, and through the wall of the Middle East had been in communication with it for two hundred years. but except for this, the most advanced member of the world family knew next to nothing about geography. The southern half of Africa, the continents of America and Oceania did not appear on any map.

The womb of Western civilization had been the Mediterranean and by the fifteenth century that culture still clung to the region which had nurtured it. The city states of Italy, mothers of the Renaissance, were the most advanced offspring. Genoa, Florence, Milan, Pisa, and Venice had grown rich and fat on the shipments of spices, jade, ivory, and silk that had begun to trickle into Europe with the opening of a trade route to Cathay during the thirteenth century. Indirectly, Italian merchants and their wealth made other Europeans venture south and west, initiating a process that was to make the Atlantic rather than the Mediterranean the world's most important sea.

The English, Dutch, French, Spanish, and Portuguese envied

the wealthy Italian cities, but their puny fleets could not compete with those of Genoa and Venice. They lacked the great commercial firms, the networks of markets, and the large banking systems necessary to vie with the Italian monopoly. To circumvent it, they had to explore the huge western sea. The Portuguese began to settle Madeira in 1418–19. By 1471 they had sailed halfway along the western coast of Africa. Spain had occupied the Canaries. English merchants engaged John Cabot to find western lands. Denmark sent Pining to Greenland in 1472.

Until the last decade of the fifteenth century, however, the obstacles of ocean and land mass had imprisoned the European in his own continent almost completely, even though he had begun to hack holes in the walls. Then, suddenly, the walls began to collapse. Within thirty-five years man learned more about his planet than he had since the dawn of time. The size of the world and much of what it contained ceased to be mysteries. Columbus discovered America in 1492. Cabot reached Newfoundland in 1497. Vasco de Gama completed the first voyage to India in 1498. Vasco Nuñez Balboa saw the Pacific in 1513. Magellan's expedition circled the globe between 1519 and 1522.

Europe had reached its critical mass. It blew up, spewing its religious concepts and social institutions over the globe. The Portuguese, the Dutch, the French, the Swedes, the Danes, the English—all contributed, but the country which influenced the course of sixteenth-century history the most, the nation which more than any other destroyed the walls imprisoning Europe was Spain. Spain financed the first expedition across the Atlantic. Conquistadors opened the vast area between the Tierra del Fuego and California. Spanish ships first sailed round the world.

In some respects, Spain was the European country least likely to contribute anything, let alone a major share, to world exploration. Whereas France, England, Portugal, and the Low Countries had a history of national unity at least a century old, Spain did not achieve this status until January of the year Ferdinand and Isabella dispatched Columbus on his first expedition to the New World. The Holy War against the Moors, a war whose final phase lasted two centuries, ended in 1492 with the fall of Granada.

Spain of 1492 was peculiarly organized. Basically, of course, the country had a carbon copy of other European national structures; it was built upon an uneducated peasant class which tilled the land and paid a tithe. On the other hand, Spain had no bourgeoisie. The Moors and Jews, who had dominated Spanish trade, were expelled at the end of the Reconquest. Moreover, the two hundred-year war left Spain's nobles unemployed—the country was full of soldiers with no war to fight.

A militant church and a spirit of militant nationalism carried Spain from its northern redoubt to control of the Iberian peninsula. The country had whipped itself into a lather of religious and patriotic fanaticism during the centuries-long effort to eject the Moor. These characteristics still motivated the nation in 1492. If its recent acquisition of national status and the lack of a middle class hampered Spain, its fervent patriotism, its military caste, and its religious consciousness favored the pre-eminent position Spain captured in the international competition for power, wealth, and land. Spain had been simmering for two hundred years. It was inevitable that it should eventually boil over.

The boiling point was reached in 1492. The last Moor had been expelled. The last inch of Spanish soil had been regained. What could siphon off the energy engendered by Spain's religious nationalism? How could Spain use its military men to express its urge for expansion? What could a resurgent but backward Spain do to rival the power of its better-organized neighbors?

Ferdinand and Isabella found a solution. It was no coincidence that the crazy Genoese navigator who proposed to sail west to Cathay should be in the Spanish court the day Granada fell, January 2, 1492. Christopher Columbus, who had traveled from court to court in Europe to find backing for a voyage, encountered his most receptive audience in Spain. The Spanish monarchs had stalled him, promising to consider the expedition as soon as they had conquered the Moors. Four months after the fall of Granada, they agreed to send the gloomy Italian into the western sea.

And so it was a foreigner who carried the Spanish flag to the New World. It was Columbus who plotted the route over which Spanish traditions, nationalism, religious fanaticism, and expansive spirit traveled to America.

Spain became the mistress of a New World Mediterranean, the

Caribbean. She expressed herself and her needs in the establishment of Spanish colonies, products of her culture. Within the limitations of a tropical climate, she built a new Spain, a replica of the old.

The Spaniard in the New World was different from explorers of other nations. He possessed intense awareness of nationality, sense of mission, pride in Spain and confidence in his race. His religious devotion, born of seven centuries of conflict with Mohammedans, was profound. Not the least important aspect of the Indian to the Spaniard was that he had a soul to be converted and brought to the true light—and if recalcitrant, better off dead.

A roll call at random of the first arrivals indicates a colorful lot: Cortés, a ladies' man, whose conquests were for some time more frequent in bed than in battle; Ojeda, a courtier and acrobat; de Bastidas and Enciso, lawyers; Pedrárias Dávila, a nobleman who had almost been buried alive while in a coma and always carried the coffin with him to remind him of his miraculous escape; and Pizarro, a swineherd. Adventurers all, they were in pursuit not of land, spices, colonies, or markets, but gold. Confident in the power of their swords, they raced across new lands to find it. It was only an accident that any of them became colonizers and producers of natural wealth. Plunder had been the legitimate reward of the soldier for centuries and plunder they sought to the exclusion of anything else.

But in the Antilles there was no plunder, except Indian girls. For the moment they had to take what they could get: land. On his second voyage Columbus declared the first division of territory in the islands, and at the same time tacitly authorized the Indian slave trade. Each colonizer received not only land, but the people who lived on it.

Indian slavery was contrary to official Spanish policy. The Indians were considered wards of the Crown, people to be befriended, taught and converted. In 1503, however, Spain's attitude hardened somewhat. Using a prize piece of reverse logic, Isabella decreed:

As now we are informed that because of the excessive liberty enjoyed by the said Indians they avoid contact and community

with the Spaniards to such an extent that they will not even work
for wages, but wander about idle and cannot be had by the Christians to convert to the Holy Catholic Faith . . . I command you,
our said Governor, that beginning from the day you receive my
letter you will compel and force the said Indians to associate
with the Christians of the island and to work on their buildings,
and to gather and mine the gold and other metals, and to till
the fields and produce food for the Christian inhabitants and
dwellers of said island; and you are to have each one paid on
the day he works a wage and maintenance which you think he
should have . . . and you are to order each cacique to take charge
of a certain number of the said Indians so that you may make
them work wherever necessary, and so that on feast days and
such days as you think proper they may be gathered together to
hear and be taught any matters of Faith.

With the best of intentions, the gentle Queen, the devout Christian, had branded the word slave across the face of America.

One need not feel too sorry for the aborigine. In many cases,
his condition changed only slightly from Pre-Conquest to Post-
Conquest times. Among the more advanced tribes the relation
between chief and subject was often that of master and slave.
Even the less-civilized Indians had a slave class of war captives.
However, the Indian made a poor slave. He refused to work and
often ran away. As early as 1500 the Spanish were importing Negroes, introducing a third racial strain into the New World.

Much has been written concerning the barbarity of the conquistador toward subject peoples, but it cannot be properly evalu-
ated except against the sixteenth-century background of atrocities committed by Indian against Indian and European against
European. Caribs used to tie a captive to a post and shoot arrows
into his body—just to see whether he'd flinch. When he died, he
was butchered. Human limbs hung from Carib larders like hams
in a packing plant. In Mexico Cortés found Indians in cages.
Their fellows fattened them like hogs, slaughtered them like cattle, and ate their flesh as if it were beef. Aztecs sacrificed youths
and maidens by ripping out their beating hearts. To exterminate
a rival's family the Inca Atahualpa had pregnant women disem-
boweled. The Spaniard who subjected Spaniard to the thumb-
screw and rack, who quartered criminals, burned heretics, and

impaled enemies, pitted his cruelty against the heartless bestiality of the native American.

For obvious reasons, the Spaniard tended to treat Indian women better than the men. The conquistador found them attractive. The syphilis rate in the islands skyrocketed. Although some Spanish women came to the colonies, not enough arrived to satiate the desires of conquistadors. The blending of Indian and Spanish blood produced a large mestizo class which at first found itself worse off than either of the parent groups. Later the more ambitious of its members formed a small artisan class.

Over all facets of life in the Caribbean fell the shadow of the Church, as a religious force for Indian conversion, as landholder, and as educator. Ferdinand and Isabella sent twelve friars with Columbus on his second voyage. The cross followed hard upon the sword, sometimes even preceding it. The first missionaries were sincere, valiant, and charitable men, motivated by spiritual considerations, and they rapidly won the affection of the Indians. It is reported that in Mexico, where the cruelty of the Spaniards had made the word "Christian" a reproach, the Indian would argue if he heard a missionary called a Christian. "No," he would say, "the man is a priest."

The members of the Church who arrived later were not so saintly. The priesthood of Spain had its corrupt branches. Celibacy was frequently ignored and some priests had concubines. For many the Church represented an avenue to wealth and prestige. When the New World became comparatively comfortable and civilized, it tempted ambitious prelates. They helped gather the wealth in real estate which made the Church a powerful economic force in the New World. The conquistadors made it a practice to contribute a portion of their plunder to religious orders, and many Spaniards, having good reason to be worried about the salvation of their souls, willed large bequests to the Church. As early as 1530 the Church figured among the principal landholders in the Antilles.

The contribution of the Church was fundamental to the intellectual development of the New World. In the Caribbean Franciscan friars established church schools for children of Europeans and the sons of important Indian chiefs. Later they gave classes to lower caste Indians, teaching reading and writing as well as various trades and skills. A Dominican university, the first in the New World, was established at Santo Domingo in 1538. In addition the Church compiled an irreplaceable record of Indian languages and cultures.

The New Spain that developed in the Caribbean was based on a slave class which worked for European lords under the guidance of the Church. This was the system transplanted to all Spanish dominions.

Christopher Columbus, Admiral of the Ocean Sea, discovered the mainland of South America on his third voyage in August 1498. The part of it he visited was the northeast coast of Venezuela. Almost anyone who can read knows the story of Columbus' first voyage. It was a feat rewarded by a triumphal return. Greeted by throngs he rode through the streets beside the King. When he announced plans for a second voyage, nobles of the court vied for the privilege of sailing with him. A fleet of seventeen ships, stocked with every possible comfort, set out to batter at the gates of the New World. The home-coming was a sharp contrast. Columbus failed to bring back the immense treasure he had promised, and what was more, he had lost all but one of the four ships in his section of the fleet. It took Columbus three years of begging to win royal backing for his third trip.

By 1498 Spaniards had learned that the fabulous Indies were more hell than gilded paradise. The monarchs of Spain had difficulty recruiting a crew. The fifteenth-century Spaniard had a natural aversion to signing his own death warrant. So Ferdinand and Isabella turned to those whose death warrants had already been signed. In an appeal to the nation's prisoners, they proclaimed:

To show clemency and mercy . . . (we) desire and order any and all males, and such of our subjects and inhabitants as up to the day of the promulgation of this our letter have committed any murder or assault, or any other crimes of whatsoever nature, except heresy and lese majesty or treason, premeditated murder, arson, counterfeiting, or sodomy, or taking gold or silver or money or other prohibited things out of our kingdoms, to go and serve in Hispaniola.

Thugs and assassins were the companions of Columbus as he sailed from San Lucar Harbor, May 30, 1498, on his third voyage to the New World—a voyage precipitated by one rumor and two suppositions. Indians on Caribbean islands had spoken of a continent to the south. João II, King of Portugal, had predicted that a great continent would be found west of Africa on the equator. Aristotelian theory preached that similar products are found at the same latitudes. Columbus reasoned that since the Portuguese mined gold in Africa, the Spanish would discover gold in a new continent at the same latitude.

Armed with these scientific bagatelles, and invoking the special protection of the Holy Trinity, Columbus traveled south to the latitude of Portugal's Sierra Leone colony in Africa. Plotting a course directly west, he planned to keep sailing until he hit land. A few days after he left the Cape Verde Islands, the wind failed and the ships drifted for eight days on an oily sea until July 22, when a breeze sprang up and carried them west. In those eight days of calm and stifling heat, water stores had been depleted.

Columbus knew what he might expect should he return to Spain empty-handed again. It would mean disgrace. It could mean prison. He sailed west as far as possible, but on the morning of July 31, 1498, he changed course and headed north to replenish his water supply at one of the Antillean islands he had discovered on his second voyage.

One can picture the Admiral on the poop deck of his flagship, a grim figure with graying locks, troubled by gout, giving the order which spelled personal disaster. Although he planned to resume the search for a continent after he procured water, the chances of finding it must have seemed very remote as his ships turned about and nosed toward the northern horizon.

Columbus, who filled his journal with lamentations bewailing the various disasters which befell him, had an infinite capacity for self-pity. On the poop deck of his ship the morning of July 31, he was probably sunk in such profound melancholy he did not notice the presence of his servant, Alonzo Perez. Suddenly Perez shouted. On the northwest horizon he had seen three specks.

Columbus fell to his knees and gave thanks to God. Writing in his journal to Spain's royal couple, he said, "At midday, as God has always been kind to me, a sailor from Huelva, my servant, came to the poop deck and saw land to the west. We were 15 leagues from it and it seemed that there were three mountains."

Three mountains indeed there were. The Holy Trinity under whose aegis Columbus had sailed had presented him with a miracle. And it was a true miracle. If Columbus had changed his course earlier or if Alonzo Perez had not glanced west at midday, the Admiral would have passed by without discovering the island or the continent which lay beyond it. He named the island Trinidad in thanksgiving and headed northwest to reach it.

The fleet still needed water and Columbus skirted the southern coast of Trinidad looking for a stream. He found one on August 1, 1498, at Erin Beach, Trinidad, and from there he first saw South America. He thought Venezuela's Punta Bombeador an island and called it "Isla Santa."

Columbus weighed anchor next day and sailed west around Punta de Arenal, the southwest corner of Trinidad, where his fleet anchored to give all hands a rest. While there the foreigners were visited by twenty-four Indian warriors in a canoe, and this boatload of curious aborigines provided Columbus with one of the many disillusionments that pockmarked his career.

To Columbus, the superstitious Christian, the island of Trinidad and the three mountains at its southeastern tip had been an omen. He reasoned that such a holy and propitious sign could mean no less than the attainment of his lifelong goal—Cathay. As the Indian canoe advanced across the water, Columbus prepared to meet the retinue of the Grand Khan or at least some of his subjects, and was deeply disappointed to find his visitors looked like natives he had seen on the Caribbean.

On August 4, Columbus set sail for a spit of land thirty-five miles to the north, diagonally across the Gulf of Paria from Punta de Arenal, Trinidad. It was the Peninsula of Paria on the mainland, but it seemed another island to the Admiral and he named it "Isla de Gracia." Arriving at the tip of "Isla de Gracia" later that same day, Columbus decided to sail west around the "island," and he began his exploration of the continental coast he did not know he had found on Sunday, August 5.

For several days the Europeans explored the coast. They passed intriguing little coastal indentations split by arroyos that led to hilly country in the background. They saw cultivated fields flanked by huts, but no inhabitants. The Indians had fled to the hills in fright. Columbus, who was anxious to take possession of the area, postponed the ceremony until he could round up some Indians to witness it. On August 6, the Spaniards captured four and marched them off to witness the official act by which the King of Spain stole their land. Columbus, who was nursing bloodshot eyes, probably did not preside at the ceremony. In fact, it is doubtful whether he ever set foot on the mainland of South America.

Following the ceremony, the Europeans gave their captives rattles, cloth, and other trinkets, and then set them free. This show of generosity brought other Indians down from the hills. They surrounded the Spanish caravels in their canoes, trading fruit for European junk. These Indians, probably members of the Paria tribe, were happy, amiable, and hospitable. In his journal Columbus remarked on their fine villages, their idyllic surroundings, and the pleasantness of the climate. But the thing he liked best about the Paria Indians was the fact that they wore pearl necklaces.

Columbus was so thoroughly pleased with the Paria tribe that he began to think he might be skirting the island fringes of Cathay after all. While he invented reasons to support this improbable thesis, however, the Admiral of the Ocean Sea was neglecting an important series of incontrovertible facts which indicated he had at last found terra firma.

Columbus had known for several days that the water under his ships was fresh and not salt. Furthermore, he had noticed strange currents upon first entering this fresh-water gulf. The water had seemed to flow in two directions. On August 11, the caravel *El Correo* made a side trip and discovered the reason for the weird conditions. Its crew returned to tell about a tremendous river disgorging a flood of water through four mouths. The river, of course, was the Orinoco and the men saw only four of its seventy-odd mouths.

Columbus, who could usually make two and two equal thirty-eight, had suddenly forgotten how to add. He proceeded to name every promontory of land in sight Isla de one thing or another.

Why was Columbus, who was ready to call almost every little Caribbean island Asia and who maintained that Cuba was Japan to the end of his life, so cautious when he actually encountered a continent? One can only guess. Bartolomé de las Casas in his *History of the Indies* claims Columbus did not grasp that a big river means a big land mass because he had never seen any of the Old World's mighty floods. Samuel Eliot Morison in *Admiral of the Ocean Sea* adds that the discoverer did not know a continent when he saw one because the alluvial deposits of the Orinoco did not correspond to his idea of what a continent should look like. In any event, Columbus was talking about "Isla de Gracia" for several days after his crew began speculating about the new continent they had discovered.

Still trying to get around "Isla de Gracia," Columbus turned about and sailed north. He wanted to investigate the pearl beds on the northern coast of the Peninsula of Paria where the Indians told him they had found their baubles. He was pressed for time, however. He felt that his colony on Hispaniola needed his attention, and on the 14th he decided to sail north. He left Venezuelan waters on August 15, 1498.

It seems strange that Columbus left the continent before he found the pearl fisheries, since he knew that a few pearls would do more for his reputation in Spain than the discovery of a new planet. Columbus himself listed his reasons. He suspected his presence was needed in Hispaniola. His ships were too large to undertake coastal exploration. His men were tired, supplies were low, and he could hardly see thanks to weeks of sleepless nights.

There was nothing Columbus would have liked better than to investigate more of the coastline. For it had suddenly dawned on the Admiral, just before he had to leave it, that a land mass so extensive could not be an island. Writing in his diary the 14th and 15th of August, he confided, "I believe this is terra firma, very large, about which until today nothing has been known, and reason aids me greatly (in this belief) on account of this great river and sea which is of sweet water, and also aids me the saying of Esdras in Book IV, chapter 6, who says that six parts of the world are of dry land and one of water. And if this is the mainland it is a thing worthy of admiration and will be, among learned men.

For such a great river comes out that it makes a sweet water sea of 48 leagues."

Columbus clearly intended to return for further exploration after a rest in Hispaniola, but he never got the chance. Accused of a variety of crimes, mainly arising from maladministration of the Hispaniola colony, he was shipped home to Spain in chains. By the time he undertook a fourth voyage in 1502 to find a passage to the Indies, adventurers had been tapping the wealth of fertile Venezuelan pearl beds for two years. In fact, when the pearl fisheries were finally discovered in 1500, Columbus was falsely accused of keeping the location a secret in order to bilk his royal benefactors and enrich himself.

On the way to Hispaniola, Columbus made a mental inventory of the observations he had gleaned during the previous two weeks. He thought about the miracle of Trinidad, the sweet-water sea, the river with four mouths, the amiable Paria Indians, and the unknown continent. At the same time he made the second of two incorrect astronomical observations which seemed to indicate that his spherical world had a bump at the point where his new continent lay. With this "information," he tried to fit his findings into the puzzle of world scientific and theological theory. The synthesis indicated to Columbus with absolute certainty that he had not only discovered a continent, but the Garden of Eden as well!

The Garden of Eden, the birthplace of the human race, the earthly paradise which man had been trying to relocate for centuries—this was the pearl Columbus gave to the world after his third voyage of discovery. It is ironical that he should have thought a jungle area so hellishly hot and unhealthy that even today it conspires against human existence a heaven on earth, but within a fifteenth-century frame of reference, the deduction made a modicum of sense.

It was said that the Garden of Eden lay on the world's eastern fringe, and Columbus argued he had found the East. The Bible says Eden has a great river which divides into four branches. The description fitted the river the men of the *El Correo* had seen. A popular conception of the times held that Eden was so high it looked as if it would touch the moon. According to Columbus' astronomical observations, "Isla de Gracia" bulged toward the sky. The conclusion was inevitable, at least for Columbus, but his theory only served to discredit him in the eyes of more prosaic thinkers in the Spanish court. It seemed fitting to them that he should return to Spain chained and manacled like a lunatic.

Columbus had a faculty for reaping misery as the reward for his accomplishments. He did more for Spain than any man before or since his time, but he never won much admiration or acclaim. It was not enough that he had discovered Cuba, Puerto Rico, Jamaica, Hispaniola, most of the Lesser Antilles, Trinidad, the South American continent, and Central America. Columbus died friendless and out of favor, forgotten by the world. Men were to name his continent after another man.

Venezuela played a part in the series of errors which caused this final indignity. To her shores came Americus Vespucci, the Florentine, and jaunty descriptions of her aborigines helped fill the thirty-two pages of the four Vespucci letters which led to the immortalization of their author's name on every map of the Western Hemisphere.

The shadowy figure of Americus Vespucci and how his life influenced the cartography of the world are battlegrounds over which generations of scholars have dueled. He has been called a charlatan, the true discoverer of the New World, a great astronomer and navigator, the perpetrator of history's most successful hoax, a talented scientist, and a professional liar.

Americus Vespucci was born in Florence, the son of a notary, in 1451. He studied Latin, mathematics, and astronomy with his uncle, a Dominican friar, and became a commercial subaltern in the banking house of Lorenzo Piero Francesco di Medici, son of Lorenzo the Magnificent. In 1492, within the month Ferdinand and Isabella agreed to send Columbus abroad, Vespucci arrived in Spain to work for the Medici in Sevilla. Then followed the years during which he is said to have made three or four trips to America. Surely, he must have learned something about the sea. For the lowly banking clerk was made the Chief Pilot of Spain in 1508.

Beyond these sketchy details, historians have the four letters Vespucci wrote about his alleged voyages to the New World. These epistles, which enchanted an era hungry for news about the lands across the western sea, were sixteenth-century best sellers.

They passed from hand to hand while the journals of Columbus remained locked in a Spanish royal vault. Vespucci's spicy suggestions of intimacies with Indian belles, his account of an island where giants lived, his description of lands untrammeled by European woes titillated the mass and captivated the scholar. Within the space of a few years, Vespucci's name became inextricably confused with the idea of a New World. Few had ever heard of Columbus. It was natural for an Italian printer to use Vespucci's name in the title of a book recounting the various voyages of discovery. It was also natural for a scholar in St. Die, France, named Martin Waldseemuller, who published a new work on world cosmography in 1507, to use the name "America" for the area which almost everybody knew Americus Vespucci had discovered.

Of the four Vespucci letters, the first is suspect. It tells of a voyage made in 1497, which would establish that Vespucci and not Columbus discovered the continent. Stefan Zweig in his book *Americus Vespucci* says that an unscrupulous printer, intent upon sales, split a letter reporting a trip to the Venezuelan coast and Lake Maracaibo with Alonso de Ojeda in 1499 into two parts, making a total of four letters instead of three. According to Zweig and most other historians, Vespucci actually did travel to Venezuela with Ojeda and made trips under the Portuguese flag along the coast of Brazil in 1501 and in 1503.

It remained for future generations to untangle the web of errors and give Columbus the immortality his discovery warranted. We recognize Columbus today as one of those rare visionaries who have enough courage and enough faith in themselves to prove their visions real.

However, it is difficult for us, with our complete geographical concepts, to appreciate the incredible fortitude it must have demanded for Columbus to sail west into the void. The man who may one day guide the first rocket ship into outer space will know precisely what that situation demanded of the Admiral. His exploit ranks among man's greatest.

As for Americus Vespucci, who died shrouded in the same oblivion which clothed Columbus, the controversy that he produced is only academic. He helped baptize America, but after the christening, the name was no longer his—any more than the New

World belonged to Columbus after he found it. The New World, America, belonged instead to the horde of adventurers, churls, pirates, holy men, farmers, slaves, and lunatics who followed Columbus out of the fifteen century, the Age of Speculation, into the sixteenth century, the Age of Discovery.

Chapter III

SAINTS AND SINNERS

FOUR ATTRACTIONS—pearls, gold, slaves and land—brought the conquistador to the continent Columbus had discovered on his third voyage. The search for these things characterized the exploration and settlement of Venezuela during the sixteenth century.

Columbus insured the early invasion of South America when he reported that the Indians on the Peninsula of Paria adorned themselves with pearls. Two years after his visit, adventurers found the pearl islands off Venezuela's coast and precipitated a fortune hunt that produced some of South America's first settlements.

The few pearls the Indians of northern Venezuela could trade for trinkets did not satisfy the avarice of the Spaniards. They shortly impressed the aborigine to comb the ocean for more. Indians perished from brutality by the thousands. They had to be replaced, and a flourishing slave trade to supply the needs of the pearl islands developed. Moreover, the Indian slave system already existing on Hispaniola consumed human flesh voraciously. In the relatively docile tribes of northern Venezuela, both the Antillean planter and the Venezuelan pearl hunter found a rich natural resource.

Gold, as well as slaves, led Spaniards inland. In pursuit of treasure, conquistadors plodded across the Andean cordillera to the llanos, over the mountain highway to Bogotá, through the jungles.

and the savannas, to almost every corner of Venezuela. Though they found the yellow metal, they did not find enough, and because they had discovered nothing more appealing, the conquistadors began to exploit the soil instead.

The interest in land and its cultivation constituted the final phase of sixteenth-century history. By 1600, the outline of a map of modern Venezuela was clearly visible. Maracaibo, Mérida, Coro, Barquisimeto, Barinas, Valencia, Cumaná, and Caracas had been founded and agriculture rather than gold or pearls sustained the Spanish lord. The colonial way of life was established.

The Spanish faculty for doing the impossible in an impossibly short span of years was dramatically evident in Venezuela. The feat of establishing the colony is a monument to the fortitude, greed, single-mindedness, and ingenuity of a strange assortment of human beings. Sixteenth-century Venezuelan history is the story of these men, vying with each other for dominion over a golden image which turned to earth.

The first adventurer to follow Columbus across the Atlantic to Venezuela was Alonso de Ojeda, a flamboyant little man who once amused Queen Isabella by catwalking a twenty-foot beam extending into space from a church tower in Sevilla and kicking one foot at the air to show his disregard for danger. He demonstrated the same disregard all his life.

Born in Cuenca, Spain, of good family, Alonso de Ojeda traveled to the New World for the first time as a member of Columbus' second expedition. A good-looking man whose diminutive stature belied his herculean strength, the young conquistador distinguished himself on the Admiral's second voyage when he and nine companions captured a recalcitrant Indian chief and brought him to Columbus through sixty leagues of hostile territory. Writing to Ferdinand and Isabella, the Admiral said, of Ojeda, "He has discovered much more than all the others."

He asked for royal permission to head an expedition of his own in 1498. With four ships, he set out from Santa María, Spain, in May 1499, and followed the route Columbus had taken to South America the year before. He sailed along the coast of the continent to the Gulf of Paria, observed the Orinoco, touched Trinidad and Margarita, visited Curaçao, and on August 9 arrived at the tip of the Paraguaná Peninsula, the arm of land behind which lies the Gulf of Venezuela and the entrance to Lake Maracaibo.

The ships proceeded into the Gulf of Venezuela and there encountered Indians whose houses built on stilts over the water are said to have caused Ojeda to name the area "Venezuela." These Indians took one look at the winged monsters which loomed on the horizon and retired to their houses. Then they packed sixteen maidens aboard canoes and delivered them to the conquistadors, four to each ship. Ojeda reciprocated with trinkets and won the confidence of the natives. Many of them swam out to feel the hulls of the ships. Suddenly an old Indian crone, standing in her doorway, began to scream. The damsels aboard the ships jumped into the water. Indian braves on shore let fly with a rain of arrows. Vengeance followed swiftly, and in South America's first battle between men of two continents the Spanish killed twenty Indians and captured five. Ojeda's good treatment of the prisoners made for a rapprochement before he sailed south to explore Lake Maracaibo.

In his nine-day circuit of the lake, the Indians of Coquivacoa feted him wherever he went, dancing for his men and giving banquets. They showered the expedition with offerings of colored feathers, arrows, birds, and animals. Ojeda himself picked up a most useful souvenir. An Indian girl, whom he named Isabel in honor of the Queen, went with him when he left. The love affair of Isabel and Alonso de Ojeda is a story which ended only with both their deaths.

Isabel was tall and beautiful with a complexion the color of wheat. She accompanied her lover everywhere, shared his privations and saved his life on more than one occasion. After the first voyage, Isabel went to Spain, where she appeared in court dressed in costly silks and European finery. When Ojeda was commissioned to make a second voyage, in 1502, Isabel became a member of the expedition, serving Ojeda as interpreter, among other things.

Ojeda had formed a partnership with Juan de Vergara and García de Ocampo in order to raise capital for the 1502 voyage. When the expedition arrived at Lake Maracaibo, the partners quarreled. Vergara and Ocampo accused Ojeda of stealing and carried him in chains to Hispaniola for trial. During the trip,

Ojeda tried to escape by throwing himself, chains and all, into the sea. Isabel had him fished from the Caribbean, and the judges of Hispaniola and the King and Queen saved him from the machinations of his partners. Cleared of all charges, Ojeda made a third voyage to the Venezuelan coast in 1505, but of this trip nothing is known.

The most important expedition Ojeda made to the continental coast began in 1509 when he sailed from Hispaniola to explore the lands between the Cabo de la Vela and the Gulf of Urabá. With four ships, three hundred men, and Isabel, Ojeda landed near present-day Cartagena, Colombia, and set out on a slaving expedition. After capturing many Indians some miles from the coast, Ojeda and his men were ambushed as they made their way back to their ships. Ojeda was the only man to escape. Exhausted, his shield pierced by three hundred arrows, he lay in the jungle, uninjured but more dead than alive, until Isabel and a search party from his ships found him. She had insisted that the crew keep looking for him long after everyone else had given up hope.

Ojeda immediately sailed west to the Gulf of Urabá. There he founded heavily fortified Villa de San Sebastián, the second Spanish settlement on terra firma. (Columbus had established the first in Veragua during his fourth voyage.)

Ojeda's little colony was ill-fated from the beginning. The expedition was critically short of supplies as well as men. Hostile Indians subjected the settlement to continual attacks. During one foray an arrow pierced Ojeda's thigh and the leader repaired to his fortress to undergo a grisly treatment. It was standard medical practice to cauterize wounds with red-hot irons, but in Ojeda's case, the wound proved so severe the surgeon refused to operate. He said the treatment would kill the patient. Ojeda, who had enough sense to realize that he would certainly die if the wound were not treated, threatened the doctor with the gallows. As the irons seared his flesh and his leg smoked, Ojeda bore the pain with what one historian calls "singular and rare serenity."

The plight of San Sebastián grew steadily worse. When Ojeda recovered he embarked with a passing expedition to seek aid in Hispaniola, instructing his men to follow him if he did not return within fifty days.

Ojeda did not return within fifty days or, for that matter, ever again. The expedition became marooned on the southern coast of Cuba, and the founder of Villa de San Sebastián wasted many of those fifty days wandering through Cuban jungles. He reached Santo Domingo months after his settlement had been abandoned. Old before his time, troubled by his wound, Ojeda prepared for death. He brooded about his epitaph (for a time he favored "Alonso de Ojeda, the Unfortunate") and sat down to write his memoirs, which have been lost. Besson, whose *History of the State of Zulia* contains long passages devoted to the career of Ojeda, pictures the failing explorer, pen in hand, reminiscing by candlelight, his three children by his side, and Isabel at his feet watching the sun of her existence decline.

Ojeda died either in 1515 or 1516 and was buried in Santo Domingo. Isabel did not outlive him very long and in death provided a perfect operatic finale to the Ojeda episode. Franciscan fathers found her lying on Ojeda's tomb one morning at dawn. In her last demonstration of devotion to her lover, she had gone to his grave to die.

Though Ojeda paved the way for future conquest in western Venezuela, most of Venezuelan history for the first thirty years after 1498 occurred in the eastern part of the country, about which Columbus had brought reports to Hispaniola after his third voyage.

In those days, the Spaniards scurried around the Caribbean looking for natural wealth whether they had any clues or not. It takes little imagination to visualize what effect Columbus' references to pearl-bedecked Indians on the new continent must have had on Spanish adrenal glands. This was no rumor. This was no suggestion. And even if Columbus were crazy, there were others who had seen Indian girls wearing pearls as big as their eyeballs. A few days, a small expedition, only a few ships, perhaps even one . . . the expense? Why, in comparison to the gain, almost nothing!

The sirens were calling and susceptible Spaniards were lured to a rocky little island called Cubagua.

Less than a year after Columbus left the Venezuelan coast an expedition from Spain found the waters from which the Paria

Indians had obtained the pearls Columbus saw. Cristóbal Guerra and Pedro Alonso Niño got the jump on everybody else because they had been preparing an expedition when the news of the pearls reached Spain. Of course, out of deference to Columbus, King Ferdinand forbade Niño and Guerra from going within fifty leagues of any land the Admiral had discovered, and of course, out of deference to the pearls, Niño and Guerra went as quickly as possible to poach on Columbus' lands.

After discovering the pearl beds near Margarita and Cubagua islands and exploring a bit of the coast, Niño and Guerra returned to Spain with a fortune. They carried it off their ships in sacks—eighty pounds of pearls as well as some gold. King Ferdinand promptly had Niño and Guerra jailed for hiding a part of the fortune to avoid sharing it with him. He could prove nothing, however, and Guerra and Niño were set free to enjoy the fruits of the era's most profitable expedition.

In 1500 fifty pearl-hungry adventurers from Hispaniola founded a settlement on Cubagua. Nueva Cádiz was the first village on territory which is now Venezuelan.

The Spaniards' eagerness for pearls amused the Indians. Though they used the pearls for adornment, they regarded them as by-products from the oysters they ate and were pleased to unload the useless trinkets on silly foreigners who would give them knives and mirrors in exchange for the white spheres even the oysters didn't seem to want. This amicable trade in which each party considered the other a sucker went on as long as the Indians had spare pearls. Then the silly European became a raving, homicidal maniac whose excesses seemed barbaric even to a barbarian.

The natives of the island were enslaved to dive for oysters, and as the fisheries grew and the Indians died, other aborigines were brought from neighboring islands and the mainland. No less an authority than Bartolomé de las Casas, protector of the Indians, attests to the sickening conditions under which the natives were forced to work. Wrote Las Casas of Cubagua in 1519:

Scarcely had the Indian pearl fishers come up from the depths of the water bringing oysters when their masters forced them to go down again without giving them time to recover strength and restore the regularity of their breathing. If the Indian, in exhaustion, delayed a few minutes, the master forced him to go down with strokes of the whip. On this account almost all died in a short time. Their food consisted of the remains of the oysters and occasionally they were given cassava bread; never did they see any liquor which might help to sustain the strength of their wasted bodies, covered with sores from the constant contact with the salt water. Their bed was a small block of wood to which they were tied, laden with chains, so that they could not escape. At dawn of the next day they returned to work; and many disappeared beneath the waters, victims of the sharks who ate them alive; others fell unconscious, others gushed blood at the mouth; most were victims of hunger, cruelty, and despair.

The island reached its economic zenith or nadir, depending upon how you look at it, in 1513, after which the production of pearls began to decline. For extra income, adventurers turned again on the Indians. By this time, the Spaniards had been in the Caribbean for twenty years and their genius for destroying human life in their implacable pursuit of wealth had all but wiped out the native populations of the larger islands. In addition, Caribbean agricultural economy was expanding. The demand for slaves was great; the price high. Cubagua maintained its vitality with a new transfusion of Indian blood. The peaceful tribes of northern Venezuela were captured and shipped to Caribbean markets, even though only cannibals and hostile Indians could legally be enslaved.

Benzoni, an Italian sailor who visited Cubagua, describes the plight of the island's victims.

During our stay in Cubagua arrived Captain Pedro de Galice with more than four hundred slaves he had captured; and, whether it was for lack of food, or excessive labors and weariness, or the sorrow of being torn from their homeland and their parents and children, the fact is that all were almost lifeless. It had happened that if one after another, under the weight of so many miseries, could not keep up, the Spaniards, not wishing to leave them behind for fear they might conspire, drove them on with blows until they fell dead. These naked, weary, beaten, hungry creatures, sick or useless, demanded pity. The unhappy mothers, weeping and bowed by sorrow, carried two or three children at their sides; all bound with ropes and chains around their necks,

arms, and hands. There was no girl who had not been raped. . . .
All were branded on face and arms with a hot iron in the shape
of a *C*, and the governors then did with them as they pleased,
giving them to the soldiers or playing for them at dice.

More than once royal authority tried to cure Cubagua of its
ills, but whatever the island had was catching. Almost every judge
the Audiencia in Hispaniola sent to check Cubagua's abuses joined
the islanders in their efforts to avoid paying the King his fifth
and to circumvent his edicts regarding the slave trade.

The Indians did not wait for the King to protect them. Carib
pirates attacked the island in 1515 but were repulsed when a
warship happened along in the middle of the battle. In 1520, a
force of Indians crossed the channel from the mainland. Though
they numbered three hundred well-armed men and had two ships,
the Spanish retired without a fight. They were back the next
year.

Cubagua continued to thrive, feeding off its slaves and its pearls,
until the late 1520's, when a series of well-deserved misfortunes
befell it. The production of pearls continued to drop while new
beds were discovered near Coche and Margarita islands. Many of
Cubagua's 1,500 inhabitants moved. Charles V applied strict penal-
ties for slaving activities during one of his blanket prohibitions
on the crime, and for once, this had a restraining effect on the
slave traders.

The perverse little colony struggled along anyway. Indians still
drowned in its coastal waters and passed through its market to
slavery overseas. The thugs still brawled, tortured, murdered, and
raped. The King ranted about his fifth and against the slave trade,
and the Indians made feeble attempts to revenge themselves. In
the end it was not man but nature which punished the island. As
a result of one of those rare historical instances when justice seems
not only poetic but divinely inspired, Cubagua perished.

The island was struck by a combined earthquake and hurricane
one morning in 1543. The sea flowed into the streets; the land
opened; falling houses crushed their occupants and those who
escaped rushed out into the fury of the elements to be swept away,
calling upon God, of all things, for rescue and answered only by
the revengeful roar of the wind. By the turn of the century noth-

ing remained of Cubagua but scattered stones and the skeletons of the Indians sacrificed to its greed.

Eastern Venezuela also had its share of saints. The Church sent a succession of dedicated priests who did their best to protect the Indians and subvert the crass materialism of the European laity. They left no impression on the course of history. They believed in turning the other cheek, and to the pearl fisherman and the slave trader a turned cheek was simply an invitation to slap it.

The first two missionaries sent to their doom in Venezuela were Fray Francisco de Córdoba and Fray Juan Garcés. The two Franciscan friars established themselves on the coast of Venezuela in 1513, built a monastery near present-day Cumaná and began to teach the natives about Jesus Christ. They won the friendship and trust of the Indians completely—so much so, in fact, that when a Spanish caravel dropped anchor nearby one morning the Indians did not dash off into the woods as they had previously done when foreigners approached, but waited with their tutors to greet the crew. The Spaniards made a favorable impression. When they were ready to leave, the chief and his official entourage went aboard ship to bid their guests farewell. With the Indians aboard, the Spaniards hoisted anchor and sped away as fast as a good east wind would take them.

Ashore the natives watched helplessly as the caravel bore the chief and his train toward the horizon. Then they fell upon the priests. Garcés and de Córdoba persuaded the Indians to grant them a reprieve. They asked for four moons in which to secure the freedom of the chief.

Fortunately for the friars, another Spanish ship appeared on the scene. Instead of seeking its protection, which they might have done, the Franciscan brothers simply asked that the sailors inform the Hispaniola authorities of the crime. The sailors did notify the authorities, and partisans rallied to the cause of the missionaries, but the judges who might have ordered the release of the chief and his train did nothing. When Garcés and de Córdoba perished four months later, it was Spanish perfidy that sentenced them to death. The Indians merely served as executioners.

Both the Franciscans and Dominicans sent missionaries to Ven-

ezuela in 1518. The Franciscans established themselves in the
monastery built by Garcés and de Córdoba near Cumaná while
the Dominicans erected a new monastery some miles to the west
at Chichirivichi. The Indians apparently had short memories, for
they welcomed the missionaries as if they had never hustled their
predecessors off to meet their Maker.

The Indians and the missionaries lived in perfect harmony for
two years until an unprincipled lout named Alonso de Ojeda
(Las Casas holds that this Ojeda was the father of the discoverer
of Lake Maracaibo) preyed upon a tribe near the Chichirivichi
monastery. Ojeda had traveled a few miles inland to purchase
corn and asked for a detail of fifty Indians to help him carry it to
the coast. There his sailors fell upon the Indians while they were
resting. In a short scuffle, the Spanish killed several but captured
the majority. Ojeda sailed away richer by thirty-three slaves.

Again the Indians revenged themselves on the friars. They
lopped off the heads of two priests at their prayers. Fortunately
most of the Dominican friars happened to be in Cubagua at the
time. As for Ojeda, he was ambushed and slain as soon as he returned to Chichirivichi.

There still remained one monastery in eastern Venezuela. The
Franciscan brothers survived this blood bath because the Indians
to whom they ministered had not been affected by Ojeda's treachery. Their turn was yet to come.

Alarmed by the Indian uprising, Hispaniola authorities sent
one of their most efficient butchers to teach the Venezuelan savages a lesson. Captain Gonzalo de Ocampo rounded out a circle
of treachery by ambushing the Indian chief who had engineered
Ojeda's murder. Then he turned on the disorganized tribe. He
hanged some Indians, impaled others and sold the survivors into
slavery to cover the costs of the expedition. Moving east, he laid
the foundations of Nueva Toledo near present-day Cumaná. It
was the first attempt to found a city on soil of the Venezuelan
mainland.

The Ocampo affair occurred just in time to thwart the most
intelligent plan to civilize Venezuelan Indians that had yet been
proposed. In the last analysis, the priests who came to Venezuela

were trying to create a productive community of men loyal to the
Spanish crown and the principles of the Christian religion. Selling the Indians for slaves was as economic as selling mahogany for
firewood, and one of the men who realized it was Father Bartolomé de las Casas, apostle of the Indians. Las Casas was motivated
by pure humanitarianism, but in addition, he understood the
extent of the economic and social crime Spain was committing
by enslaving the Indians. A man of sharp insight and transcendent
idealism, Las Casas developed ideas which we are only beginning
to value today.

A member of a noble family, Bartolomé de las Casas was born
in Sevilla in 1474. He was educated at the University of Salamanca
and shortly after leaving it set sail for the New World. In the
Caribbean, he was revolted by Indian slavery and took holy orders,
the first to be granted in America. He made his initial plea for
Indian rights before King Ferdinand in 1515 and as a result was
named head of a commission of priests to study means of correct-
ing the abuses.

He continued his antislavery campaign throughout his life,
both in Spain and America. Curiously, his love of the Indians led
him to be an enemy of the Negro, whose slavery in place of the
American aborigine he advocated for a time. On account of this
idea, which he later repented and stoutly fought, Las Casas has
been blamed for the introduction of Negro slavery to the New
World. Yet Negroes were used as slaves before his time. That the
Negro would never have been a New World slave had Las Casas
not advocated the practice for a short time is manifestly absurd.

Las Casas was a prolific writer. His *History of the Indies* is one
of the more valuable sources on early American history. He died
in 1566 at the age of ninety-two.

Out of his passionate desire to improve conditions for the Indian
came Las Casas' plan for civilizing him. He asked Charles V for
a grant of a thousand leagues of land which he might govern
without any interference from soldiers or officials. He wanted to
found a colony with several hundred workers, specialists in all the
crafts, who could teach the aborigine the practical side of Western
civilization. Because Las Casas wished to use his colony to redress
former crimes against the Indian as well as to prevent the perpetra-

tion of any new ones, he urged that Indians enslaved in the Caribbean be sent to his colony for resettlement.

Las Casas thought he could pacify the territory under his control within two years. He enchanted the King with visions of regular revenues which would increase as the colony became more productive. In 1520, he secured authorization to govern an area from eastern Venezuela to Santa Marta, Colombia.

This sixteenth-century Point Four Program could not succeed at a time when only Las Casas seemed to understand its merits. The plan failed before it got under way. The laborers who were to teach the Indians began to desert as soon as they reached the Caribbean. Only weeks before Las Casas landed near Cumaná to befriend the Indians, Gonzalo de Ocampo had increased hatred of the Spaniard to a new high. When Las Casas arrived in Venezuela, survivors of Ocampo's blood purge had fled into the interior. The coastline was deserted. Those laborers who did come with Las Casas sailed away with Ocampo a few days after their arrival, leaving their leader to civilize the area almost single-handed. Even this he tried to do, but when he made no headway, he took ship for Hispaniola to seek help, which he did not get. He never returned.

Las Casas left Francisco de Soto to guard his interests. De Soto hardly waited until Las Casas had gone before subjecting the terrified Indians to a new orgy of Spanish cruelty. He had been given two ships and sufficient personnel to guard the Indians from the slave traders. Instead de Soto himself used the ships to hunt slaves.

Once again the Indians retaliated. This time they burned the one remaining monastery on the Venezuelan mainland, that of the Franciscans, and killed a missionary who had not escaped in time. Several hundred of them launched an attack on Cubagua itself. It was 1520, the year when the Spaniards, well equipped as they were, quit the island rather than face them. The attackers sacked the city and returned to the mainland to enjoy a short-lived period of freedom from Spanish incursions.

The Spanish returned in 1521. Under Jácome Castellón, they treated the Indians to another massacre. Castellón secured the Spanish position on the mainland by overseeing the construction of a fortified city where Las Casas had begun to found his colony. When the fort was finished in 1523, Castellón called the settlement Nueva Córdoba. Today we know it as Cumaná.

Thus ended the initial phase of the struggle to humanize the Conquest of Venezuela. Humanity surrendered unconditionally. The slavers continued to pursue their prey all along the coast.

Of the three forces that worked to protect the Indians, none was effective, nor did they ever become effective at any stage of the Conquest. The King was too far away. The Church had no troops. The Indians themselves lacked the means to combat the advanced techniques the Spaniards employed in battle. Now and then the King would succeed in asserting his authority or the Indians might win a battle, but in the long run, nothing availed against the methods of the conquistador. He had the power and he used it as he saw fit. It was he who made the history of sixteenth-century Venezuela. He plotted the course of it, and Venezuela still suffers as a result.

Chapter IV

CONQUEST

THE BEACHEAD FOR Spain's invasion of Venezuela was the western part of the country near Maracaibo. Though neglected while easy fortunes could still be made on Cubagua and Margarita, western Venezuela drew increasing numbers of traders and sleazy entrepreneurs as the demand for Indians in the Antilles grew.

Slave hunting was profitable in western Venezuela. Spanish adventurers could roam the swamps and desert lands around Lake Maracaibo breaking whatever laws they chose. The nearest officials were hundreds of miles away in Santo Domingo. For the first thirty years after the discovery, the area was an open preserve. Hundreds of docile savages were captured, branded, and shipped to the Caribbean.

To rectify the situation, the Real Audiencia in Santo Domingo decided to found a colony on the mainland near Lake Maracaibo. In 1527 they sent a representative to choose a site.

He was Juan de Ampúes, sagacious, efficient, and incorruptible. Landing near the neck of the Paraguaná Peninsula in early summer 1527, de Ampúes and his sixty men initiated the operation by making friends with surrounding tribes.

They wandered around the barren, scrubby plain south of the Paraguaná Peninsula until they found a suitable location for a settlement. On July 27, 1527, they laid the foundations for Santa

Ana de Coro, three miles from the Gulf of Venezuela. The city was western Venezuela's first.

De Ampúes never had a chance to enforce the law in western Venezuela. One year after his arrival, Charles V replaced him. The new rulers of Coquivacoa weren't even Spanish. For the next eighteen years, most of Venezuela belonged to a German bank.

Charles, the ruler who succeeded Ferdinand, was ambitious. When the title of Holy Roman Emperor fell vacant, he could think of no one better suited to wear the mantle of the Caesars than himself. Unfortunately for him, Francis I of France could. In fact, with some judicious bribes, the young French monarch had convinced most of the electors that he was extremely well qualified. Charles reasoned that if the electors could be bribed once, a higher price would change their minds. Thus began a shameless battle for an auctioned dignity. Europe was treated to the spectacle of two great kings outbidding one another four and five times. Charles won, but he had mortgaged his realm to bribe his way to the German throne. Two German banking houses, the Fuggers and the Welsers, had lent Charles the money he needed. The Welsers had caught the treasure-hunting infection which irritated the New World. In partial payment for the loan, they asked Charles for Coquivacoa. He gave them an indefinite lease.

Germans, not Spaniards, guided the destiny of western Venezuela from 1528 to 1546. They conducted the explorations which first revealed the riches of Venezuela's interior.

Since they did not know how long their indefinite lease would run, the Welser governors and the Spaniards they commanded were not interested in the future of the province. They behaved like pirates rather than colonizers, sacking thoroughly every league of country they explored. For a while things were as bad in western Venezuela as in Cubagua.

Charles himself had recognized that his favor to the Welsers was potentially a dangerous move. He attached conditions to the grant. He obligated the Welsers to found two cities and three forts during the first two years of the lease. He retained his right to a fifth of all profits and ordered that only hostile Indians be enslaved. But an ocean away, the Welsers, in their hectic race against time, chose to ignore him.

As Coro's first German governor, the Welsers picked Ambrosio Alfinger (Ehinger), a heartless little despot whose only aim was to produce booty for his employers. He sacked the area around Lake Maracaibo and the region west of it, leaving a trail of dead Indians, burned villages, and ruined crops behind him. In a few months, he had stolen sixty thousand pesos worth of gold ornaments.

Because the booty encumbered his party and because he needed supplies and reinforcements, Alfinger decided in 1530 to send twenty-five men back to Coro with the loot while he waited in eastern Colombia for them to return. Commanded by Captain Iñigo de Vascuña, the treasure party and its slaves started for Coro. South of Lake Maracaibo they lost their way. Neither the gold nor the slaves, nor any of the soldiers—except one—were ever seen again.

The story of the one soldier, Francisco Martín, is worth telling. It exemplifies the sufferings, endurance, and fantastic experiences of those men who explored the New World and survived.

Famished after wandering for days through the wilderness, Vascuña's party stumbled along the bleak, uninhabited slopes of the Andes, and when desperation had overcome all scruples, the Spaniards fell upon the Indian slaves who carried the treasure. They killed, cooked, and ate them. When there were no Indians left, the Europeans began to eye one another, until in sheer terror of each other they decided to break up and strike for Coro in small groups.

Martín and three companions struggled as far as the River Chama, which flows north into Lake Maracaibo. There they met four Indians who gave them maize and roots to eat. The white men wolfed the food. Then they attacked the Indians, all but one of whom escaped. The hapless one was eaten raw.

Fearful of vengeance, Martín's three companions fled toward the mountains. Martín, who had been wounded in the leg, swam to a log in the river and was carried downstream. Friendly Indians later fished him from the water and the chief of the tribe, amused and astonished at the sight of a man with fair skin and hair, invited him to remain with his people. Martín became the medicine man and after distinguishing himself in battle won the hand of the chief's daughter and automatic succession to the leadership of the tribe. Two years later, an expedition found Martín, painted like a savage and running nude through the woods. They took him back to Coro.

As for Alfinger, he broke camp after waiting a year for Vascuña. Heading south, he skirted the banks of the Magdalena River, swung toward the southeast across the Colombian llanos and scaled the Andean cordillera. Near present-day Cucutá, Colombia, he received his just deserts. In an Indian ambush he fell wounded and died three days later. His men wandered back to Coro.

The stories of Alfinger and Francisco Martín epitomize the next twenty years. The routes of later expeditions changed and manners and morals occasionally improved, but the sufferings from disease, hunger, and wounds, and the audacity and endurance necessary to survive them, remained the same. So did the aim, the pursuit of wealth; and the end, failure or early death.

After Alfinger, Hans Seissenhofer (called Juan Alemán by the Spaniards for obvious reasons) became governor. Later explorers were Jorge Spira (George Hohermuth of Spiers), Nicholas Federmann, and Philip von Hutten.

Seissenhofer scarcely set foot outside Coro during his short term as governor. The careers of Spira, Federmann, and Hutten were more colorful. Striking out east of Coro, they all turned south-southwest near the sources of the Apure River and marched along the Andes into the heart of the country just south of Bogotá. All of them were looking for "El Dorado."

Leaving Coro in 1534, Spira followed this golden dream as far as strength and endurance could carry him, fighting strange animals and savage tribes. Nature used every weapon to thwart him. Once during the rainy season in the llanos, his men were marooned on a hillock. Ravenous jaguars, trapped with them, surrounded the camp and tore several men to bits. They spent three fruitless years wandering among the mountain tributaries of the Orinoco and Rio Negro. Only eighty of Spira's four hundred-man expedition reached Coro again in 1539. Perhaps weakened by the ordeal, Spira died the next year.

Nicholas Federmann, Spira's lieutenant governor, was luckier. When his expedition reached the Colombian Andes in 1538, he learned that Don Gonzalo Jiménez de Quesada, an indefatigable pursuer of El Dorado, and Sebastián de Benalcazar, a captain in Pizarro's army, had arrived at the valley of Bogotá almost simultaneously. Quesada had marched south from Santa Marta while Benalcazar had come from Peru. Both claimed the rich and fertile valley of Bogotá. Federmann led his army into the valley and blithely put in a claim of his own. There was an eruption of intrigue and cross intrigue, but a temporary truce was arranged. Federmann received four thousand pesos in gold as a token of his rights, and the three leaders agreed to let Charles apportion the conquest. They sailed for Europe, heads buzzing with projects for outwitting each other in Spain. Charles took years to make up his mind. Before he could approve anyone's claim, Federmann died.

The governor who followed Spira was a Spaniard and a bishop. Coro had become the seat of a bishopric in 1531, although the first bishop, Rodrigo de Bastidas, did not arrive in Coro until 1536. In 1540 the Audiencia of Hispaniola found him a logical choice for the interim governorship. He had a strong influence in the colony, and had supported the Welser administration when other Spaniards tried to undermine it.

As Bastidas' lieutenant the Audiencia chose Philip von Hutten, the last of the German conquistadors in Venezuela, and the least offensive. He was young, amiable, and courteous, and a close relative of the Welsers.

In 1541 Hutten left Coro for "El Dorado." Word of the "exact" location had filtered back from Bogotá through Federmann's men. Bastidas, though a good bishop up to a point, could not resist backing Hutten's expedition and sold five hundred slaves to cover the cost.

Southeast of Bogotá Hutten thought he was about to find the elusive city. He had made friends with the Guayupe Indians, who told him of a fabulous country further south. It turned out to be the domain of the Omegua Indians, whose fertile valley, while not El Dorado, was desirable enough to make the Omegua fight very hard to keep it. In the battle Hutten was wounded by an Indian lance thrust deep in his chest. To save Hutten's life, one of his soldiers performed a most bizarre experiment. He took an Indian and jammed a lance through the part of his chest where

Hutten had been wounded. Then he dissected the subject to find out how close the lance had come to the heart. The Indian died, of course. But the soldier now knew how to operate on Hutten.

While Hutten was in the wilds of southern Venezuela and Colombia a new governor had been sent from Spain. Stopping off at Santo Domingo on Welser business, he dispatched his lieutenant, Juan Carvajal, to Coro. Carvajal forged credentials and presented himself at the city gates as the new governor in person. Like any legitimate governor, he immediately set out to explore the interior. He had decided to found El Tocuyo when Hutten arrived at the site on his way back to Coro. Hutten took the usurper's arms and horses away from him, but when Carvajal promised to behave, he gave them back. Carvajal then trailed Hutten and his men as they marched toward Coro, took Hutten prisoner and beheaded him on the spot.

This callous murder, as well as previous bad feeling between Germans and Spaniards, stirred the court to action. Charles revoked the Welser lease and restored Spanish authority in western Venezuela. Because Carvajal cut off a German's head and provoked the return of Spanish rule, he has sometimes been painted as a hero. Spain obviously did not agree. In one of his first official acts Juan Pérez de Tolosa, the new Spanish governor, had the good sense to hang Carvajal from his own gallows in Tocuyo.

The new Spanish administration both suffered and profited from the sins of its predecessors. Thanks to German explorations, Spaniards knew what to expect of Venezuela, but on the other hand, these expectations were not as bright as they had been in 1527. The Germans had denuded the province of what little movable wealth it had possessed. They had envenomed relationships between Indians and Europeans. Whole tribes had moved from the coast to inland fastnesses, leaving the Spaniards without enough labor to exploit the most important resource the Germans had left untouched—the soil.

Juan Pérez de Tolosa, the new governor, concerned himself with land development. Unlike the Welsers, he could make long-range plans. To stimulate agriculture and reward some of his subordinates, he distributed what few Indians remained near El Tocuyo in encomiendas and sent his brother to find more fertile lands. With one hundred men Alonso Pérez left Tocuyo in February 1547. The expedition discovered lush Santiago Valley where the city of San Cristobal was later built. The governor dispatched another party to the area around Lake Valencia. As a result the town of Borburata, a port on the Caribbean, was founded in 1548.

From then on, the Spaniards had a choice. They could seek treasure they were not sure existed or they could settle down to torment Indians into extracting wealth from the land. Many of the less impatient Spaniards contented themselves with an encomienda. The development of land had begun.

The Spanish had a system for choosing the sites of towns. First they would detail an expedition to cover an unexplored area. If conditions conducive to economic development and enough Indians to do the work were found, a second expedition to the favored location was assigned to establish a settlement which would serve as a center for encomiendas. The city was then laid out. Encomiendas were apportioned. The work of molding a community began. In this manner the Spaniards settled Nueva Segovia (later Barquisimeto) in 1552 and Valencia in 1555.

Near Barquisimeto explorers found the gold mines of San Felipe and eight years later they discovered the Los Teques mines. One would expect this wealth to push all prosaic thoughts about farming from the minds of the settlers, but the gold was easier to find than to get out. The Los Teques mines were an outpost in the wars with the Caracas tribes and were alternately occupied by Spaniards and Indians for twenty years. At San Felipe Negro slaves working the mines revolted. They fled to the hills, established a miniature kingdom, with high priest, monarch, and anointed heir, and declared war on Barquisimeto. No sooner had Diego de Losada crushed them than the Jirajira Indians began a concerted effort to drive the Spaniards from the area. They were not completely subdued until 1628.

The interest in land received a major boost with the extension of Spanish power into the rich farming lands of the Carib tribes in the valleys of the eastern Andean cordillera. Slowly the Spaniards invaded the plateau that slopes toward Lake Valencia, inched through the lush, stream-fed canyons to the east of it, hurdled the mountains, conquered the series of tillable valleys that begin at

Caracas and plunge in terrace-like succession eastward to the sea. Farming would pay well in these valleys of volcanic soil and one of the first men to perceive this was Francisco Fajardo.

Fajardo is an important figure not only because of what he did, but because of what he represented. Born on Margarita, the mestizo son of a conquistador and a cacique's granddaughter, Fajardo spent his life making the most of his double heritage. As the son of an Indian princess he commanded the allegiance and obedience of many tribes, and as the son of a Spaniard he was assured the protection and help of Spain. Recognizing his singular qualifications, Francisco Fajardo determined to subjugate his mother's people, whose traditions and languages he knew.

In 1557 with his mother, a handful of Europeans and one hundred Indians, he sailed eastward along the coast of the mainland to a place called El Panecillo where he received a warm welcome from the Indians. The caciques offered Doña Isabel, Fajardo's mother, any land she cared to claim, and Fajardo set out to obtain Spanish authorization for establishing a colony called El Rosario on the lands which he and Doña Isabel chose. But Indians and Spaniards began to quarrel. Doña Isabel and several other settlers were killed, the Indian chief was hanged in reprisal, and the settlement had to be abandoned.

Fajardo returned to the mainland in 1559 and performed the intrepid feat of traveling from the site of El Rosario to Valencia, through entirely hostile and unconquered territory, with only five companions. He sought the help of Governor Collado, who made him a lieutenant general and gave him thirty men to conquer the valleys inhabited by the Caracas tribes. Triumphing more often by persuasion than by force, Farjardo led his tiny force eastward to found an outpost called San Francisco, near present-day Caracas, and a settlement, El Collado (later Caraballeda), on the coast near what is now La Guaira.

The mere presence of the Spaniards in the vicinity provoked an uprising of the Teques tribe under the leadership of Guaicaipuro. Battle was joined between Spaniards and Teques. Guaicaipuro and his confederation won the preliminary skirmishes, forcing the Spaniards to abandon San Francisco and El Collado. When Fajardo returned to the mainland once more, he was hanged in

Cumaná by an unscrupulous Spanish magistrate who feared his power.

The life of Francisco Fajardo marked the beginning of a new era. Fajardo had bulldozed a path to the most desirable lands in Venezuela and in doing so had crystallized Indian hostility into determined resistance. It was ironic that Fajardo, the native conquistador who preferred diplomacy to force, should have helped provoke the Indian wars. But the mestizo was a settler, and more than the slaver, the gold hunter, and the explorer, the settler spelled enemy to the Indian.

Early in the Conquest Venezuelan tribes tolerated the Spaniards. Even after slaving activities had begun on a large scale, the Indians simply fought to protect themselves and rarely resorted to tactics designed to drive the intruder out of Venezuela altogether. It was only when the Spaniards started to settle that the Indians realized the extent of their danger. The result was a war which seriously hampered the conquerors for twenty years.

The Indians of Venezuela were tenacious adversaries. Unlike the Incas and the Aztecs, who reigned over many subject peoples, Venezuelan tribes were all independent. In Venezuela, the conquistador could not ally himself with the minions to defeat the master. Instead of one big entity, he had to fight a multitude of little ones.

When Fajardo was expelled from the Caracas valley and the adjacent seacoast, Spanish headquarters in El Tocuyo retaliated promptly. Diego de Losada marched eastward with 150 men and fought two battles before he reached the site of San Francisco, near which he built a fort in 1567. He called it Santiago de León de Caracas. It was to become Venezuela's capital and largest city.

Losada believed Indian resistance in the Caracas valley would dissolve if the Spanish could capture or kill Guaicaipuro. He besieged the chief's camp at night. Caught off guard, Guaicaipuro, his wife and twenty-two warriors fought to the death. Scarcely daring to believe they had actually killed him, the Spaniards fled from his body in terror.

His death did not simplify the task of subjugating Guaicaipuro's army. The problem multiplied. Instead of one hostile force, a dozen confronted the conquerors. They had to subdue the tribes one after another. By 1570 two of the strongest, the Gandules and Mariches, were defeated, and within the next few years most of the Caracas confederation tribes, including the powerful Teques, came to acknowledge Spanish rule. Spain owed the final establishment of her hegemony in the valley of Caracas to Garci-gonzalez de Silva, a one-man army.

Once when Garci-gonzalez and three companions were treacherously attacked in their sleep by supposedly friendly Indians, Garci-gonzalez awoke, seized a flaming brand in one hand and a spur in the other, and fought with such effect that the Indians fled in panic, knocking down one wall in their haste to get out of the hut. Outside Garci-gonzalez battled until beaten to his knees. Resorting to his wits, he suddenly shouted as if to allies in the surrounding darkness, "Come on! Let's finish these animals off!" The Indians turned and ran.

Bleeding from several wounds, Garci-gonzalez returned to the hut, got two wounded friends on their feet, loaded the other on his back, and started off for Teques' territory three leagues away, with his assailants hot on his heels. The Teques, who disliked their neighbors even more than they did the Spaniards, gave Garci-gonzalez and his friends sanctuary.

On another occasion he trapped the Indian chief Paramaconi in an isolated hut on the edge of a steep cliff, and while other Spaniards came to grips with Paramaconi's bodyguard, Garci-gonzalez attacked the chief. Paramaconi leaped over the cliff to escape. Garci-gonzalez leaped after him, and the two, bruised but still alive, grappled at the bottom of the gorge until Garci-gonzalez gave Paramaconi a blow which split his chest open. Leaving the chief for dead, the Spaniard had his men pull him up the cliffside with ropes. A year later Paramaconi, with a scar from shoulder to thigh, appeared in a Spanish camp with all his subjects to offer his allegiance to the white man whose reckless valor had vanquished him on the night of their duel.

The Indian wars were characterized by a series of battles between a few hundred Spaniards and as many as twelve thousand Indians. Outnumbered frequently thirty to one, the Spaniards won most of the time by dint of superior armaments, courage, and sheer determination. They also had a psychological advantage. When they captured or killed an Indian chief, his tribe nearly always made peace. Each Spaniard, on the other hand, considered himself a general and fought to the end.

This capacity for independent action had its drawbacks. In 1561 the Spaniards were forced to suspend hostilities against Venezuelan Indians to defend themselves from one of their countrymen, a traitor who wanted to be King of Peru.

Lope de Aguirre was a madman suffering from paranoia. One of Pizarro's conquistadors, he left Peru in 1560 with an expedition bound for El Dorado. They sailed down the Amazon from its headwaters in Peru, and seven hundred leagues downriver Lope de Aguirre revolted. He had decided to lead the expedition around the northern shoulder of South America, across Panama, and south to wrest Peru from the King of Spain. He believed the New World should be ruled by those who had conquered it. Killing the expedition leader, he and his men stole the ships. In 1561 Aguirre arrived at Margarita Island. He kidnaped the governor and kept him hostage while his three hundred men terrorized the inhabitants for months. They stole gold and silver from the Real Hacienda and plundered Asunción, slaughtering as they robbed. Aguirre ordered a priest killed for refusing to give him absolution following confession. In another fit of temper he had a woman of good family hanged and ordered his men to use her body for target practice while she was strangling. Aquirre's excesses did not stop with the Margariteños. Since he suspected everyone of treachery, he sometimes executed members of his own expedition without apparent provocation. Once he killed a crew member who was incautious enough to ask him whether land they were approaching was an island or the mainland. He hanged another sailor who complained of ill health because he wanted no weaklings in his crew.

Haunted by religious and political delusions of grandeur, Aguirre wrote a letter to Philip II, painting himself as a fervent Catholic ridding Venezuela of dissenters. It was a letter in which he alternately defied the King, scolded Philip for not appreciating his efforts on behalf of Spain, and threatened him with hell-fire.

In other equally demented outpourings he styled himself "Lope de Aguirre, Traitor," a title which both terrified him and filled him with pride.

Aguirre's long stay in Margarita gave Spaniards in Panama plenty of time to prepare for his invasion of the isthmus. When the traitor left the pearl island, he had to abandon his plan for the conquest of Peru. He sailed for the mainland of Venezuela instead. He sacked Borburata and marched on Valencia. Spanish troops from all over Venezuela converged on the area. Aguirre moved on Nueva Segovia (Barquisimeto). Government forces, aware of the fear Aguirre's men felt for him, scattered promises of amnesty around the city and retired to the surrounding hills. The device worked. Upon arriving in Barquisimeto, Aguirre's soldiers grabbed the passes and deserted in droves. Faced with certain defeat, Aguirre stabbed his daughter to save her from possible reprisals and rape, and then surrendered. As two of his own men prepared to shoot him, Aguirre placidly appraised their marksmanship. To one who winged him in the arm, he said, "Bad shot." To the other, whose bullet pierced his heart, he commented, "That's a good one," and fell dead. After feeding Aguirre's dismembered body to the dogs, the Spaniards marched off to fight the Indians again.

By 1575 the Spanish had almost unbroken sway from the Andes to Caracas. The government of Santa Fé de Bogotá had conquered the lands as far east as Mérida, founded in 1558. The only territory the Spanish did not control between Bogotá and eastern Venezuela was the area east and south of Caracas.

Barring the road to Cumaná were two principal tribes, the Quiriquire and the Cumanagoto, both well-organized and warlike. Garci-gonzalez fought the Quiriquire in 1578 and the Cumanagoto in 1579, effectively weakening both. But the enemy which finally destroyed the Indians of the center was not man but disease.

In 1580 a Portuguese ship arrived at the port of Caraballeda carrying, among other things, the first shipment of smallpox germs ever to arrive in Venezuela. By the time the authorities discovered cases of the plague aboard ship, it was too late. The killer had

begun to stalk across the province, raging in the bodies of a people whose racial strain had built up no resistance to it. Hundreds
of Spaniards died, but Indian deaths totaled tens of thousands.
Bodies littered ravines and forests, whole settlements perished,
entire Indian nations vanished without a survivor. At least the
majority of Venezuela's Indians died. When the plague began to
diminish in 1581, the decimated Indians ceased to give the Spaniards serious trouble.

During the century that ended in 1600, Venezuela had under-
gone profound changes. From an unexplored frontier it had become a territory spangled with busy little communities. All across
the country along the curving arc of the Andes from Cumaná to
Mérida networks of haciendas began to spread over the land, trans-
forming Indian villages into laborers' quarters and the savage himself into a peon.

The Spaniards who had followed Losada or Garci-gonzalez or
any one of a dozen others had received their reward in encomiendas
and had settled down to make them pay. This ex-conquistador
felt his own importance. He had carved out a hunk of the New
World for Spain and now he owed it to himself to make his hacienda and his Indians pay.

The encomendero won the right to the services of the Indians
in exchange for certain benefits he was supposed to provide. According to the laws affecting encomiendas, he had to protect the
Indians from injustice, make them live in villages and observe
civilized social mores governing family life. He was ordered to
instruct them in the Christian religion, organize domestic government under the authority of the Indian chief, direct their work,
and destroy all savage habits and inclinations. For their part, the
Indians owed the white lord a prescribed number of workdays
a year, or a tribute in produce or money. The encomendero could
employ his Indians any way he wished, building, mining, or farming, but under the encomienda system, he did not own the Indians.

Spain used the encomienda as a means to pacify the Indian when
no other was available. As more missionaries arrived in Venezuela and the Church grew strong, she no longer needed the
planter to civilize her wards. As a result, encomiendas were no

longer granted in Venezuela after the seventeenth century and those already existing soon ceased to be legal. The pattern, however, had become well enough established so that in some cases Indians who owned no land continued to work for the master of a hacienda, while others began to eke out a livelihood on land which the Spaniard disdained. To the encomendero the end of the system created little inconvenience. Long before the middle of the sixteenth century he had started to buy African slaves over whom he could have absolute control.

The little strand of towns that dotted sixteenth-century Venezuela existed for the most part to serve the encomendero. By 1600 Asunción, Cumaná, Coro, El Tocuyo, Barquisimeto, Valencia, Mérida, Caracas, Trujillo, Maracaibo, Carora, San Sebastián, Guanare, Borburata, La Guaira, and Caraballeda were thriving with the first vigor of settlement. Ports had begun to handle a small export trade in hides, cacao, flour, and cotton. Tocuyo had developed a specialized cotton weaving industry. Some communities like Coro, which had only been important as a springboard, had passed their historical zenith. Others, like Caracas, which had been the capital since 1578, enjoyed unusual prosperity. All but a few burgeoned with the colony's agricultural economy. Together they formed a colony which had grown large enough to agitate for special privileges.

In 1560 Sancho Briceño won four concessions for the colony at the Spanish court. The King agreed to send at least one ship each year under reduced customs duties, to allow two hundred Negro slaves to enter the colony duty free, to dispatch additional monks, and to give the cabildos (town councils) of the province the right to govern their districts independently in case of the absence or death of the governor. In 1590 Simón de Bolívar, an ancestor of the Liberator, had these privileges renewed.

Venezuela had also reached the stage where its settlers defended their rights against the encroachments of royal authorities. The citizens of Caraballeda abandoned the settlement in 1586 rather than permit the governor to usurp their right to elect two members of their cabildo.

A new generation was growing up. A generation born in Venezuela, to whom strange names like Barquisimeto and Caracas were more familiar than Sevilla and Aranjuez, whose skin was darker, whose features more Indian, than those of their fathers, whose ties were to their own lands and their own little cabildos rather than to Spain. Spanish colonists were beginning to feel like Venezuelans.

Chapter V

PIRATES AND PROFITEERS

PERHAPS THE WORST thing that ever happened to Spain was the discovery of gold in the New World. Far from benefiting the nation, the sacked treasures of the new colonies practically ruined it.

The gold Spain bought with blood destroyed her economy, enriched her enemies, made her the prey of seafaring robbers, and encouraged her to involve herself in a series of disastrous wars. The combination weakened her to the point where she could not take care of her colonies and couldn't do much about it when they decided they could take care of themselves.

At the time of the discovery, Spain was a poor country, neither populous nor well developed. Spaniards had struggled for centuries to free themselves from Moorish interference and had wasted their resources in European struggles as well. With the establishment of Spanish rule throughout the country, the unified nation did itself irreparable harm by banishing the Jews and the Moors, whose commercial talent and experience a resurgent Spain desperately needed.

Nevertheless Spain's economy had begun to develop along healthy lines in the fifteenth and early sixteenth centuries. Textile factories and iron foundries sprang up in scores of cities. Annual fairs to foment commerce were held. In Catalonia great quantities of cloth were manufactured. Valencia produced cotton goods. Agri-

culture flourished. Spanish commercial concerns had branches in
the principal centers of Europe.

Then, as the sixteenth century waxed, Spain began to manifest
peculiar symptoms. When Charles V ascended the throne, Sevilla
had 15,000 or 16,000 textile plants employing 130,000 workers,
but during the sixteenth century, the number of her textile factories plummeted first to 400, then to 60. The same dismal
pattern of falling productive capacity reached every segment of
Spain's economic life. Silk production in Granada dropped. The
glove industry was ruined. Agriculture decayed. The bulk of
Spain's laborers and farmers faced unemployment.

This diseased condition beset the richest nation, by sixteenth-
century definition, that the world had ever seen; a nation which
commanded a new hemisphere hungry for anything she could
produce. Overseas colonies gave her sugar, tobacco, cacao, hides,
and cotton. Fleets of treasure ships docked at her ports regularly.
Endowed with everything a nation wanted, Spain was nevertheless a pauper, and she sank deeper into penury with each day.
What had happened to Spain? What illness had her economy
caught? The sixteenth-century Spaniard did not know, and everything he tried to do brought fresh disasters because of his ignorance.

The prevailing sixteenth-century economic philosophy was mercantilism. Based on the fallacy that national economics duplicate
on a large scale the problems of the individual, mercantilism
preached that a nation, like a person, is rich when it has a lot
of money. The mercantilists assumed gold and silver had an
intrinsic and invariable value. The production and conservation
of precious metals was the only economic problem. Spain realized
the goal of mercantilism; she bathed in a sea of gold and silver.
But that was the trouble: she was drowning in it.

Today we know that the laws of supply and demand apply to
money as well as to goods. With increases in the amount of currency in circulation values of monetary units fall and prices soar.
The economic health of a nation is not measured in terms of its
treasury surplus but in the productive capacity of its entire population. These elementary economic truths escaped the merchant
of the sixteenth century. He believed precious metals would re-

main precious even though they should become as common as blades of grass.

As treasure ships plied between America and Spain, the amount of gold and silver in European circulation increased ninefold. By 1600 price levels were also nine times higher than they had been before the discovery. Nine pieces of gold bargained in 1600 for the same quantity of goods one gold piece purchased a century before. Because Spain received most of America's precious metal and received it first, her prices climbed faster and higher than those of other European countries.

This inflationary spiral wrecked Spain's industrialists and farmers. Goods from countries lacking gold were cheaper than those produced at home. Foreigners prospered while Spanish factories closed and her crops withered in the fields. Though Spain imposed strict trade regulations and tariff barriers, large-scale smuggling took the place of legitimate international trade as the Spanish consumer continued to buy the best product at the lowest price.

France and England benefited by mercantilism. They were forced to develop their economies so that they could earn the gold and silver they too thought would make them rich. A quirk of history made France and England strong. "If these means had fallen into the hands of England and France," says Eduardo Arcila Farías in *Economía Colonial de Venezuela*, "these nations would have adopted the policy Spain followed; and we should have seen Spain forced to develop its national production in order to snatch from them (France and England) through the medium of commerce, part of their metallic riches. History would have been different. Today we would be confronted with an England worn-out and backward, and a prosperous Spain."

Working on the principle that gold is desirable no matter how one finds it, France and England not only built up their industries to win it from Spanish markets but did their best to steal it before it ever reached there. Fortunately for them, they did not steal enough to injure their growing productivity. However, their efforts colored the history of the Caribbean area for two centuries. The sixteenth and seventeenth centuries were heydays of the privateer and freebooter.

The first professional pirate expedition to reach the shores of

Venezuela seems to have been a French fleet of three ships which appeared off Cubagua in 1528 and bombarded the island, but failed to take it.

It was also the French who first used piracy as an instrument of national policy in the Caribbean. Francis I of France, whom Charles had outbid for the Holy Roman Empire, sent freebooters overseas to harass the Spaniards and enrich himself. When one of his mercenaries, a Florentine named Giovanni da Verrazano, managed to sack a fleet carrying treasures stolen from Moctezuma, freebooting received an impetus that launched a score of tiny fleets manned by Brittany fishermen and "sea dogs" from Devon.

During the last half of the sixteenth century French and English privateers harassed the shores of Venezuela with the regularity of commuters. In one year, 1567, five fleets totaling forty ships touched at Venezuelan ports.

These late sixteenth-century pirates were often just seagoing blackmailers. Impeded by Spanish law from trading with the colonies, French and British merchantmen frequently threatened Spanish-American cities with destruction unless they agreed to exchange goods. Given the opportunity to make a legitimate profit, this type of sea dog seemed to prefer it to pillage. One of the most successful of the sixteenth century hold-up artists was John Hawkins, the merchant who fathered British piracy.

Under the protection of Queen Elizabeth, Hawkins headed a slave-running venture. He purchased Negroes in Africa, sailed to the Caribbean and, like a traveling salesman, peddled them from port to port.

In 1565 he sailed into Borburata harbor with a cargo of Negroes, cloth, and wine. He politely solicited permission to trade and the governor, Alonso Bernáldez, granted it. Hawkins unloaded his wares, paid the legal duties on them and sailed away with his pockets full of the governor's personal fortune, as it later proved to be. Angered by the governor's disregard for her laws, Spain fined Bernáldez the total value of the merchandise sold by Hawkins.

French freebooters of the era also employed the Hawkins gun-point technique. In 1566 Jean de Bontemps arrived on the Venezuelan coast to offer for ransom a Spanish ship he had captured. The next year Captain Jacques Sorel demanded a thousand pesos from the citizens of Borburata, threatening to burn the city if they denied him. In 1567, Nicholas Valliers did burn Borburata and sacked Coro when the governor refused him permission to trade. In 1570 Jean de Bontemps, who had visited Venezuela every year since 1566, burned Borburata again. After this last assault Borburata's citizens, tired of rebuilding their city, packed up what was left and moved away.

Until 1670 these roving Frenchmen and Englishmen were not pirates except in the eyes of Spain. They traveled under letters of marque and with the full approval of their governments, who more often than not were at war with Spain. During peacetime France and England winked at their wayward boys, whom they often publicly denounced or imprisoned briefly to convince Spain they meant well. With the signing of peace in 1670, however, letters of marque were withdrawn. Though the privateers continued to terrorize the Caribbean, they did so without the endorsement of their governments, which had grown rich enough to find them inconvenient. France and England eventually had to help crush the Caribbean piracy they had originated.

The most famous pirate of them all was Sir Francis Drake. Drake, who had served his apprenticeship under Hawkins, was a hero to the English. Aboard the *Golden Hind* he sailed around the world. He helped destroy the Spanish Armada and he filled the coffers of England with Spanish gold. He was the greatest Englishman of his day. But to the Spaniards he represented the devil incarnate. Drake became a hero at their expense.

A devout Protestant who yearned to cure the Spanish of a "Papist infection," Drake sailed the seas for God and Queen Elizabeth, praying to one and worshiping the other. And when Spaniards heard his name they crossed themselves and told their beads. For Francis Drake, the robber captain, was the avenging sword of the heretics. He hated Spain whose Inquisition tortured English bodies and disfigured English faces. He retaliated by shipping sacred treasure from Catholic shrines to grace the homes of London parvenus. Describing his capture of Santo Domingo he wrote, "We burned all the wooden images, we broke and destroyed whatever we found in the churches, and we took much silver, money, and pearls that had been hidden in wells and other places."

Such was Drake's fame that when an English corsair raided
Caracas in 1595, Spanish historians assumed the culprit was Queen
Elizabeth's robber knight. For two centuries Venezuelan writers
dutifully reported that Francis Drake had vented some of his hate
for Spain on Caracas. It was not until the nineteenth century that
scholars checked the yarn with English history and found that
a pirate named Amyas Preston had violated a city called Santiago
de León de Caracas in 1595 and that on the date of the attack, Sir
Francis Drake was hundreds of miles away.

At any rate, the sacking of Caracas was carried off in the best
tradition of Drake. Like Sir Francis, Preston favored flanking
attacks. After taking La Guaira he made preparations to cross
the range to Caracas, ostensibly via the Spanish road. Faithful
Caraqueños gathered their arms, marched through the gates of
the city and climbed the mountain highway, but Preston foiled
them by following a hazardous and little-used trail over the Avila.
By the time the citizen army, arrayed behind excellent fortifications high above Caracas, realized what had happened, Preston
was inside the city. Only one old man resisted Preston's entry.
Alonzo Andrea de Ledesma, too proud to run away, grabbed his
lance, struggled on to his horse, and rode out to challenge the
British, advancing on the city with their pennants flying. Touched
by the quixotic valor of the old conquistador, Preston ordered
his men to avoid killing him. This just insulted Ledesma. He
spurred his horse and charged the British. Reluctantly, the cor-
sairs shot him in self-defense. The first thing the British did in
Caracas was bury Ledesma with full military honors. They stayed
in the city for ten days, plundering from house to house.

Men like Amyas Preston and particularly Sir Francis Drake
launched the juggernaut of English power in the Caribbean. They
weakened Spain abroad while English merchants, factory owners,
and workers built an economy which inevitably expanded into
Spain's New World Mediterranean. Tiny Britain became mighty
and arrogant. Symbolic of their country's growing prominence in
the Caribbean were two other famous Englishmen who invaded
Venezuela—the poet-soldier Sir Walter Raleigh, colonizer of Vir-
ginia, and the pirate Henry Morgan, who came to the Antilles as
a slave and left them as a lord.

Sir Walter Raleigh, sometime favorite of the Queen, was in the Tower of London when he first conceived of an expedition to Guiana and the Orinoco. His aim? Manoa, city of gold, whose image filled his mind during lonely months in a dungeon. Raleigh decided he knew where to find the hidden city and clamored from his cell for the right to look for it. Elizabeth, in whose temporary disfavor he had fallen, relented and sent him to Guiana. There he saw trees, lizards, Indians, snakes, crocodiles, and jungles, all of which proved to him beyond any doubt that El Dorado was in the area—up the Orinoco, as a matter of fact. Since he lacked the men to pursue the search Raleigh returned to England, burning Cumaná on the way because its inhabitants refused to supply him with provisions.

His second expedition to Venezuela also began in the Tower of London. Jealous James I had imprisoned Raleigh following the death of Elizabeth, but he proved as gullible as his predecessor. Again Raleigh was released and again he set sail for South America. In 1617, at the age of sixty-five, he sent an aide, his son and 250 men up the Orinoco to El Dorado. Instead the expedition spent itself at the Spanish city of San Tomé where the governor and his troops tried to sink the English fleet and did kill Raleigh's son. Though the English routed the Spaniards and burned the town, they were too weak to continue. Raleigh returned home to lose his head. His life was sacrificed to satisfy Spanish complaints about the Orinoco raid.

During the seventeenth century the English did not stop at stealing Spanish gold. They also robbed a few islands, among them Jamaica and Barbados. To populate her Caribbean possessions and work in the fields, England sent her own riffraff and Irish Catholic boys and girls captured during religious wars. The need for labor in the new possessions was great. White slaves brought high prices, and the traders took to kidnaping anyone in sight. They abducted intoxicated adults and children who had strayed too far from maternal apron strings. Henry Morgan is believed to have been one of these child slaves, sold into indenture to pay his passage to the Caribbean.

The early life of Henry Morgan may have been humble, but his later years formed a career that for merciless sadism, for bloodthirsty arrogance, remains virtually unchallenged in the annals of piracy. Morgan was the buccaneer's buccaneer—heartless, dashing, audacious and brave. He ruled a pirate kingdom in Jamaica where bearded rovers tortured prisoners for sport and drank themselves insane during respites. Port Royal was the pirate's Caribbean capital and Henry Morgan was its most illustrious citizen.

Morgan raided the Lake Maracaibo region in 1669, initiating the attack with an eight-day reign of terror in Maracaibo itself. Though Maracaiberos had fled their city when they first got wind of the dreaded Englishman's approach, Morgan's cutthroats soon flushed them out of the woods and began brandishing their torture instruments. None of the prisoners seemed rich, but Morgan tormented them all—men, women, and children. First he burned them with matches. Next he removed hunks of flesh from their bodies. Then, in sequence, he cut off hands, arms, and legs. Finally, fitting a cord around their heads, he tightened it until the eyes popped out. In Maracaibo this procedure failed to yield much loot, not because the subjects were able to bear this treatment stoically, but because most of them had no valuables to surrender. The rich, as the pirates learned, had fled to nearby Gibraltar.

There Morgan's methods proved more effective. Enough citizens had gold and jewels to trade for their arms and legs so that Morgan was kept unusually busy. After a five-week inquisition, he made survivors ransom their city to save it from destruction and sailed away with Gibraltar's last ounce of wealth.

Meanwhile, Spaniards at Maracaibo had been preparing their revenge. A force of six ships under Alonso del Campo y Espinoza had blockaded the exit from Lake Maracaibo and a fort which Morgan had rendered ineffective when he entered the lake had been remanned and re-equippd.

Morgan's plight was desperate. His largest ship carried only 14 cannon while the Spaniards boasted three ships of 30 to 40 cannon each. To offset this physical superiority, Morgan relied on his ingenuity. He prepared a fire ship. Manned by a few doughty sailors, the explosive-packed ship was steered toward the anchored flotilla off the Maracaibo bar. When it reached the point where it would do the most damage Morgan's men lit a fuse and abandoned it. Seconds later the ship blew up, setting fire to two of

the biggest Spanish craft. Simultaneously Morgan's fleet attacked
a third. Within an hour the Englishmen had routed the entire
Spanish force. Captain Henry Morgan, who was to be knighted
and become Jamaica's lieutenant governor, sailed merrily across
the Maracaibo bar and headed for Port Royal.

Closely related to the history of piracy was the development of
smuggling in Venezuela. Freebooters of the Hawkins variety were,
of course, more smugglers than pirates. They initiated at gun
point a practice which Venezuelans in later years needed no such
inducement to employ. The Venezuelan planter wanted a multitude of goods—slaves, tools, luxury items, manufactures of various
kinds. And he had the wherewithal to buy them. His cacao, tobacco,
and hides brought good prices in any market. So when ships arrived to offer him things he wanted in exchange for things he
had, the Venezuelan did not stop to inquire what flag the captain
flew. That Spain forbade trade with foreigners did not seem important. The captain took cacao, the planter slaves, and both went
away happy.

Spanish policies gave smuggling its biggest impetus. Spain believed countries should monopolize the trade of their colonies,
even preventing them from trading with each other. It seemed
like a good idea and it was one which Britain later used to advantage with her North American colonies. But eighteenth-century
Great Britain, the era's greatest producer of manufactured goods,
could give her colonies the articles they wanted. Spain, weakened by her ruined economy, could not even supply her own
needs, let alone those of Spanish America. On top of this,
the Crown exacted high tariffs on both sides of the Atlantic,
sold items at ruinously high prices and offered to buy colonial
products at fractions of their market value. Britain, France, and
Holland sold and bought at prices Spain neither could nor cared
to match. Smuggling naturally thrived. It is estimated that at least
25 per cent of Venezuela's annual trade was carried on clandestinely. In war years, when Spain could not send many ships to
the Caribbean, this figure sometimes rose as high as 90 per cent.

Spain, of course, rapped colonial knuckles. She maintained a
coastal patrol and meted out harsh sentences for smuggling. Nothing availed, however, against the irrepressible urge to sell goods

to the highest bidder. Foreign vessels from Martinique, St. Thomas, Curaçao, or Tortuga, unloaded goods on the Venezuelan coast under the noses of the customs officials and the Barlovento armada.

Smugglers were nearly always abetted by the colonists, and even on occasion by the officials charged with upholding the trade laws. Many Venezuelan merchants maintained correspondence with foreign firms, placing orders which could only be delivered illegally. Upset by the tolerance of government officials toward illegal trade, the King wrote to Venezuela in 1692, "The repeated incursions which the Dutch and other foreign nations have made in your part of the country follow from the tacit permission which the governors of the Indies give them to trade, or from the little diligence which on their part they apply to hindering it." A scandalous case in 1673 revealed that functionaries of the Royal Treasury itself had permitted smugglers to trade at Venezuelan ports.

The principal goods involved in this secret traffic were cacao and tobacco, the two most important crops Venezuela produced during the colonial period. Frequently four-fifths of Venezuela's annual cacao crop left the country illegally. Goods smuggled into Venezuela included foodstuffs, cloth, metalware, and especially Negro slaves.

At first Venezuela's economy was diversified. The land was fertile. The country's variegated climate equipped it to grow crops characteristic of both the tropic and temperate zones.

As the colonial period progressed, however, economic activity began to be dominated by the production of tobacco and cacao, the crops which yielded the greatest returns. This specialization caused decreases in the outputs of other products. By the eighteenth century the practice of "monocultivo" was such a pronounced feature of Venezuela's economy that during the War of the Spanish Succession, when colonial trade was seriously disrupted, acute shortages of maize, yucca, beans, flour, and wheat existed, even though the province was capable of growing these staples.

Cacao held an especially important place in Venezuela's economy. By 1620 Venezuela was sending five ships a year to Veracruz, and the Mexican trade became a virtual Venezuelan monopoly at the end of the seventeenth century when the colony obtained an exclusive concession to carry cacao to Mexico. This steady trade was immensely valuable. Mexicans not only provided an outlet for Venezuelan production but paid for cargoes with badly-needed currency. During the sixteenth and seventeenth centuries Venezuelans were so short of coins they had to use pearls as money.

These profitable cacao and tobacco crops tightened trade links with the mother country. During the early colonial period the yearly or bi-yearly fleet to America had not touched at Venezuelan ports, and colonists traded with Spain through Santo Domingo, Puerto Rico, Cartagena, and the Canaries. With the beginning of the seventeenth century and the exploitation of cacao and tobacco, however, trade with Sevilla itself was established. This direct trade was often interrupted, but not because Spain chose to neglect her colony. Spain of the seventeenth and eighteenth centuries was a nation almost perpetually at war.

These constant wars forced Spain to alter her monopolistic policies. As Spanish merchantmen were sunk by enemy warships, excess produce piled up on Venezuelan docks. To help the colony survive the War of the Spanish Succession (1701–1713) Spain awarded a contract to a French company authorizing a limited slave trade. The French exchanged Negroes for Venezuelan crops and smuggled in other goods as well. At the end of the war, a British company took over the French concession.

These experiments with alien companies strengthened Venezuela's foreign ties. The French and English took advantage of Spain's disorganized state after the war to make deep inroads into rich Caribbean markets. Foreigners were taking more goods out of Venezuela than the Spaniards, who had neither the material, the ships, the men, nor the money to interfere.

The success of the British and French companies gave Spain an idea. A Spanish company might satisfy the trade needs of the colonists and prevent foreign exploitation at the same time. In 1728 the Compañía Guipuzcoana, staffed and financed principally by Basques, was formed.

Awarded sweeping control over Venezuelan economic life, the Compañía Guipuzcoana profoundly affected the country's history for more than fifty years. Its ways of doing business produced deep cleavages between economic classes, made Venezuelans more conscious of their rights, and created an atmosphere of hate and distrust that revolutionaries later exploited. The Compañía Guipuzcoana gave Venezuelans their first experience in active resistance to authority.

According to its contract, the Compañía was to send at least two ships a year to Venezuela. It agreed to supply the colonists with what they needed and buy what they had to sell. Though the King reserved the right to extend similar privileges to other companies, he never did. In effect, the Guipuzcoana received a total monopoly over Venezuelan trade.

Trouble between Venezuelans and Basques started immediately. Caracas had a grudge against the Guipuzcoana because its cabildo had not been consulted before the contract was signed. Venezuelans resented company efforts to combat smuggling and curtail trade with other Spanish possessions.

Feelings rose to a high pitch in 1738 when the Company tried to usurp Venezuela's Mexican cacao monopoly. Infuriated planters refused to sell the Company any cacao to ship. The Veracruz trade reverted to Venezuela and the Company gained nothing but the hearty enmity of great landowners like the Marqués del Toro, the Marqués de Mijares, and the Conde de San Javier.

Though the Basques provided a trade outlet and insured a steady flow of goods from abroad, the Company paid badly and extracted fat profits. Between 1728 and 1749 it manipulated the price of cacao per fanega from twenty pesos down to nine pesos, whereas the cost of cultivation to the grower during this period remained the same. In its role as merchant, the Company sold goods to the colonists at higher prices than prevailed in the Caribbean. From time to time, negligently or intentionally, the Guipuzcoana created a scarcity market by allowing vital goods, such as flour, to fall into short supply. The Company profited while Venezuelans suffered.

At times Venezuelans fought back. Four years after the Company arrived, a group of Negroes and mulattos rebelled and established an armed camp on the coast from which they traded with the Dutch in Curaçao. In 1741 citizens of San Felipe mutinied because the Company tried to install one of its men as Chief Judge of the city. Cabildos were swamped with complaints concerning Guipuzcoana outrages. By 1749 the Company had alienated practically everybody. And when Juan Francisco León led a full-scale revolt in that year the sympathies of the entire province were with him.

In the beginning the movement was not a rebellion at all. León was an assistant lieutenant of the armed forces and commission judge in the little town of Panaquire. Replaced without reason by a Basque connected with the Company, he decided to make a protest march upon Caracas. En route other malcontents joined him. Planters, merchants, campesinos swelled the parade. The character of the demonstration broadened. From the dramatization of a personal gripe, it became a movement to drive the Company from Venezuela. León wrote to the governor during the march and demanded the Company be liquidated, its ships barred from Venezuelan ports, and its officials plus any other Basques in the province expelled. Arriving in Caracas, he camped in the principal square, now the Plaza Bolívar, and insisted that an open meeting of the cabildo be held to discuss the Company's conduct.

The cabildo agreed that the Company was prejudicial to Venezuelan interests and should be dissolved, and when the governor promised to act accordingly León retired. With the immediate threat removed, the governor wrote to the King representing the movement as a revolt. Santo Domingo and later Spain sent troops. An investigation was held, but when authorities learned how large a percentage of Venezuela's population had been involved, they threw up their hands and declared a general amnesty.

At the beginning of 1751, a new governor ignored the amnesty and proceeded to throw followers of León into jail. León was forced to fight. Against well-disciplined troops, the rebels had no chance. In February 1752, León surrendered. He was sentenced to death and shipped to Spain where the King eventually pardoned him on condition that he fight for Spain in Africa.

The revolt was not completely futile. It did inspire several effective reforms. These included the cancellation of all Company privileges not contained in the original charter. The governor was instructed to see that the Company sold merchandise as cheaply as possible. Most important of all, a committee formed by the governor, a member of the cabildo, and a Company official was empowered to fix prices to ensure the cultivator a fair return.

Conditions in Venezuela improved, not only because of these reforms, but also as a result of changing policy in Spain. To combat "monocultivo" Spain encouraged a diversified agricultural pattern by lowering duties on coffee, sugar, cotton, and indigo. In 1777 restrictions on the importation of Negroes were abolished. The same year, the government opened Venezuela to restricted foreign trade and allowed colonials to pay for foreign imports with any domestic product except cacao. It was also at this time that the Intendancy, an agency specifically charged with stimulating agriculture, was established.

Appointed by the King, the Intendant had dictatorial authority over economic matters, and in his sphere, more power than the governor. Under his surveillance came agriculture, trade, colonization, and the administration of public income and military budgets. He could change the fiscal system, examine government accounts, insist upon reduction of various administrative expenditures and impose or remove taxes.

Spain charged him with cleaning the Augean stables of colonial administration. Many officials were bought lackeys of the Compañía Guipuzccana; others took advantage of position to slice their own taxes and evade the law. Port authorities collected nonexistent taxes from inbound ships and let others, which bribed them, pass without paying any dues.

The first instructions for the Intendancy exemplified the intelligence of current economic thought. They included projects for the settlement of colonists on unused land to increase Venezuela's population and level of production. Colonists would hold the property only as long as they made good use of it. The government threatened to reappropriate neglected holdings.

The Intendancy helped bring about the final dissolution of the Compañía Guipuzcoana. It had assumed most of the Company's original functions and the first Intendant, Abalos, a man of great energy and integrity, never missed an opportunity to complain in his dispatches that the Company was trying to keep Venezuela in a state of economic infancy. Overextended and in debt both in Spain and Venezuela, the Company had suffered severe competition from Venezuelan merchants, who had been granted privileges it once enjoyed alone. The War of 1779 dealt it a final blow. Some of its ships were taken by the hard-pressed Spanish government in payment of debts, some were captured by the English; and worst of all, Spain granted Venezuelans the right to trade with Dutch and French colonies when war caused shortages in the province. Hit by these multiple disasters, the Compañía Guipuzcoana folded in 1784.

The dissolution of the Company, the establishment of the Intendancy, and changes in Spanish policy heralded the inauguration in 1789 of free trade between Venezuela and other Spanish possessions. Venezuela was the last of the colonies to receive this concession, although in practice it had been trading under the new conditions since 1781, owing to the War of 1779.

With the introduction of freedom within the family circle, Spain reduced restrictions on international trade as well. In the War of 1779 she permitted French and Dutch vessels to dock at Venezuelan ports. By 1797, when Spain was again at war with England, she extended this provision to include ships of any foreign neutral. An incidental feature of this development was the establishment of commerce on a fairly large scale with the United States.

Strangely enough Spain's abolition of her rigid trade restrictions produced violent opposition in Venezuela as well as violent enthusiasm. Planters benefited by the new competitive market, buying supplies cheaply and selling their crops to the highest bidder. But merchants saw their control of the Venezuelan import-export market vanishing, and with it their "200-per-cent" profits. The free-trade issue increased bitterness between the two powerful minorities and widened a cleavage which persisted into the Venezuelan Revolution.

When Spain granted modified free trade in 1797, merchants from all over Venezuela gathered in Caracas on October 4 to protest. On November 7 the landowners called a counterdemonstration, labeled the merchants oppressors and profiteers, and begged the intendant to pay no attention to them. As they ranted, their passions carried them far beyond a simple economic issue. They saw more clearly than ever how dependent was their welfare upon the caprice of Spain. She was their real enemy. Between the lines of a manifesto prepared by the landowners at their protest meeting rumbled the political artillery of a coming revolution.

To demand, as our merchants do, that because the motherland cannot trade, because it cannot ship its products and manufactured goods to America, America must be hampered in the export of its fruits and the supplying of its needs by foreign hands, is to demand that our laws relative to trade be established for the sole benefit of Spain: that those laws, protective of all parts of the State, should protect one only. . . .

It is time to break the veil of silence, to confront the oppressors of these countries, to give them to understand that we are acquainted with their intrigues, to procure the means of undoing their usurer's ideas, and, in a word, to state clearly that this most remarkable, rare, and unexpected action of some of our merchants has its root in the spirit of monopoly with which they are animated, that same spirit beneath which this Province has been chained, has groaned, and still groans sadly.

Chapter VI

THE SOCIAL PYRAMID

VENEZUELA IS A half-breed, the child of a many-blooded marriage. European whites, African Negroes and American Indians contributed their bodies, superstitions, languages, temperaments, and attitudes to form a distinct national culture pattern completely different from any of the civilizations that produced it but nevertheless reminiscent of them all.

Venezuela's racial history may be seen in the faces of her citizens, which range from pure types to mixtures reflecting every possible quantitative combination of the three blood strains. The mingling of the races may be seen, too, in folkways and customs influenced by two and sometimes by three distinct ways of life. Venezuelans still eat Indian cassava bread. To celebrate Catholic feasts, communities of Negroes employ pagan ritual and translate the intricate and sensual rhythms of tree-trunk drums into ecstatic dances their ancestors once used to placate African gods.

Besides coloring Venezuelan life, this interaction of civilizations and races created peculiar problems during the history of the country. Interracial contact welded rigid class lines, extreme regard for social station, and hysterical attitudes which impede the kind of social and economic integration a country needs in order to progress. Intermarriage has helped combat social disunion in Venezuela, but two centuries ago, when the process was less com-

74

plete, the racial segments which formed the province's population were separated by distrust and fear. In fact, they hated each other.

It has been estimated that Venezuela's population in 1800 totaled approximately 700,000.[1] The breakdown by races was roughly 140,000 whites, 100,000 Negro slaves, 70,000 Indians,[2] and 400,000 pardos [3] and free Negroes. A white minority, which comprised only 20 per cent of the total, dominated this variegated society. Numerically weak and economically powerful, the whites straitjacketed the country's social order so that Negroes, Indians, and pardos could not threaten the prerogatives of the ruling class. According to colonial law, only Spanish gentlemen whose racial backgrounds contained no Jewish, Moorish, or Negro antecedents could join the royal army, attend the university, or take religious orders. White *criollos* controlled the cabildos. They generally had the right to trial before special courts—ecclesiastical, hacienda, or military—and always formed the bodies which judged the rest of the population. So zealous was the white Venezuelan in his efforts to restrict the freedom of others that he himself became a prisoner of caste.

A Venezuelan white *criollo* was a very self-conscious gentleman —twice as scrupulous a gentleman, in fact, as a Spanish gentleman of comparable rank. He lived by an ironbound code which governed the kind of occupation he chose, dictated his dress and made it imperative that he place his social position above even his natural inclination to fall in love with whomever he fancied. The *criollo* class was composed of those who had, or claimed, "hidalguía," and could use the partitive "Don" to decorate their Christian names. An hidalgo (literally the "'son of something") exuded those ineffable qualities of intellect and behavior which special family ties were thought to convey. Since the "hidalguía" of most Venezuelans was traceable only to some bad-mannered conquistador who won rank in return for distinguished service, Venezuelan hidalgos comported themselves with all the studied

---

[1] All population figures for this period are guesses.
[2] This figure reflects only those partly civilized Indians who fell under Spanish influence.
[3] This term refers to all peoples of mixed blood.

elegance of people anxious to prove they are really elegant. At least a dash of Indian blood sullied the purity of most *criollos*. So preserving, or more often feigning, an antiseptic family background and behaving as the member of an antiseptic family should, became all the more important.

A cardinal tenet of the *criollo* class was abhorrence of manual work. An hidalgo could honorably serve society as a priest, an army officer, a doctor, or a lawyer, but any other capacity was thought to demean him. He could not be a merchant, a carpenter, or a farmer. Though the principal source of *criollo* wealth was land, an hidalgo only owned it; he never worked it. In fact, he considered a display of interest in his land unbecoming a gentleman. He lived in town, visited his hacienda for a vacation, and occupied himself with leisurely pursuits. His passion for being a gentleman exceeded even his regard for wealth. To maintain the illusion of superiority, *criollos* whose neglected land could not support a nonworking owner sometimes sold their property rather than depreciate their social standing by paying more attention to it. Priests, army officers, and lawyers were frequently impoverished hidalgos who had been forced to seek profitable sinecures.

In his private life, the *criollo* also lived by rigid standards. He married in his own class at an early age. Official courts could prevent him from choosing a socially inferior wife. *Criollos* secluded their women and demanded that they be modest, retiring, and sexually ignorant. He venerated their ability to do almost nothing and found them so dull that he had to amuse himself with women of the lower classes.

The philosophy of the gentleman befouled many facets of Venezuelan life. One of the clearest presentations of its evils has been delivered by a Venezuelan who saw it in action. Discussing Venezuelan education of the late eighteenth century, Dr. Miguel José Sanz said:

Good faith, tranquillity, affection, trust, cannot exist in a country where each strives to distinguish himself from the others by birth and vanity; where, instead of being inspired to just emulation of the virtues of his good countrymen and horror at the vices and crimes of the bad, the child is taught, or at least from the lips of his parents hears, only that Pedro is not as noble as Antonio, that the family honor of Juan is marked by such and such a stain, and that Diego's family wore mourning while Francisco's cut it short. . . . In Caracas the system of instruction is generally bad. The child has not even learned yet to pronounce his letters well and can only scribble and read without understanding when there is put in his hands the *Grammar of Nebrija,* without taking into consideration that if he does not know how to speak his own language well, how to read, write, and calculate, it is ridiculous for him to learn Latin and dedicate himself to the branches of knowledge which the university teaches. . . . Generally it is judged that no knowledge exists outside of that contained in the *Grammar of Nebrija,* the philosophy of Aristotle, the *Institutes* of Justinian, the *Curia Philippica,* the theology of Gonet and Larraga; it is believed that it suffices to know how to write briefs, say mass, wear doctor's bands or sport the habit of monk or priest; that decency prohibits working the land and orders a disdain for the mechanical and useful arts. Out of pure ostentation the Venezuelan puts on military uniform; he translates French to make Castillian ugly; he obtains the degree of lawyer to gain his daily bread, takes clerical orders to acquire consideration, and the vows of poverty in a monastery precisely to be rid of poverty. . . . Everybody wishes to be a gentleman or live in idleness, given over to the ugly vices of sensuality, gambling, intrigue, and calumny. On this account lawsuits multiply, the wicked flourish, the good are discouraged, and all is corrupted.

At least a small segment of Venezuela's white population in 1800 remained relatively uninhibited by *criollo* manners and morals. There were many "poor whites" who regardless of their racial purity had to work with their hands to keep alive. In addition, first-generation Spanish immigrants had no income to live on. They profited by the white Venezuelans' refusal to work and some became wealthy running stores and businesses of which the hidalgo code disapproved. However, colonial folkways were pernicious enough to infect even healthy European attitudes toward business. Writing of retail merchants in 1804 François Depons, the French Agent in Caracas, said, "The usual profits of the retail merchants are 25 to 30 per cent. To judge by this, few careers would lead more quickly to riches, and this would be true if the sales of any store were sizable. But as the life associated with this profession is very sedentary, and consequently suits the Spaniards very well, shops multiply and sales are divided up to an infinite degree; the same thing happens to the profits, and there remains to each only what he needs to maintain his family and sustain himself decently. Hence, this class which elsewhere progresses quickly here maintains itself without advance and one sees more bankruptcies than fortunes."

Supporting the extravagances of the province's white *criollos* were 100,000 African Negroes. The slaves carried the colonial social pyramid on their backs. They tilled the soil and did onerous household chores, producing the time and the wealth which many of Venezuela's masters squandered on foppery.

Throughout most of the colonial period, Venezuelan slaves served their masters as beasts and were often treated as such. Their condition, of course, depended upon the kind of owner to whom they belonged, and more particularly, to the attitude of his overseer. Sometimes they received the attention of valued property; more often they were neglected like the land itself. Slaves dwelt, as a rule, in miserable, unsanitary hovels. They rarely received medical care. They supplied their own food, working small private plots in free hours. They could be lashed if they disobeyed instructions. No one bothered with their education beyond teaching them to say their prayers and observe Catholic ritual. On the other hand, owners in Venezuela treated their slaves no worse, and sometimes better than the British and French.

Slaves in Venezuela enjoyed a few advantages their counterparts in North American colonies were denied. Spanish law vouchsafed the Negro the right to insist that his master sell him to someone else should he consider his treatment unsatisfactory. If he had saved an amount of money equal to the price his owner originally paid for him, he could buy his freedom, which could cost, according to the law, no more than three hundred pesos. Venezuelan slaves earned money by doing extra work or by selling excess produce from their small private plots.

Somewhat better off than the Negro was his predecessor in the fields. When Spain got around to applying its laws regarding Indians, she made up for lost time. By 1800, the Indians whom the whites had partially civilized lived in their own villages and tilled their own land, unless like those of the llanos they supported themselves by cattle raising. Spain favored segregating her wards from the whites, and the best minds of the Consejo de Indias had devised ingenious laws to protect the Indians from Spaniards. In the courts they were considered minors. No contract made with them could be held valid. Those who committed crimes against them were punished more severely than if a Spaniard had been the victim. They were assured title to the lands they held when subdued. The villages where they lived were governed by men of their own race, and when Spain learned that Indian chiefs were inclined to oppress their tribesmen, she appointed officials charged with protecting the average Indian's interests.

Like the civil authorities, the Church treated the Indian as a child. If his confession were incomplete, his church attendance irregular, his inclination to incest or drunkenness disturbingly profound, the Church understood and broadened her strict tenets to keep him technically, if not actually, on the right side of God. One apologist went so far as to declare for the Caribs' benefit that the eating of human flesh was not in itself a sin.

The paternalism of church and state had an obvious effect. The Indian, who was neither educated nor stimulated, did not grow up. He saw no reason to work, stole when it suited his purpose, and found in aguardiente a means to make himself physically, as well as intellectually, torpid. In church, completely nude or dressed only in a few rags, the Indians listened to sermons from reclining positions, sometimes stretched prone on the floor. Many were openly skeptical or contemptuous of Catholicism and did not hesitate to voice their objections during services. At mass, it was not uncommon for an old crone to argue with the points the priest made in his sermon. If he spoke of the goodness of God and his power, she would ask, "Why, if he is so good and so powerful, doesn't he give us food without our working for it?" When hell was the subject, she wanted to know, "Have you seen it? Who told you so? Who has come back from there?" Should the sermon dwell on the mortification of the flesh and abstinence, the voice challenged, "Why doesn't the good father practice what he preaches?"

The three pure types—Negroes, whites, and Indians—had produced by 1800 a fourth social class which lacked the definite status of its progenitors. Venezuela's pardos, the largest racial group in the country, numbered about 400,000 before the revolution. Technically free men, they enjoyed only the restricted liberty of a modern Negro in the southern United States.

The Venezuelan philosophy of white superiority imposed limits on a pardo's economic and social aspirations. Professions were monopolies of the whites, although in the eighteenth century a shortage of doctors forced the *criollos* to allow the pardo to practice medicine. Many pardos, of course, turned to the trades and crafts which the whites despised. Some became storekeepers and merchants.

At the end of the sixteenth century, royal cedulas had assured the pardo the same honors and privileges that any Spanish citizen possessed. He could hold public office or enter the Church. In the first fifty years of the seventeenth century, however, other cedulas withdrew these rights, and, in addition, prohibited him from taking the degrees of notary or serving in the royal army. He could only join the militia, which was especially formed so that the man power of the pardo class might be utilized without contaminating *criollo* forces. The pardo, and particularly his wife, were subjected to strict sumptuary laws. A woman with a single drop of Negro blood could not wear silk, gold, pearls, or a cloak— symbols of the well-to-do. Pardos could not have Indian servants.

By the end of the eighteenth century most of these restrictions had fallen into disuse. Moreover, an ambitious family might buy from the King a "Dispensa de Color" which by royal decree purged their blood of any unwelcome racial strain. Displaying commendable contempt for Venezuela's artificial and hypocritical social code, the King also peddled "authentic" hidalguías for 107,000 reals and the title of "Don" for 1,400. While the pardo could buy *criollo* privileges, it rarely did him any good. The white would not accept him. Consequently, few pardos bothered to improve their financial position, which frequently bordered on penury. It seemed senseless to work very hard when the offices and status on which society put the highest value were forever closed to him.

Naturally, it was between the pardos and the whites that the bitterest racial feeling developed. Resentful of the discrimination to which they were subjected, the pardos agitated for improvements. Spanish officials, who lacked the prejudices of Venezuelan *criollos,* sometimes listened and occasionally encouraged the advance of talented pardos to civil office and posts of distinction. The struggle of the pardo for recognition and Spain's willingness to grant it embittered relations between white planter and pardo merchant, already at odds over the question of free trade, and gave the *criollos* another reason to harbor resentment toward Spain. The intensity of the white Venezuelan's hate for the pardo is eloquently expressed in a document drawn up by the Caracas cabildo in 1796, protesting the sale of hidalguías and titles to those of mixed blood. The cabildo declared,

"[This sale] is frightening to the inhabitants and citizens of America, for only they know from birth on or through the experience of long years, the immense distance which separates whites and pardos, the advantages and superiority of the former, and the baseness and inferiority of the latter." Pardos, said the cabildo, should not have "the education which they have lacked till now and should lack in the future. . . . Mulatto students will swarm to classes, clamor to enter the Seminary, ask for offices on the council and for public office . . . and the sad day will come in which Spain perforce will see herself served by mulattos, zambos, and Negroes, whose doubtful loyalty will cause violent upheavals." Objecting to the pardo's preference for trade over agriculture (the cabildo suggested he be forcibly put to work in the fields) they argued, ". . . being free to work when they will, to adulterate metals at their pleasure, to set their prices on their work and to cheat everyone . . . they do not care to apply themselves to other ends, for they despise . . . field work and serving those who have land."

The instrument which helped the *criollo* preserve his power was the cabildo. Through it, he could influence Spanish legislation and the attitudes of Spanish officials in the colonies.

Responsibility for Venezuela's welfare was, of course, the King's. To supervise the affairs of his colonies, he had the Consejo de Indias, a lawmaking and regulating body, which had jurisdiction over colonial courts, the army, the development of commerce and trade, and recommended candidates for all the principal political and ecclesiastical offices in the colonies. Among the appointees the Consejo recommended were the chief executives of the four

viceroyalties and six captain generalcies into which the Spanish
New World was politically subdivided.

In 1777 Spain established the Captain Generalcy of Caracas,
including most of present-day Venezuela, which had been a mere
province under outside jurisdiction prior to that year. Administering the Captain Generalcy of Caracas were the Captain General, who was chief authority and supreme military commander;
the Intendant, who controlled economic and financial matters;
and the Audiencia, the supreme judicial court, which also advised
the captain general on administrative matters. Under the Spanish authorities came the local cabildos—the municipal governing
bodies, and the only political institutions in Venezuela which in
any way represented colonial interests.

Besides administering local affairs the cabildos acted as courts
in their districts and, through protests and recommendations to
the captain general, influenced his decisions. Though the only
governmental body which derived its power from Venezuelans,
the cabildo represented the wealthy and not the population as
a whole. While two of its members (the alcaldes) were elected, they
were chosen only by other members of the cabildo. These, who
numbered from six to sixteen depending on the size of the community, generally bought their posts. A needy or retiring cabildo
member might sell his seat to whomever he pleased provided the
candidate was acceptable to the king. With this system in force it
was easy for the Venezuelan *criollo* to make the cabildo a private
club.

Most powerful of Venezuela's cabildos was the one which sat in
the capital. Until Spain established an audiencia at Caracas in
1786, the Caracas cabildo was the governor's or the captain general's most influential adviser on colonial affairs. After 1760, it
had price-fixing powers affecting the entire province. It was the
Caracas cabildo which engineered the overthrow of outside power
and the establishment of Venezuela's first independent government in 1810.

The menace of white supremacy, which the cabildo strengthened and helped perpetuate, damaged Venezuela to the point
where even today she has decades of work ahead of her before all
of its evil effects will be eradicated. Spain may have oppressed Vene-

zuela, but she never matched the oppression which the *criollo* imposed on his countrymen. If she was guilty for allowing her Inquisition to prohibit the hidalgo certain books, he was guiltier for preventing the pardos, the Negroes, and the Indians from learning to read at all. Spain's neglect of her colony's welfare compares favorably with the *criollo's* indifference to the land and the living conditions of his Negroes or his bastard children in the pardo class. When he joined the ranks of Venezuela's revolutionaries, he ruled a society which treated the Indian as a child, the Negro as an animal, and the pardo as a family disgrace. He kept them all in a state of abject ignorance so that one generation remained as infantile as the last. In judging a man by his color instead of his ability and establishing limits to his attainment, he removed all incentive to work and to learn. As the self-appointed model of acceptable conduct, he set an example for idleness and irresponsibility. He made the siesta a national dream. The result for the population as a whole was misery, ignorance, lack of industry, and the neglect of civic and moral values.

Condemnation of Venezuela's aristocracy does some outstanding members an injustice. In any moneyed class, certain individuals use their leisure to improve themselves and contribute to a nation's culture and welfare. Simón Bolívar, Francisco de Miranda, Miguel José Sanz, Andrés Bello and Simón Rodríguez, to mention a few, were unusually gifted men with advanced political and social views. Aristocracy allowed Venezuela to have an intellectual life far out of proportion to its scanty population.

Nor did Venezuelan aristocrats have a monopoly on irresponsibility. Social injustice existed in all parts of the world and aristocrats as a class were everywhere indifferent to it. The callousness of French aristocrats had cost them their heads twenty years before. The United States constitution established the inviolable right to own property. This meant, among other things, the right to own slaves. As for Venezuelan colonial society, it was not unique. The evil effects of a similar social structure may be seen in the southern United States today.

Nothing better illustrates conditions in Venezuela at the end of the eighteenth and the beginning of the nineteenth centuries than the description of Caracas which François Depons included in his account of Venezuela following a tour of duty in the country as the French Agent. Though he perhaps lacked the insight of a native Venezuelan, he commanded a breadth of experience which permitted him to compare Venezuela's capital city—the richest, biggest, and most advanced in the land—with the principal centers of the world. The following account of Caracas in 1804 is composed of excerpts from Depons' description.

This city, situated at 10°31' latitude N and 69°3' longitude W of the meridian of Paris, was founded by Diego de Losada in 1567; 47 years after Cumaná, 39 after Coro, 33 after Barcelona, and 15 after Barquisimeto.

Its Prerogatives

It is the capital not only of the Province of Venezuela, but also of the immense territory occupied by the Governments of Maracaibo, Barinas, Guayana, Cumaná, and the island of Margarita, as it is the seat of the Captain-Generalcy, the Royal Audiencia, the Intendancy and the Consulate.

Temperature

Its temperature does not correspond at all with the latitude in which it is found. Rather than an insupportable heat, such as one would think one ought to feel at so short a distance from the equator, spring reigns there almost constantly. It enjoys this advantage thanks to its height of 3,025 feet above sea level.

However, there is not a day in which the sun does not attempt to exercise in Caracas the rights which it exercises in all regions situated in the same latitude; but the topographical location of the city disputes with it successfully.

Situation

Caracas rises in a valley four leagues long, running from east to west, between the mountains which border the sea from Coro to Cumaná. It is in a sort of hollow of this same chain, for it has to north and south mountains of equal height. The area of the city is 2000 paces squared. Its land is as nature made it; art has done nothing to level it or flatten its accidents. For this reason, there are very few streets in the city on which one does not have to climb or descend. Principally in the north-south direction the slope is very pronounced.

WATERS

It enjoys the waters of four little rivers. The first, called the Guaire, borders it to the south without penetrating the city. Although not sufficiently powerful to merit the name of river, it is enough so to merit one more honorable than that of arroyo. The second, called Anauco, runs through the western part; and the point where it comes closest to the city is Candelaria, where there is a lovely bridge which facilitates communications with the valley of Chacao. The third is the Caroata, whose bed, stony and bordered with shacks, follows a north-south course in the west part of the city and separates it from the barrio called San Juan. The two parts of the city are joined by a stone bridge of considerable solidity. The fourth is named Catuche; the city owes to it the existence of an infinite number of public and private fountains, whose waters come from this stream.

These four rivers, having served for all the domestic uses of the city, meet in a single bed, cross the valley of Chacao, which abounds in fruits, viands and commercial produce, and finally mingle their waters with those of the Tuy, which flows into the Ocean.

STREETS

The streets of Caracas, like those of all modern cities, are rectilinear, oriented by the four cardinal points, more or less 300 feet apart and about 20 wide. This is the only regularity, the only symmetry which is noted in this fairly large city, which is nevertheless passably well constructed.

SQUARES

There are only three worthy of the name, nor are those free of irregularities. The so-called Plaza Mayor, which ought to be the best proportioned, is made ugly by some huts constructed on the south and east corners, which are rented to merchants for the profit of the Ayuntamiento. This plaza occupies a space of about 300 feet square. It is well pavemented and in it is carried on the sale of all provisions. Vegetables, fruits, meats, fish, fowl, game, bread, monkeys, parrots, sloths, birds, everything is sold there. It has two entrances to each side. The position of the cathedral on the east side is not in symmetry with the square.

The second square is that of Candelaria, surrounded with fair regularity by an iron fence planted in a rubble-work base of uneven height. The square, though not paved, has a clay floor mingled with sand which substitutes for the best pavement; as a whole it presents a most agreeable aspect, not, indeed, owing to the buildings which surround it, for none of these is worthy of attention. Only the church of Candelaria serves it as adornment; and if there is no geometric agreement between the square and the church, the latter has a pleasant façade which does not detract from the square.

The third is that of San Pablo; its only regularity is in its square form, and its only adornment a fountain placed in the center. On the southeast corner rises the church of San Pablo, which harmonizes with the square only in forming one of its sides.

Houses

The private houses are lovely and well built; there are many of two storeys in the city, with very fair appearance. Some are of bricks, but most are of mud walls with brick reinforcement.

The houses of the notables of the city are generally furnished with decency and even with richness. In them are seen beautiful mirrors, scarlet damask curtains in the windows and interior doors, chairs and sofas of wood whose seats, of leather or damask, are stuffed with horsehair, and which are worked in gothic style, though with excessive gilding; high beds whose raised canopies show an excess of gilt, covered with lovely mattresses of damask and many feather pillows with cases of rich mousselines adorned with lace; nevertheless there is only one bed of such magnificence in each big house; usually it is the nuptial bed which is only a showpiece.

One's glance also lingers on tables with gilded feet, chests of drawers on which the gilder has lavished the resources of his art, beautiful chandeliers hung in the principal apartment, cornices which seem to have been drowned in gold, superb carpets which cover at least the part of the room where the seats of honor are; for the furniture is arranged in the salons so that the sofa, essential part of the furnishings, is placed nearest one, with chairs to right and left, and at the other end the principal bed of the house, in a room whose door is always open, unless it is in an equally open alcove.

This sort of apartment, always extremely clean and very well decorated, seems forbidden to the inhabitants of the house. It is only opened, with very few exceptions, when someone comes to carry out the sweet duties of friendship or the weighty ceremonial of etiquette.

Public Buildings

The only public buildings of Caracas are those dedicated to religion. The Captain General, the Real Audiencia, the Intendant, and all the tribunals occupy rented houses. Even the military hospital is in a private house. The Counting House or Treasury is the only edifice belonging to the King, and its appearance hardly indicates the majesty of its owner.

The same cannot be said of the barracks; it is new, attractive, built elegantly, and placed on a site whence it dominates the city. It has two storeys and two patios. It can conveniently lodge 2000 men. It is occupied by troops of the line. The Militia have their barracks—that is, the house which does duty as such—at the other end of the city.

Archbishopric

The Archbishopric of Venezuela has its seat in Caracas. Its diocese is very extensive: on the north the sea limits it from the Unare River to the jurisdiction of Coro; on the east the province of Cumaná; on the south, the Orinoco; and to the west, the bishopric of Mérida. I have already said that it became an Archbishopric in 1803. Its annual rent depends on the abundance of the harvest and the price of the articles on which the tithe is collected.

Cathedral—Churches

The Cathedral does not merit description except for its position in the hierarchy of temples. It is a cause for surprise not to find, in a city so populous as Caracas and which so venerates the Christian religion, a Cathedral which corresponds in reality to the importance of the Archbishopric and the city itself. If lovely tapestries and gildings ennoble the interior of the church; if the priestly vestments and sacred vessels show richness which suits the temple to which they belong; its construction, on the other hand, its architecture, dimensions and proportion have nothing majestic, imposing or regular about them.

The architectural humbleness of the principal church has, however, its cause. I should explain it in order not to humiliate the

Caraqueños. The bishopric was transferred from Coro to Caracas in 1639; consequently up until then the Cathedral of Caracas could not exist, and when they began to execute the plan of a sumptuous temple, on June 11, 1641 at 8:45 A.M. there came a strong earthquake which caused much damage in the city; and it was considered as a warning of Providence that the edifice should be more suitable for withstanding catastrophes of this sort than for awakening admiration in the curious. From then on they thought no more of magnificence; indeed, they outlawed it to give the church more solidity.

In general the churches of Caracas are well built. The parish church of Altagracia is the best of all and its construction would honor the principal cities of France. The right of virtue to public esteem and admiration obliges me to state that the free pardos living near that church built and adorned it at their expense, aided by some contributions from whites.

RELIGIOUS PRACTICES

Like all Spaniards, the Caraqueños are proud of being Christians, and they are not wrong; but they are mistaken in thinking that to be Christians it is necessary to be ostentatious about religious practices. Surely God is not so well pleased by pomp as by the humility of his creatures. Charity, or the love of God and one's neighbor, is enough to make a man a Christian and a citizen. The Spaniards are very assiduous at divine service, that is to say, at mass on the prescribed days, at sermons and processions; for, though it is difficult to believe, they do not include vespers among their religious exercises, contrary to what is customary in France and in Spain itself.

The dress of the men for church-going is more or less similar to what we use. However, they have to go in a coat or wear cape or overcloak. Neither color nor social position exempt the wearing of one of these three habits.

The dress of the women, rich or poor, principally of the white women, must be rigorously black. It consists of a black skirt and cloak. Only the slaves are allowed to wear white cloaks.

The object of such a dress was to require the use of the veil, and with it outlaw from the church scandalous displays of luxury, seductive coquetteries, impure desires and lascivious glances, and, furthermore, to establish uniformity before the eyes of the Lord and prevent riches or social degrees from profaning the sanctity of the site. But this wise custom, like everything which comes from man's hands, has been corrupted with time, and of its primitive purity there remains today only the black color of dress.

If the latter, in the beginning, was to be the same for all women, and surely of inexpensive material, it is today much more varied and costly. The gauze cloaks reveal the traits and charms of the woman who wishes to delight herself in them. This dress, merely religious, for it is exclusively used to go to divine office, made of silk or velvet and adorned with rich lace, costs at least 400 to 800 pesos fuertes. If anyone is ashamed to have her poverty known, wearing less rich clothes, she imposes on herself all sorts of privations to rival the others.

Those who do not have the means to get adequate clothes to attend the ceremonies have to go to the masses which are said before dawn, whose object is precisely the comfort and spiritual benefit of those who lack sufficiently decent clothes to appear in church during the day.

HOLIDAYS

The Spaniards know no other holidays than those marked by the Roman calendar. In Caracas these are so many that very few days of the year are not celebrations for some saint or the Virgin. They are indefinitely multiplied because each fiesta is preceded by a novena, consecrated only to devotions, and is followed by an octava, during which the faithful of the quarter, and even the rest of the city, mingle public prayers with public diversions like fireworks, music, dances, etc. Nevertheless such holidays are never transformed into banquets. The feastings which, by the etymology of the word, should be the soul of feast days, and are truly so anywhere else, appear unknown to the Spaniards. This race is sober even in the delirium of pleasure!

The most brilliant features of such holidays are the processions. In general they take place in the afternoon. The saint, natural size, is richly dressed. They take him in very well decorated litters, followed or preceded by other saints of the same church gotten up less sumptuously. The men go in two rows. Each of the principal ones carries a candle; then comes the music, the clerics, the civil authorities, and finally, the women hemmed in by a barrier of bayonets. The cortege is always very large. Wherever the procession is to go the windows are adorned with floating hangings, and they give the barrio a pleasant festival aspect. In the windows shine forth women who have come from all over the city to enjoy so agreeable a spectacle.

The principal and almost exclusive devotion of the Spaniards is the Holy Virgin.

THEATER

The theater is the only public diversion of Caracas. There are performances only on holidays. The entry price—a real—is low enough to indicate the quality of the actors and the convenience and beauty of the spot. The works, very bad in themselves, are in addition very badly presented. Declamation is a sort of stammering monotone, like the tone in which a child of ten might repeat his badly learned lesson. Neither grace nor action nor inflection of the voice nor natural gestures; in a word, nothing of what constitutes an up-to-date actor. The comic actors of Caracas can be compared to those clowns who go from fair to fair, living not off the pleasure of their spectators, but off their pity.

Presumably nobody, after the description of such a spectacle, could imagine it other than always deserted or frequented by the basest populace, completely lacking in taste and education. However, I must undeceive him of such an error; rich and poor, young and old, hidalgo and peasants, governors and governed, all assiduously attend this theater.

SPORTS

In describing the public diversions of Caracas, I must not overlook the three courts on which are played ball (jai alai) with racket or bare hand. The Basques introduced this game, but have abandoned it to the inhabitants of the country, who observe the rules closely and, without developing so great a skill as their teachers, practice it well enough to amuse the fans who attend their matches.

A few deteriorated billiard tables, scattered around the city, on which nobody plays, form, so to speak, the remaining diversions of Caracas.

One would be mistaken, however, if he deduced from this scarcity of diversions that the Spaniards did not like gambling; this passion dominates them much more than us. One can justly call them temerarious gamblers. Neither when they gain nor when they lose do they show signs of impatience or pleasure. The sensations which good or bad luck produce in them are concentrated in their souls. In reality, only when they gamble do they seem to despise money. Until 1800 the authorities pursued the big gamblers who, to escape their vigilance, were obliged to move their meeting place frequently and to admit to their group only those who made up the game. But in the last three or four years only the poor are pursued by justice, imprisoned and condemned to fines for gambling. Among people of distinction the tacit right to ruin each other is enjoyed without the intervention of authority.

If Caracas possessed public walks, lyceums, reading rooms, cafés, now would be the time to speak of them. But, to the shame of this large city, I must say that here these characteristics of the progress of civilization are unknown. Each Spaniard lives in his house as in a prison. He goes out only to church or to fulfill his obligations. Nor does he try to sweeten his solitude with cultured games; he enjoys only those which ruin him, not those which might distract him.

POPULATION

According to the church census of 1802, the city of Caracas has 31,234 inhabitants. But, because of the inadequacy of this census, it may be calculated at 42,000 persons. This population is divided into whites, slaves, freed slaves and very few Indians. The whites constitute approximately a quarter of the total; the slaves form a third; the Indians a twentieth, and the rest are pardos.

Among the whites are six Castillian titles: three marquises and three counts. All the whites claim the title of hidalgo; but one should take the hidalguía of about a third of these at least as "titulo de inventario" (i.e., purchased). In reality, a white Spaniard never passes for a commoner except when he is in poverty.

All the whites are hacendados or businessmen, soldiers, clerics, or monks, court or treasury employes. None dedicates himself to mechanical arts or trades. The white Spaniard, and principally the Criollo, feels dishonored if he gains his living by the sweat of his brow or if he owes it to the callouses on his hands. He endures hunger, thirst, the inclemencies of the weather with admirable stoicism, moved only by horror of work; nothing, according to his criterion, can degrade a man so much as labor. He judges it impossible to maintain his dignity and honor his ancestors duly except with pen in hand, sword at belt, or breviary before his eyes.

WHITE EUROPEANS

In this city the Europeans form at least two clearly differentiated classes. The first comprises the employes from Spain. They give cause for complaint from the Criollos, who consider unjust the man who employs others and not themselves. The luxury in which these employes live also rivals that of the Criollos.

The second class of Europeans resident in Caracas is composed of those whom industry or the desire to make a fortune have brought to this spot. Almost all are originally from Basque country or Cataluña. Both are equally industrious, but the Basques without so much effort administer their businesses better. The Basques as well as the Catalans are distinguished among their fellow Caraqueños by their good faith in business and their promptness in paying.

The Canary Islanders, who, more out of necessity than ambition, abandon their native land to establish themselves in Caracas, are as hard workers as the Basques and the Catalans.

WOMEN

Ornaments of Caracas are its women, enchanting, gentle, simple, seductive. There are few blondes; the majority have jet-black hair and skin like alabaster. Their eyes, large and open, speak expressively that language common to all countries, but not to all ages. Their scarlet lips blend agreeably with the whiteness of the skin, and contribute to form that combination which is called beauty.

It is a pity that the stature of the Caracas women does not correspond to the harmony of their features. Very few are above middle height and many are below. Rare are those who have small feet. As they spend most of their lives at the window, one might say that nature has wished to beautify only the part of the body which they most frequently allow to be seen. They dress with considerable elegance. They lack much in manner, walk and grace.

In Caracas little is done for the education of men and nothing for that of women. There are no girls' schools. They therefore have no other education but what their parents give them, which is limited to much praying, bad reading and worse writing. Only a youth inflamed by love could decipher such scrawls. They are not taught music or dance or sketching. What they learn is summed up in routinely playing a little guitar or piano. Very few have even the first notions of music. Despite their defective education, Caracas women somehow manage to unite social graces with virtue and the art of coquetry with the modesty proper to their sex.

These observations are applicable only to those women whose fathers or husbands have some of fortune's goods or exercise lucrative employments, for the white women of Caracas whom fate has condemned to earning a living have no other available means than provoking the passions. More than 200 of these unfortunates spend the day covered with tatters in the depths of their small huts, which they are careful to keep always closed, and go out by night to earn by vice their crude sustenance. Their dress is usually a white skirt and cloak, with a cardboard hat covered with cloth and adorned with false flowers or sequins. This means of gaining a living is accompanied, or rather followed, by begging alms. Finally they dedicate themselves exclusively to begging when age or illness no longer allow them to count on the products of libertinage.

House Slaves

House slaves are very numerous in Caracas. It is believed that the wealth of a household is proportionate to the number of slaves in it. In each house there must be four times more than are really necessary. Anything else would pass for stinginess displaying poverty, and this must be hidden when possible. Any white woman, even though her fortune may not permit it, goes to mass followed by two mulatto or Negro women slaves. The truly rich take four or five slaves, and if someone else from the same house goes to church he or she takes along the same number. In Caracas there are houses which have 12 or 15 slaves, not counting the servants of the men.

Pardos and Freed Slaves

In proportion to other social classes probably there is not in all the West Indies a city with more pardos or descendants of freed slaves.

These exercise all the offices disdained by the whites. All the carpenters, woodworkers, masons, ironworkers, craftsmen, locksmiths and goldsmiths are pardos or descendants of freed slaves. In no office do they excel; for as they learn their trade by routine, they lack the principles of the art. On the other hand their natural indifference extinguishes in them the emulation to which the arts owe their progress. However, in carpentry and masonry they show a certain progress; but woodworking is still in swaddling clothes. All these artisans work very little, and though this appears contradictory, their work is much cheaper than that of the European worker. They live only thanks to their great sobriety in the midst of all sorts of privations. In general, overburdened with family, they live in poor houses, sleep on leather hides, and feed off the products of the country. The exceptions are very rare.

Their poverty is such that one cannot charge them with any work without their asking for a down payment. The ironworker never has iron nor coal, nor the carpenter wood, and they need money to get them. What happens, if one wants something done, is that one begins by compromising with the worker and becoming dependent on him. Nor can one thereafter have recourse to another, because one would run into the same difficulties. All one can do is get after them, keep an eye on them, and even then, there are the holidays, illnesses and trips, to strain the best-tempered patience to its last limit. So that one is very badly served, and above all, with much slowness.

UNIVERSITY

The education of the youth of Caracas and of the archdiocese as a whole takes place in the joint College and University. The founding of the College preceded that of the University by more than sixty years and was due to the pious zeal of Bishop Antonio Gonzalez de Acuña, who died in 1682. In the beginning only Latin was taught, and only lectures on Theology and Philosophy given.

With the growth of the city was born the idea of endowing it with wider and more varied means of instruction. The foundation of a university was solicited and granted by the Pope on August 19, 1722, and confirmed by Philip II [sic]. The installation took place August 11, 1725. The statutes were dictated and the King approved them May 4, 1727.

From this date and in virtue of these titles the city of Caracas possesses a university to which, as I have said, is annexed a college.

In this double institute there is a school of writing and reading.

Three Latin classes, in one of which Rhetoric is taught.

Two professors of Philosophy, one a secular or lay priest and the other a Dominican friar.

Four professors of Theology.

A professor of Civil Law.

A professor of Canon Law.

A professor of Medicine.

All the degrees of Bachiller, Licenciado and Doctor are received at the University.

At the University and College of Caracas there were present in 1802 64 students living in residence and 400 living out, divided thus:

Lower classes, Rhetoric included	202
Philosophy	140
Theology	36
Canon and Civil Law	55
Medicine	11
School of Plain Chant	22

From this greenhouse come the ministers of the church, the magistrates of justice and the defenders of the people.

POLICE

Among all known peoples, the Spanish are those who give the police least to do in maintaining public order. Their natural sobriety and, principally, their phlegmatic character, abhor the frequency of quarrels and tumults. In the streets of Caracas there is never noise. All go by silent, melancholy, grave. Three or four thousand persons come out of a church, and make no more noise than turtles crawling in the sand. In the same circumstances Frenchmen, weary of the silence they must observe during divine service, react in the opposite manner leaving church. Men, women and children with their conversations form a noise which can be heard at a good distance. Four times the number of Spaniards produces only the buzzing of a beehive.

But, if the magistrate does not have to fear noisy misdeeds, he cannot on this account be less vigilant and active. Murders, thefts, frauds, infidelities, require so much diligence and investigation, the employment of so many means, that they put to the proof the most acute zeal and the most penetrating sagacity.

Far from being free of it, the Spaniards feel perhaps more than any other race that vengeful spirit whose greatest danger lies in choosing the shadows to aim its blows and hide its rancour under appearances of friendship, in order to find more easily the opportunity to satisfy it.

When one who, by his social rank, should take personal vengeance, receives an affront, scarcely does he let his anger be seen, or hides it completely, but from that moment on he lets no chance pass to plant a dagger in the breast of his new enemy, and then immediately takes refuge in a church, so that the ecclesiastical court can present his premeditated crime as a happenstance, and this despicable homicide as a pardonable thing.

Almost all the murders in Caracas are the work of European Spaniards. Those imputable to the Criollos are as infrequent as the thefts attributable to the former. The white Criollos, or pretended whites, who have been drowned in abjection and filth by laziness and the vices engendered by it, and the freed slaves, to whom working for a living seems excessively laborious, are the only authors of Caracas thefts.

The adulteration of weights and measures, the falsification and adulteration of fruits and provisions, are also frequent crimes, because they are considered rather proofs of skill than pilferings.

Doubtless this would be enough to give work to the most vigilant police force. Many other things are in their charge: the feeding of the city, for example. Would you believe that Caracas, capital of provinces where enough cattle are raised to supply all the foreign colonies of America, often lacks butcher's meat? But so it is: Caracas, residence of a captain general, seat of an Archbishopric, of a Royal Audiencia, of the principal courts, with more than 40,000 inhabitants and a garrison of more than 1,000 men, suffers scarcity in the midst of abundance.

If in its (Caracas') streets garbage does not accumulate, it is the work of the rain, and not the care of the police, to which it is due.

In all countries, the police have to deal with begging. The police of Caracas seem to pay no attention to it at all. The streets swarm with poor of both sexes who live only by charity, and prefer to live by this means rather than work. Religion, very wrongly interpreted in this respect, prevents the Spaniard from inquiring whether the beggar, by his faculties, age or health, can gain a living without begging. He believes, or at least behaves as if he believed, that the Bible in praising charity recommended the man who begs it.

As soon as someone begins to beg he puts himself under the protection of the police rather than under its vigilance. At any hour beggars enter the houses. The crippled and the robust, the old and the young, the blind and he who enjoys good sight, all have an equal right to charity. Each gives or denies alms according to his own purse and not in accord with the need of him who begs.

Foreigners find it difficult to reconcile the blind charity of the Spaniards with the disagreeable picture of the poor stretched out in the streets during the night, in the shelter of the walls of the churches and the archbishop's palace, without any protection against the night air, so dangerous in the torrid zone, nor against any other inclemency of the weather. One has the impression of being in a barbaric country. But if one examines the matter closely, one understands that such disorder comes from an excess of piety. Those who seem in misery are only beggars whose drunkenness prevents them from seeking better shelter, and who do not go to sleep in the hospitals because, as these shut their doors early, they would not be able to spend on aguardiente what they have gathered during the day. The police know very well what goes on, but cannot oppose it, for if they did so it would be judged lack of charity. The livery of God which the beggar wears exempts him from obeying any regulation at all, shelters him from all censure, makes him inviolable.

To get some idea of the number of street beggars, it suffices to know that the Archbishop distributes a general alms every Saturday, each beggar receiving a half esquelino, or the sixteenth part of a peso fuerte, and that each time there is spent in this from 75 to 76 pesos fuertes, which corresponds to a minimum of 1200 beggars. In this list are not included the really poor, whose number is still greater, and among whom Don Francisco Ibarra, worthy Criollo prelate of Caracas, secretly divides his income.

COMMUNICATIONS WITH THE INTERIOR

Caracas, center of all the political, judicial, fiscal, military, commercial and religious affairs of its dependencies, is naturally the center also of all means of communication. The extent of the country and its small population indicate the state in which the roads may be found. The majority of them are only traced. The obstacles, the inundations, the lack of bridges and boats to cross the rivers, make the roads impassable during the rainy season, although indeed there is no period in which they are comfortable. They usually measure the distance by days and not by leagues. From my own experience, the day is calculated in ten leagues of 2,000 geometric paces each.

Such was Caracas in 1804—a provincial city of forty thousand, socially divided against itself, the little-known capital of a thinly populated province. Nevertheless, it was this Caracas which gave birth to and helped shape one of history's most important movements—the South American Revolution.

This South American Revolution, a war for liberty and sovereignty, was to fail in some of its more glorious aspects. Conditions like those which existed in Venezuela limited the results. For the most part, Latin Americans only succeeded in trading old oppressors for new ones. In Venezuela where the liberators suspected liberty, where domestic tyranny dwarfed tyranny from abroad, where education deformed rather than formed society, true freedom could not flourish. Unlike the United States, where citizens fought to preserve the considerations they had enjoyed as Englishmen for 150 years, Venezuela fought to acquire a political status for which it had no training. Ignorance and social disunion confounded the efforts of Venezuelan idealists who dreamed of Athens on the Caribbean.

Venezuela could sign a Declaration of Independence, but it could not sign away three hundred years of oligarchy. The sewer of political, social, economic, and moral corruption in which Venezuela had stagnated for three centuries could not be purified by ink, or even by blood.

Chapter VII

THE EVE OF REVOLUTION

IN THE BEGINNING the Venezuelan Revolution was a civil war. Only reactionary *criollos* and a few sincere idealists favored independence. The pardo, recognizing the *criollo* as an enemy, long remained loyal to Spain. The Indian and the Negro, indifferent to the fate of a country they did not regard as theirs, ignored the revolution until they found that fighting bore profits. Then they battled for whichever side offered the most booty. In this conflict of ideals and interests, one-third of the country's population perished.

Minor insurrections had occurred several times during Venezuela's colonial history. In the 1790's there were uprisings of Negroes in Coro and pardos in Maracaibo, but like most of the early revolts these had been motivated primarily by desires for personal rather than national freedom. The first armed conspiracy against Spainish rule did not evolve until 1797. In that year, two educated *criollos* organized a rebellion of dissatisfied planters and army officers.

José España and his friend Manuel Gual hatched plans for their abortive revolution with the help of four Spanish insurrectionists. The Spaniards had been shipped to dungeons in La Guaira for trying to start a "French" revolution in the Peninsula. Not a whit abashed, they spent their time in jail converting the guards,

99

the governor of the fortress, and any Venezuelans they could reach, including España and Gual, into republican patriots like themselves. Their friends arranged an escape on June 4, 1797, but the Spaniards fled to English sanctuaries and left the Venezuelans to stew in their own revolution.

The 1797 revolt was squashed before it began, thanks to a talkative conspirator. While being shaved one morning the indiscreet *criollo* suggested that the barber join the insurgents. A few days later the barber mentioned the incident to his confessor; the confessor hustled to another cleric, both to the provisor and the provisor to the captain general. The barber's client was imprisoned and his papers, incriminating other conspirators, were seized. In 1799 executioners hanged six of the top conspirators. Forty more were condemned to dungeons in Puerto Rico and Spain. Gual, who escaped, was poisoned in 1800 by a fanatical royalist. As for España, captured a year after the revolution fizzled, the Spaniards dictated an especially grisly sentence, one they reserved for revolutionary leaders. His sentence read:

It is commanded that: without the slightest delay except to grant the ordinary ministrations to his soul, he be taken from prison, tied to a horse's tail and dragged to the scaffold, the town crier shouting his crime along the way. Dying naturally at the hands of the executioner, his head is to be cut off and his body quartered. His head is to be carried in an iron cage to the port of La Guaira and put on top of a 30-foot spike that is to be driven into the ground at the entrance to that port from the town of Caracas. One of the quarters is to be displayed at the entrance to Macuto, where he hid other traitors to the state whom he took from prison and for whom he arranged an escape. Another of the quarters is to be put in Vigía de Chacón where he hid the said rebels to the state. Another is to be put in the place called Quitacalzón, up the river from La Guaira, where he took the oath of rebellion against the King. The remaining quarter is to be put in La Guaira where he planned to unite the people he proposed to command.

España's death insured him a martyr's halo. On the scaffold in what is now the Plaza Bolívar, he said, "The fire of Caracas is not extinguished. It will not be long before my ashes will be honored."

He was right. On the day Venezuela published its Declaration of Independence, July 14, 1811, Caraqueños paid homage to his sons on the very spot where twelve years before their father had been hanged.

Such eruptions in the colonies indicated that the remoteness of South America had not immunized it from the ideas which had freed the vast new United States and, through France, had cast Europe into turmoil. For this reason the España revolt seemed particularly important to one errant Venezuelan, who had lived for years in revolutionary centers and had preached South American liberty to such a strange assortment of powers as Catherine the Great, The French National Convention, Alexander Hamilton, and William Pitt. In 1806 he would bring the ideas and the might of North America and Europe to the shores of Venezuela.

Francisco de Miranda was an enigmatic figure. Disdained by the *criollos* of Caracas as the son of a merchant, yet acclaimed in all the capitals of Europe for his brilliance, erudition, and elegance; luxurious and infallible in his taste in clothes, houses, and books—bought with other people's money; a solitary exile who convinced hardheaded statesmen that he had but to land for the inhabitants of Venezuela to rush to his standard; fawned over by Philadelphia matrons, a favorite of Catherine the Great, a connoisseur of continental bordellos who had two children by his London housekeeper; a man who nourished grandiose illusions about his role and found them franked by history itself— each facet of his life adds to the complexity of his character.

Born in 1750 of a wealthy Caracas family, he attended the University of Caracas and completed his formal education in Spain. He decided to become a soldier and bought a captain's commission for forty thousand pesetas. Distinguishing himself in the Oran campaign of 1774 he won high praise from one of his commanders, Don Juan Manuel de Cagígal. On the other hand, he was three times arrested by superior officers who charged him with "disobedience," "insubordination," and neglect of duty. Through army estimates of his character one sees a highly intelligent officer, well aware of his own merits, dissatisfied with subordinate positions, and despising those who did not measure up to his intellectual, social, and cultural pretensions. His difficulties in Spain encouraged him to seek transfer to America. In 1780 he was detailed to the Caribbean with a detachment Spain sent to harass the British during the American Revolution. He helped besiege Pensacola and won the rank of lieutenant colonel.

When Miranda returned to Havana his old friend and army patron, Don Juan Manuel de Cagígal, now captain general of Cuba, appointed him his aide-de-camp. In this capacity Miranda made a semiespionage trip to Jamaica where it seems he paid for data on English forces by helping his informant smuggle English goods into Cuba.

Out of this incident arose a crisis which changed the course of his life and made him first a renegade and later Spain's archenemy. Rival officers spread a report that he had shown an English general Havana fortifications (false); and that he had helped smuggle contraband from Jamaica (probably true). The Spanish general Gálvez informed his government that Miranda exerted an evil influence among the soldiers and stimulated the jealousy of military commanders. In August 1782, Miranda was arrested and charged with smuggling. Declared guilty, he was deprived of his commission, sentenced to a heavy fine, and banished to Oran.

Miranda hadn't waited to hear the sentence. He had left for the United States, motivated at this turning point in his life by a disgust for Spain's treatment of him, a lifelong dream to further his education by a grand tour of North America and Europe, and a letter written in February of 1782. This letter, signed by Juan V. Bolívar (the Liberator's father), Martín de Tovar, and the Marqués de Mijares, said:

. . . we send you the information which we believe necessary in order that in our name and in that of our entire province you may make compacts or contracts with our full power and consent. Lastly, if you judge it convenient, you may treat with foreign powers in order to redeem us from this cursed captivity.

Though Miranda had told Cagígal on leaving Havana that he planned to lay his case before the king in Spain, a year later he was visiting Alexander Hamilton in New York and laying before him a plan for the liberation of Venezuela. The project interested Hamilton and other influential North Americans. Miranda's diary of acquaintances reads like a Who's Who of post-Revolutionary America: Baron von Steuben, Anthony Wayne, Gouverneur Morris, astronomer David Rittenhouse, George Washington, Thomas Paine, Samuel Adams, and Lafayette. He circulated in the best society of Charleston, Philadelphia, New York, and Boston, and when he left America for London in 1784 he had built a springboard which would help fling him at the throats of his enemies twenty-two years later.

After a short visit in England Miranda set out on a grand tour of the continent. He crossed the channel, admired the statue of Erasmus in Rotterdam, accepted an invitation to dine with King Frederick William in Prussia, sampled a brothel in Prague, inspected a letter written by Hernán Cortés in Vienna, chatted with Joseph Haydn in the gardens of the Esterhazy Palace in Hungary, browsed through the Medici library in Florence, saw the Pope celebrate mass at the Vatican, rode horseback through Athens, and tried to force his way into the Sultan's palace in Constantinople.

It was from Constantinople that Miranda embarked for Catherine the Great's Russia. When his ship reached the Crimea on December 31, 1786, "Count Miranda"—as he now styled himself—contrived to meet Gregory Potemkin, Prince of Taurus, the one-eyed paramour of Catherine.

Miranda enchanted the chief minister of Russia and the two were soon touring the Crimea together. Potemkin's intimate relations with Catherine smoothed the way for Miranda's presentation at the Czarina's court. The Venezuelan "count" bought a blue suit and a sword, traveled to Kiev, and kissed Catherine's hand on February 25, 1787. At dinner that night the Czarina plied the traveler with questions about the Spanish Indies and the Inquisition. Glib-tongued Francisco de Miranda charmed the fifty-eight-year-old monarch with practiced ease. Within two months Catherine was talking "about his person with the tenderness of a mother." (Legend has it that her affection was more than maternal.) She urged Miranda to stay in Russia and promised to make it worth his while. When he finally took his leave in late 1787, she gave him one thousand rubles and a letter in which all Russian ministers abroad were instructed to give him asylum should Spain try to molest him.

Sweden, Denmark, and Switzerland completed his circuit of Europe. He reached England in 1789. At this point he took a belated step. Miranda, who had been plotting against Spain for six years, put his feelings in writing and renounced his king.

The renunciation indicated that Miranda had been reassessing his relation to Spain as he made his flamboyant junket through the continent. The cause of South American liberty had preoccupied him constantly. He filled the ears of Catherine the Great and other notables with lurid accounts of Spanish excesses. In Italy he apparently contacted exiled Jesuits. The powerful Jesuits had performed important work converting and teaching uncivilized tribes in the Venezuelan llanos and jungles, among other places throughout the world; and when Charles III, under the influence of church-hating eighteenth-century enlighteners, banished the Jesuits from his entire realm in 1767 for reasons he refused to divulge, the Spanish crown made enemies of Jesuit supporters. This residue of hate was a resource which Miranda eagerly tried to tap.

Shortly after his return to England friends arranged a meeting with William Pitt, the Prime Minister. During the first six months of 1790 communications between the two were frequent. Among the many memoranda Miranda sent to Pitt was a proposal for governing the new South American nation he planned to found with England's help. It was to be called Colombia and would embrace most of South America, all of Central America, and the part of North America west of the Mississippi. Miranda favored a hereditary constitutional monarchy which would be restricted in its powers by a two-chamber house of representatives. This ideal of government became more centralized after Miranda witnessed the excesses of France's First Republic and grew more dubious of Latin America's capacities for democracy.

England saw in South American independence a means to weaken Spain and open profitable markets for English goods. In 1790 war with Spain seemed imminent. Pitt encouraged Miranda until October 1790, when Spain and England settled their controversy peacefully.

Disappointed at the breakdown of his negotiations with Pitt, Miranda took passage for France. Louis XVI was about to lose his head. Republicanism was rampant. Miranda wanted to know what liberal-minded Frenchmen would do to further the cause of South American liberty. The French were interested in Miranda's ideas, but war in Europe was sapping all their energies. If Miranda would lend his military talents to beleaguered France, the government would consider the plight of South America once the emergency had passed.

In 1792 Major General Miranda joined the French forces fighting Austria and Prussia in the north. In October he received the rank of lieutenant general and the command of eight divisions. By this time Louis had been executed; the Terror had begun. When Miranda failed to take Maestricht in Belgium and his men fled at Neerwinden, French authorities arrested him and hauled him before a Revolutionary Tribunal as a traitor.

At the trial Miranda saved his life—a rare feat in the biased courts of revolutionary France. Impressed by the testimony of witnesses in his favor, among them Tom Paine, and the fervor of the accused's eloquence, the jury unanimously declared him innocent. Even so, Miranda was not out of danger. The same month he won his acquittal the Girondists fell and the extremist Jacobins came to power under Robespierre, who loathed Miranda.

By July 1793, Robespierre had maneuvered Miranda into jail on a charge which was never stated. For the next eighteen months Miranda languished in La Force and Madelonnettes, improving his time by reading and talking to fellow prisoners. Resolved never to die by the blade in front of a cheering rabble, he had equipped himself with poison. At one point Robespierre personally inscribed the Venezuelan's name on an execution list. But it was Robespierre, not Miranda, who ended up in the Place de la Guillotine. In midsummer 1794 vengeful insurgents lopped off Robespierre's head. Fanatical French officials kept Miranda shuttling in and out of jail for the next two years on one pretext or another and when the Directoire included his name on a list of persons to be deported to Guiana in 1797, Miranda skipped to England.

Pitt welcomed him enthusiastically. France had declared war on England and trouble brewed with France's traditional ally, Spain. Miranda assumed this meant England would help him fit out an expedition. He sent a Cuban patriot to South America to report that aid could be expected at any moment. In February 1799, he wrote encouragingly to a Venezuelan exile in Trinidad, "The generals who are to command the expedition have been to see me about the affair," but by April he had to confess that the destination of the expedition had been changed and no one knew where it was going. Despairing again, he asked for a passport to go to the West Indies. When it was refused he made a short trip to Napoleon's France, where he was arrested and driven once more to English sanctuary.

For the next five years he continued to plead with successive English governments to abet South American revolution. Though England thought the project worth while and considered Miranda valuable enough to pay him a £700 annual living allowance, she never stopped hedging. In 1804 Miranda got fed up. England and Spain were fighting. The United States had started to grumble at Spain as well. Miranda had no time to waste on British hesitance. In September 1805, he embarked for the United States en route to South America.

Miranda had a fantastic plan. With or without official help, he had determined to drive Spain from the New World. In New York, he scurried about, contacting old friends. He painted florid verbal images of South American patriots trussing up Spain in her own chains. His magnetic manner, immaculate appearance, compelling arguments—his passion and his zeal—made cautious businessmen behave like romantic schoolboys. Samuel Ogden, a merchant, gave Miranda $20,000 to buy equipment. Colonel William Smith, Surveyor of the Port of New York, busied himself recruiting men and eventually entrusted his own son to Miranda's capricious care.

Nothing could stand in the way of Francisco de Miranda. When President Thomas Jefferson and Secretary of State James Madison told him they would not tolerate acts of hostility against Spain on U.S. territory, Miranda walked away from the conferences convinced that the American government had given him its tacit consent and would wink at his preparations to attack South America. This capacity for self-delusion was the tragic flaw in Miranda's character. His passion had destroyed his memory. While he talked of Spanish oppression, the glories of liberty, a new republic of free men, he seemed to forget that South America was not the United States, England, or France. The homeland he had not seen for thirty years was racked by internal hate, divided loyalties, and political immaturity. He dreamed of thousands flocking to his side on Venezuelan beaches—an ecstatic mob bent upon chasing the foreign tyrants into the sea. But true patriots, even counting those whose revolutionary motives were reactionary rather than liberal, numbered in the hundreds, not in the thousands.

Miranda and his American friends were confident. During the winter of 1805–06 they began to arm a ship. Military supplies were ordered. Meanwhile, Miranda dodged Spanish agents and tried to keep out of sight. The recruitment of a military force was carried on clandestinely. Duped by promises of good pay and other rewards, young men enlisted for duty "in the President's Guard" or to hunt for treasure in the Caribbean. Two hundred men, mostly callow youths, eventually signed up for an expedition whose purpose few, if any, of them knew.

On February 2, 1806, the 187-ton *Leander* put out to sea with its motley crew of adventurers. In the hold were 582 muskets, 16 blunderbusses and 29 cannon, as well as ammunition, cutlasses and sabers. A spanking northwest wind carried the *Leander* through the Narrows to the sea. At its masthead appeared a yellow, blue, and red standard, the flag Miranda had designed for his "Colombia."

Back in the United States, the Spanish ambassador had guessed Miranda's motives and the *Leander*'s destination. He warned his government and protested to Madison. The United States moved against Smith and Ogden in New York and indicted them for helping Miranda, a charge of which they were eventually acquitted.

The *Leander* bobbed toward the Caribbean. Several days out, General Francisco de Miranda, dressed in red gown and slippers, appeared on deck for the first time. He turned his personality on the recruits, regaling them with stories of his past and describing his ideas on politics. His friendly and fatherly attitude won him their respect and admiration. On the other hand, Miranda shocked them by engaging in a verbal brawl with the ship's captain. Commented one young witness to the scene, "A great deal of indecent warmth was shown on all sides, but in the highest degree by the general himself, who appeared, before the storm was over, more fit for bedlam than for the command of an army."

By this time, the purpose of the expedition had become known. "Colombian" soldiers who so recently had been studying or hauling freight or running errands in New York pored through manuals on the Art of War. They paraded around deck, responding to the uncertain commands of hastily appointed drill sergeants. They became artillerymen, riflemen, and light dragoons.

At Santo Domingo, where the ship tarried a month, Miranda procured two small vessels, the *Bacchus* and the *Bee,* as well as a few more recruits. His soldiers scattered among three poorly equipped ships, Miranda made his way toward the South American coast. The "Army of Liberation" reached Aruba on April 11. Miranda and his giddy crew attended to final details and prepared to strike a blow for freedom. Less than twenty-five miles away lay Venezuela.

Successive delays had given the defenders time to prepare. Spanish ships ranged the coast, waiting to annihilate Miranda, and on the night of April 27 off Puerto Cabello the revolutionaries sailed into a trap. Two Spanish vessels caught the expedition as it maneuvered to disembark. Outmanned and outgunned, the "Colombians" turned about and fled after forty minutes of fire. Pursued by the faster Spanish ships, Miranda's men dumped arms and ammunition overboard. The stratagem saved the *Leander,* which slipped away, but the smaller *Bee* and *Bacchus* were soon engaging the Spanish at close quarters.

The sixty Americans aboard held out tenaciously for thirty-six hours. They surrendered on April 29. Three months later the captors hanged ten of the lads, and decorated ten poles with their heads. The rest received prison sentences of eight to ten years.

Aboard the *Leander* Miranda sloughed off defeatism, rallied his dissatisfied and near-mutinous men, and led the crippled force to Trinidad. There, he convinced the authorities his venture had the support of the British government. Admiral Cochrane, anxious to win new markets for his country, promised British naval protection for Miranda's next landing and permitted him to recruit men in Trinidad and Barbados. With 300 soldiers, including 190

British militiamen, and an escort of English warships, Miranda landed under heavy coastal fire near Coro on August 3.

By the time he reached Coro, the city was deserted. Royalist officials, fearful that slaves might defect to Miranda, had evacuated the area. Miranda established himself in the city, published bold pronouncements calling "Colombian citizens" to his colors, and ordered the Spanish government to cease functioning at once. Not quite so confident as he sounded, he lived near the city gate, protected by a bodyguard and with a saddled horse close by to whisk him away in case the Spaniards attacked.

Miranda waited several days for his countrymen to rally round his standard. Not only were Venezuelans not flocking to the "Colombian" flag, they were instead subscribing money to defend themselves from the "perfidious traitor" and enlisting by the hundreds in a force which was rapidly being assembled to drive the invaders from Venezuelan soil. When a Spanish army of 5,500 began to slip through the hills toward the coastal plain surrounding Coro, Miranda hastily retreated to the coast. A Spanish vanguard of regular soldiers supplemented by Negro and Indian recruits chased Miranda back to his ships on August 13. The General sailed to Aruba and then to Grenada.

Still anxious to attack, Miranda had to admit final defeat when the British refused to extend him more aid. At Grenada "Colombian soldiers" enthusiastically discarded their uniforms and badgered destitute Miranda for back pay. The owner of one of the ships clamored for his money. Miranda had to disappoint his creditors. He was bankrupt. After a year in Trinidad, he sailed sadly back to England and his Grafton Street home.

So Venezuela remained in 1806 firmly attached to the dynasty of Spain, despite the promises of help some of Miranda's countrymen had held out to him. His arrival had been more of a surprise to patriots than to the Spanish officials, who had been informed. Moreover, a certain number of the *criollos* suspected Miranda's British connections. They weren't willing to exchange Spanish rule for English. Phrased by an Argentine patriot of the era, their cry was, "We want the old masters or none."

As it turned out, the cause of Venezuelan Independence received its greatest assist, not from armed invasions nor from *criollo* conspiracies, but from Napoleon Bonaparte. His imperial eagle was spreading its wings over the continent of Europe and nation after nation was disappearing into their shadow. Traditional friendship protected Spain no more than traditional enmity protected Prussia. Spain with its feeble king and degenerate heir offered tempting grounds for bloodless conquest, or so it seemed. Napoleon's attempt to control Spain set off several chain reactions. One of them ended with his own downfall while another ended in the final dissolution of Spain's continental empire in the New World.

Charles IV of Spain was an incompetent fool. He was married to a scheming, unfaithful, and selfish woman who completely controlled him. Charles IV entrusted Spanish affairs to a useless opportunist named Emanuel Godoy, whose only recommendation for the post of Chief Minister of Spain seems to have been his capacity to keep the Queen entertained after dark. While María Luisa of Parma and Godoy frolicked and the King looked the other way, Spanish power and prestige descended to new depths. By 1795 Godoy's ineptness had made Spain a virtual minion of France. Such was Napoleon's contempt for Spain that he ceded Trinidad to Britain without even consulting Madrid and sold Louisiana to the United States despite his explicit promise never to yield the territory except to Spain.

Naturally enough, Charles IV was not popular with the Spaniards. In 1808 some of his subjects revolted at Aranjuez. They made Charles abdicate in favor of his son, Ferdinand.

Napoleon had Spain where he wanted her. Spaniards were confused, the royal house divided. The French Emperor made the most of it. He refused to recognize the abdication on the grounds that it had been forced. The old King and Queen repaired to his camp at Bayonne. French troops took Madrid. Only one twist of the screw remained—or so Napoleon thought—before Spain would be undone.

With specious promises he lured Ferdinand to Bayonne. Presiding smugly as Spain's royalty vied with each other to degrade themselves before him, Napoleon ordered Ferdinand to give the crown to his father, and after he was physically beaten, Ferdinand complied. In that instant Spain's monarchs gave their birthright

to France. For Charles accepted the crown from Ferdinand only
to hand it to Napoleon, who passed it on to his brother Joseph.
The king of Spain was now a Bonaparte. Charles and Maria were
pensioned. Ferdinand was jailed.

Shocked and angered by this summary treatment of their monarchs, many Spaniards refused to accept Joseph as their king. The
Spanish people, who had never figured in Napoleon's calculations,
became his nemesis. They formed local governments to work for
the restoration of Ferdinand. They built local guerrilla forces to
fight the French. These scattered troops allied themselves with
England; the local governments named a central executive, the
Junta Central, in 1808, and the Peninsular Wars began. Instead of
a docile mob to ply as he wished, Napoleon had a hostile citizen
army to contend with. He never really defeated the valiant Spanish people whose resistance helped destroy his European empire.

Three thousand miles away Venezuela drowsed in the tropical
sun, unaware as yet of the events shaking Spain. Early in the summer, distressing rumors began to spread through the province.
No one paid much attention to them until July, when French com-
missioners arrived in Caracas to seek recognition of the new Spanish king.

The captain general, Don Juan de las Casas, was in a quandary.
The French domination of Spain had been achieved with every
semblance of legitimacy. He had no official reason to oppose the
usurpation. On the other hand, he could imagine what Venezuelans might do should they learn the whole story. In the end the
people, as in Spain, did the deciding. Learning from an indiscreet
French officer that the royal family were actually prisoners of
Napoleon, they crowded before Las Casas' home, forced him to
swear allegiance to Ferdinand, and hunted the French commis-
sioners out of Venezuela.

Public tension was further heightened when an English warship arrived with the news that a Central Junta had been formed
and had made an alliance with Great Britain. The captain general, unable to decide whether he should support France or England, consulted with a citizen's committee. Members of the committee couldn't make up their minds either. Meanwhile, Las Casas

veered from indecision to imprudence by arresting three important *criollos* on suspicion of fomenting rebellion, by rejecting the proposition of the Caracas cabildo that a junta like that in Spain be set up, and later by arresting and exiling from the city another group of responsible citizens who proposed the same thing.

At this point Las Casas was replaced by Vicente Emparán, former governor of Cumaná. Emparán, though a loyal subject, capable soldier, and able administrator, soon made as many mistakes as his predecessor. He too attacked prominent members of the colony for revolutionary leanings, encouraged anonymous denunciations, and irritated both the cabildo and the Audiencia.

Most Venezuelans were still loyal to Spain and anxious only to see some decisive measures taken for the liberation of the motherland and the restoration of Ferdinand. The captain general's refusal to act strained public patience. The moment seemed ripe for those who had been talking and thinking independence. These men wanted complete freedom, not just a junta loyal to an imprisoned Spanish king. However, they had the sense to realize Venezuela was not yet ready to support independence. The formation of a junta connected with Spain only by a tenuous link constituted a huge stride toward the ultimate goal. Ferdinand might still rule Venezuela in name, but the actual power would be wielded by members of the *criollo* class.

Only Emparán stood in their way. In early 1810 the *criollos* plotted to kidnap the captain general but Emparán frustrated the attempt. In April, the revolutionaries received another assist from Napoleon.

The French had overrun Spain. The Junta Central had fled, charging a five-man regency council with its duties. The Regency Council, though loyal to Ferdinand, ruled an imaginary realm. Except for Cádiz and the island of León the French controlled the entire peninsula.

Venezuelans learned of this sequence of events on April 17 when a ship arrived at La Guaira with two Spanish officials seeking Venezuela's recognition of the Regency Council. Emparán published the news the next day. The word streaked through Caracas. Loyal Spaniards were disturbed. Revolutionaries moved into action and lobbied in the streets. Spain had been destroyed and the Regency

Council represented nobody, they argued. Why should Venezuela obey its orders?

Community leaders met to make plans on the night of April 18. They decided to form a Venezuelan junta, still faithful to the imprisoned king but independent of any existing Spanish authority. The Caracas cabildo was delegated to meet with the captain general.

The cabildo waved aside legal procedure and called the meeting, despite the fact that it was the captain general's prerogative to convene all sessions. Moreover, they asked Emparán to appear before them.

It was Maundy Thursday morning, April 19, 1810. The cabildo attended church together and retired to their meeting rooms across the square. Ignoring the cabildo's slight to his dignity and position, a serene and confident Emparán marched into the chamber. He calmly listened while members campaigned for the formation of a Venezuelan junta. Then he answered their arguments. He claimed Spain had an adequate government in the Council of Regency and chided the cabildo for speaking of anarchy in a province like Venezuela where opposing parties and enemy bands did not exist. His arguments carried such weight that many members of the cabildo were satisfied. Emparán left to attend mass.

As soon as the captain general quitted the room, the cabildo suddenly realized what it had done. Opponents of Emparán's autocratic views had bared their revolutionary tendencies. He now knew who they were and might order their arrest. The captain general was at that moment walking briskly toward the cathedral where army officers and other royalist officials had gathered to hear mass. But on the cathedral steps a patriot named Francisco Salías grabbed Emparán by the arm and ordered him to return to the meeting. People in the plaza began to shout. A platoon of soldiers nearby started to ready its arms when an army officer, a revolutionary himself, ordered the soldiers to relax. Shocked and flustered, Emparán allowed himself to be led back across the square. As he passed through the square a corps of soldiers, his erstwhile subordinates, did not bother to salute him. Totally disconcerted, Vicente Emparán entered the council chamber.

The cabildo sat down once more to defy the will of Spain, but the members didn't know how. No sooner had they formed the Junta Suprema than they proposed to make its most effective opponent, Vicente Emparán, president of the body. As junta president, Emparán would again be in a position to destroy them all. The cabildo had begun to draw up the official act when into the room burst a self-styled "representative of the people," a priest who had come to save cabildo members from themselves.

Cortes Madariaga, a Chilean and the Canon of the Caracas Cathedral, had been listening to confessions across the square as the cabildo meddled with Venezuela's fate. From passers-by he heard what the cabildo was about to do. Gathering his robes about him, he dashed from his confessional and hustled through the plaza to the cabildo chamber.

He was passionate, an eloquent orator, a sincere liberal. Employing every stratagem at his command, Cortes Madariaga denied all Emparán had said. He claimed he had letters from Spain to prove that the captain general had been hiding the truth. He asked for Emparán's removal. It was the will of the people and the clergy, he said.

Madariaga swayed the cabildo. The captain general had only one recourse left. He decided to appeal to a crowd which had gathered outside the chamber in response to the excitement. Confident of the common man's loyalty, Emparán went out on the balcony and asked the citizens below if they were satisfied with his rule. Madariaga had appeared behind him. Shaking his head and gesturing "no," the Canon prompted the crowd. Patriots below followed his lead. *"No le queremos,"* ("We don't want you") they chanted. The crowd, influenced by what seemed to be a universal sentiment, took their cue. *"No le queremos,"* they yelled. *"No le queremos!"* Surprised and hurt, Emparán replied with dignity, "Then I don't want to command." Cabildo secretaries wrote his remark into the minutes as a voluntary resignation. Venezuela had no captain general. The first round of the revolution was over. A few days later the patriots, observing full military honors, packed Emparán aboard a ship bound for the United States.

Chapter VIII

PRISONERS OF HOPE

To MOST VENEZUELANS the formation of the Junta seemed a guarantee of continued loyalty to Ferdinand. But the Junta was *criollo* dominated. Many of its members believed a return to Spain, even a Spain free of Napoleon, pointless and against their own interests. Posts of first importance were given to patriots whose loyalty to independence was unquestioned. Many former officials were dismissed or banished. To consolidate its popularity, the Junta wiped out the most irritating traces of Spanish rule. It removed duties from articles of prime necessity, abolished the head tax on the Indian population and formed a society to encourage agriculture.

At the same time, the Junta sent representatives to Coro, Barinas, Maracaibo, Barcelona, Margarita, and Cumaná to convince the people of those provinces that the new government had acted for the welfare of all Venezuelans. Margarita, Cumaná, and Barinas quickly supported the Junta, but Maracaibo, Coro, and eventually Barcelona declared for the Council of Regency. In Maracaibo and Coro the delegates from Caracas were arrested and turned over to the Spaniards.

While strengthening its position at home, the Junta turned its attention abroad. Manifestations of loyalty to Ferdinand and an offer of asylum to any Spaniards wishing to escape the French were addressed to Cádiz. With an eye toward strengthening its position against possible retaliations by Spain, the Junta prepared to send a mission to London. Venezuela wanted assurances that Great Britain would protect it from common enemies and would mediate to keep the peace between Spain and her rebellious empire should trouble develop. For this important piece of diplomacy the Junta chose Colonel Simón Bolívar and Luis López Méndez. Andrés Bello, poet and scholar, was named secretary to the mission.

In London, the Venezuelans wrung nothing but vague promises from the English government. Spanish-American independence had become a touchy subject in England. To bolster its anti-Napoleon campaign, the British government had made alliances with the free Spaniards. The Prime Minister obviously could not make explicit arrangements with Bolívar and López Méndez, whose government had defied England's ally, the Council of Regency.

The London mission had one tangible result. It precipitated the return of Francisco de Miranda to Venezuela.

The old conspirator had holed up in his Grafton Street home following his naïve attempt to invade Venezuela. During subsequent years he wrote prolifically about Latin-American independence. When Bolívar and his friends arrived in London, Miranda was one of the first persons they contacted. It was impetuous Bolívar, acting without approval of his government, who invited Miranda to return. Despite objections of the British, who feared the General's trip to Venezuela might prejudice their relations with the Council of Regency, Miranda prepared to leave.

Miranda's return posed a problem for the Junta. Since it seemed contradictory to govern in the name of Ferdinand VII and give asylum to the foremost exponent of Latin-American independence, the Junta decided to bar the General from Venezuela. Later it relented in response to public protest. Miranda, dressed in the blue tunic, white trousers, black boots, sword, and two-cornered hat of a French general, disembarked at La Guaira on December 12, 1810, to the cheers of a crowd waiting to greet him. A few hours later, followed by enthusiastic patriots and well-wishers, he rode into Caracas on a white charger. The Junta, forgetting its earlier attitude, appointed him a lieutenant general. Miranda was the man of the hour. And the hour was critical.

In 1810 and 1811 enemy forces threatened Venezuela both from within and without. The French still menaced the Spanish Indies. Spain's Council of Regency lent an unappreciative ear to the province's declarations of loyalty to Ferdinand, considered the Junta a band of rebels, and ordered a blockade of Venezuelan ports. Spain issued licenses to privateers and subjected Venezuela both to naval raids and the more ruthless depredations of pirates.

Venezuela itself seethed with discontent, counterrevolution and intrigue. Conspiracies had been formed by Spanish residents to overthrow the Junta. Royalists in Maracaibo, Coro, and Guayana plotted to destroy the patriots and the first blood of the revolution was shed in Coro during November 1810 when three thousand Venezuelan troops attacked the pro-Spanish center.

Even within those areas where it exercised nominal control the Junta faced grave threats to its existence. It could not count on the support of the people in whose name it governed. Some citizens were bewildered royalists, some eager republicans. The great mass didn't care.

Public tolerance of the government was severely strained when the Junta issued paper money backed only by the revenues from its tobacco monopoly. Depending as the money did on a good crop and the chance of getting a good price for it, the people had no confidence in the bills. Because no one wanted to exchange goods for paper, prices rose, materials became scarce, and those on fixed incomes, the soldiers of the patriot army in particular, suffered severely.

To strengthen public morale the Junta abdicated its power to a more representative body. In March 1811, the first Venezuelan congress, composed of representatives from Caracas, Barinas, Barcelona, Cumaná, Mérida, and Trujillo, convened in Caracas. A distinctly confused body, without any practice in parliamentary methods or any firm conception of what its duties were, the Congress spent four months sorting out rules of procedure and practicing its authority on minor issues before it came to the great question which had been fermenting in the minds of its members and their constituents alike.

In early July the issue of independence raged in the halls of the Federal Palace. Excitement in Caracas was intense. Young idealists under the leadership of Francisco de Miranda and Simón Bolívar had been waging a propaganda campaign for months. They promised peace and plenty to the man in the street, blaming Spain for all of Venezuela's ills. A majority of Congress favored a declaration of independence, but many members wanted to wait until the government was stronger. To the cheers and hisses of the galleries crowded with spectators, supporters and enemies of an immediate declaration alternately took the floor. The republicans wished to finish the debate and take a vote on July 4th so that Venezuela might declare its independence on the same date as the United States. The Fourth of July came and went. The debate continued until July 5th when congress voted. Thirty-eight of the forty-four deputies signed the declaration. By solemn act, Venezuela became a confederation of free, sovereign, and independent states.

The document based its argument for independence on Ferdinand's abject transfer of his powers and his subjects to Napoleon at Bayonne. The Founding Fathers claimed Ferdinand had forfeited the right to rule over free men. Spain, the document reads, "despite our protests, our moderation, our generosity and the inviolability of our principles, against the will of our European brothers, declared us in a state of rebellion, blockaded us, combated us, sent agents to set us against one another, and tried to discredit us in the eyes of all the nations of the world, seeking their aid to subjugate us." Thus driven by events, Venezuela, first of all the Spanish colonies, proclaimed its separation from Spain.

For the province of Barcelona this irrevocable act was signed by the deputy from Pao, Francisco de Miranda. The veteran conspirator had taken an active role in the shaping of the Venezuelan Republic. From the moment he stepped once more on Venezuelan soil until the tragedies of 1812 destroyed him, his destiny was inextricably linked with the fate of the young nation. Largely through the efforts of Bolívar, who had installed Miranda in his own household and had introduced him reverently to the ardent and noble patriot youths of the colony, the lonely adventurer of Coro to whom Venezuela had offered not a single recruit became the Father of his Country and the patron saint of independence. Miranda eagerly accepted the role for which all his life had been a rehearsal. It was Miranda who inspired the club of revolutionary youths whose violent diatribes on behalf of freedom had finally goaded Congress into action; it was he who chose the flag of the new republic, the same yellow, blue, and red banner under which he had landed at Coro.

The Declaration of Independence did not make Venezuela a free, united, and sovereign nation. It only said so. After the signing of the document the government had as many enemies and was threatened from as many sides as before. Priests, Spaniards and pardos ranted against the republicans and argued for the restoration of Spanish rule. Six days after Congress voted to declare Venezuela's independence sixty Canary Islanders rode on horseback through the streets of Caracas, cursing the revolutionaries, hailing the Virgin and shouting royalist slogans. The government arrested the demonstrators, hanged the ringleaders a few days later, and displayed their bloody heads at prominent locations throughout the city.

In July Congress learned that Venezuelan royalists had seized Valencia. When the Valencians later repulsed troops sent to reconquer the city the government reluctantly asked Miranda to take over command of the patriot forces. It was a belated appointment. Miranda, the former French lieutenant general, had a more spectacular military record than any officer in the republic. However, the aging conspirator who had lived so long on British funds also had many enemies. The government preferred to employ commanders in whose affiliations and talents patriots had complete faith.

Though Miranda accepted the assignment, he attached a peculiar condition. He insisted that Lieutenant Colonel Simón Bolívar not participate. No one knows what caused this estrangement between two men who were only a few weeks before fast friends. Yet in view of their competing talents—their vanity, their ambition, their inclination to lead—the fact that misunderstandings arose is not surprising.

Miranda and the Marqués del Toro, who had effected a compromise by naming Bolívar his adjutant, marched on Valencia during the third week of July. In a month-long campaign the patriots forced the rebels to capitulate, but Miranda received no congratulations from Congress for the victory. Disturbed by charges of harsh discipline, shedding of unnecessary blood, and the levying of forced contributions, the government demanded an explanation and ordered the General to Caracas. As in France, Miranda's eloquent presentation of his point of view spiked his critics, at least temporarily.

With the impetus produced by the Valencia victory, the republicans might have chased their weak and ill-equipped royalist opponents in Coro and Maracaibo out of the country. Instead all the patriots, Miranda and Bolívar included, repaired to Caracas for debates on the kind of constitution the new country ought to have. Both Miranda and Bolívar favored a strong central government, but a majority of the convention sought to model the infant state on the United States of America. At a time when the nation desperately needed unity, Congress approved a federal form of government with seven locally autonomous states, and a national administration charged with powers affecting only the mutual interests of the constituent entities. Emphasizing the inappropriateness of the model, Rafael María Baralt and Ramón Diaz in their *Resumen de la Historia de Venezuela,* point out:

"The United States of North America was a republic before its separation from the mother country; there, the participation of citizens in public affairs and in the payment of taxes, the responsibilities of public officials, the administration of justice by juries, the entire theory of liberty was learned, practiced, and perfected during the Colonial period. . . . What similarity was to be found then between the people of North America and the people of Venezuela? Not the slightest." Of the First Venezuelan Constitution, the same authors say, "No ancient or modern political code could have conceded to the Venezuelan of 1811 more in philanthropy of principles, in consecrated respect for individual or popular rights, in precautions taken against despotism. But never did any nation adopt a constitutional law less suitable to the circumstances, more in contradiction to its interests, or less revolutionary in its results."

This Venezuelan constitution, the first of twenty-two (to date), lasted exactly three months. In April 1812, Francisco de Miranda became Venezuela's first dictator. While the patriots had been writing and signing the constitution, the royalists had strengthened their positions in both eastern and western Venezuela. Reinforcements had arrived from Spain's Caribbean bastions. By the time the constitutionally endowed Congress met at Valencia, the new capital, on March 16, the royalists had already taken the offensive. The day before Congress convened an inexperienced naval captain named Domingo Monteverde led a band of royalists into the settlement of Siquisique near Coro and claimed it for Ferdinand. Six days later he occupied the more important village of Carora.

Conditions favored the royalist cause. Venezuelans, even some of those who had originally supported the patriots, were fed up with government mismanagement. Paper money, internal disruption, and Spanish blockades had reduced the country to an economic shambles. The rabble remembered the relative prosperity and peace of the colonial period and proceeded to blame the government for conditions it could not control. Compared to the swelling multitude of dissatisfied slaves, disinterested Indians, hostile pardos, disillusioned republicans, and avowed royalists, the patriot ranks seemed slimmer than ever. Then, on March 26, 1812, the unpopular and threatened First Republic of Venezuela received its coup de grâce.

The morning and early afternoon of March 26, 1812, brought beautiful weather to the mountain valleys of Venezuela. The sky was clear; the air calm. It was Maundy Thursday and religious Venezuelans flocked to mass. Toward four o'clock in the afternoon, the heat became oppressive. A few drops of rain fell from a cloudless sky. At seven minutes after four, an earthquake began to shake the ground from La Guaira to Mérida. Cathedral roofs crashed. Public buildings tumbled. Whole neighborhoods disappeared. In twenty seconds, the most important cities of Venezuela were rubble. The screams of the injured rent the dust-filled air in Caracas, Valencia, Barquisimeto, Trujillo, and Mérida. Only three houses remained standing in La Guaira. San Felipe vanished. At least ten thousand Caraqueños died. Survivors picked through mutilated remains to find their loved ones. Others, fearful of a new tremor, rushed from the cities to surrounding hills. Thieves began plundering partly damaged shops and homes.

The tremors had hardly stopped before priests and royalists began to point out that the earthquake had occurred on Maundy Thursday. The republicans had usurped the power of the captain general, Vicente Emparán, on Maundy Thursday, 1810. God had visited an earthquake upon Venezuela to punish it for betraying the King. To the credulous, this seemed obvious. They knelt among the ruins, begging God and King Ferdinand for forgiveness. They ran through the streets, cursing the "traitors." Men and women gathered in the plazas and on rubble-strewn street corners to hear priests alternately pray to God and anathematize the patriots. The Church also used the occasion to impress the ignorant populace with the wickedness of sin in general. As a result, more than five hundred repentant couples went to Caracas altars within the next three months.

Word soon reached Caracas of the disasters in other cities of the republic. The theory that the earthquake had been caused by heavenly wrath gained added plausibility. Royalist centers like Coro, Maracaibo, and Guayana escaped unscathed. Even in affected cities the tremors seemed to make a distinction between royalist and republican strongholds. Eight hundred patriot soldiers in Caracas perished when their quarters collapsed. Troops in La Guaira and more than five hundred volunteers in Barquisimeto suffered the same fate.

In ruined Valencia, the Venezuelan Congress did what it could. The government issued manifestos explaining the catastrophe in rationalistic terms. It appealed to foreign countries for food and clothing. On the streets and in the plazas patriots tried to counteract church propaganda. Among them was the future liberator, Simón Bolívar.

Like other Caraqueños, Bolívar had rushed into the street when the first shocks began to rock the city. He helped dig out people trapped beneath toppled masonry and led others to safety. When he saw a monk preaching royalist propaganda to a crowd, he threatened to kill the cleric if he didn't keep quiet. Meeting a well-known royalist on the street, Bolívar yelled defiantly, "If nature opposes us, we will fight her and bend her to our will."

But the first Venezuelan Republic needed more than brave words. She needed brave men—thousands of them. Domingo Monteverde, the unknown naval captain, was moving on Barquisimeto, driving his ill-clad, hungry soldiers toward the heart of shattered Venezuela.

An uncouth, unlettered, and unprincipled man, Domingo Monteverde was to pyramid insubordination into the captain generalcy of Venezuela. The obscure officer from the Canaries had violated his instructions by marching on Carora after his capture of Siquisique. He continued to ignore these original orders until he had forced the republicans to their knees.

In the wake of the Maundy Thursday earthquake, Monteverde moved on Barquiṣimeto. Priests rushed out to meet him, welcoming him as a savior. He took the devastated city without firing a shot on April 7.

Congress debated what to do. Republican soldiers were deserting. Mérida and Trujillo declared for the King. Drastic action was necessary. On April 23 Congress scrapped the constitution and gave Venezuela to Francisco de Miranda. Awarded unlimited powers to cope with the situation, Miranda chose the title of "Generalissimo" instead of "Dictator," and set up his headquarters in Maracay.

The work of reorganizing the republican army began immediately. Miranda sent ragged troops to stem Monteverde's advance at Valencia. Requests for men and equipment were despatched to Cumaná and Barcelona. On May 3, Monteverde took Valencia. Afraid of rapidly-mounting royalist sympathy among Valencianos, the republicans had evacuated the city without giving battle.

Monteverde had bluffed himself into a very uncomfortable position. No one had been more surprised than he at his easy conquest of western Venezuela. His troops were untrained and ill-equipped. An expedition organized to capture one insignificant village had pushed more than eighty leagues into enemy territory. Strong republican detachments at Puerto Cabello and Barinas could easily outflank Valencia. Only a few hours march away stood the main force of the republican army, led by a famous and experienced commander.

Disaster had been Monteverde's ally. So had disloyalty in republican ranks. At a place called San José on the road to Valencia, he had faced certain defeat by a larger Venezuelan force. He won the battle when part of the republican army deserted to him. In Valencia, however, Monteverde began to shake at his own temerity. After one excursion outside the city limits his army was reduced to 500 men. Only 4,000 bullets remained. Coro, the nearest royalist center of any strength, was several days' march away.

Things were almost as bad in the republican camp. Gathering his scrubby and unhappy soldiers around him, Miranda prepared to drive Monteverde from Valencia. He sent out an advance guard to clear the way, but when he learned that these units had been defeated on May 8 following the desertion of several companies, the Generalissimo called the remnants back to Maracay where he could keep an eye on them, and decided to give his army some belated training. He drilled his rough horde and introduced it to discipline. He concentrated on making his position at Maracay impregnable.

But the royalists had resorted to flanking movements. Monteverde took the heights above Maracay and forced Miranda to abandon his prepared positions on June 17. Though the General routed Monteverde before La Victoria, he could not follow up his advantage. For three weeks a force of royalist bandits had been threatening Miranda from the south. These royalists had captured San Juan de los Morros on May 23. They unleashed a reign of terror in the area, killing innocent women and children as well as republican soldiers. They had outflanked Miranda three weeks before he evacuated Maracay and probably influenced his decision to retreat. At La Victoria he was in a better position to protect Caracas from both Monteverde and the royalists in the south.

Miranda's inept defense of the First Republic gives his critics plenty of ammunition. They jeer at his efforts to train his army and provide it with enough backbone to keep it from running away. They shake their heads at Miranda's reluctance to attack. Certainly the gallant old man's military exploits of 1812 can inspire no admiration. On the other hand, they seem partially explicable in view of the prevailing conditions.

Miranda had an army on which he could not rely in battle. Many of his officers openly opposed him. Field battles with the royalists seemed to serve only as a vehicle for republican desertions. The patriot cause had lost public support. The people wanted peace to rebuild their cities and nurse their wounds. It seems unlikely that any tactics could have saved Venezuela in 1812, though a more imaginative, aggressive and daring officer might have preserved the life of the First Republic longer than Miranda did.

Miranda showed a tendency to overestimate the strength of the enemy. His raw and unreliable troops outnumbered the royalists, who though more reliable were no less raw. The republicans had five thousand men. The royalists, even at peak strength, had only about three thousand. The patriot forces might have been expected to win, by sheer weight of numbers, a deciding free-for-all, if not a battle which would please the trained eye of a European general. However, it seems just as possible that the republican penchant for desertion might have upset the statistics before the first shot of this hypothetical battle was ever fired. Whatever Miranda's motives in retreating may have been, they could not have been inspired by cowardice. The man who in 1806 had dared to assault a united Spanish America with a few hundred mercenaries and some borrowed ships could scarcely have lost such audacious zeal and patriotic devotion in six years, though he might with increasing age have exhausted some of his competence to deal with an overwhelming situation. At any rate, he appeared less competent as the situation became more overwhelming. Finally, when Venezuela stood on the brink of disaster, Miranda shrugged and philosophically pushed her over the edge.

The Generalissimo had delegated the defense of Puerto Cabello to Simón Bolívar. Puerto Cabello was strategic. Its main fort, San Felipe, held many political prisoners and a large store of ammunition.

On the 30th of June, Puerto Cabello was stabbed in the back. A republican officer named Lieutenant Francisco Fernández Vinoni had been dickering with royalist prisoners for some time. With Bolívar in the city itself, Vinoni seized the fort and ran up the Spanish flag. The fort trained its guns on Puerto Cabello and opened fire.

The coup had deprived the republicans of Puerto Cabello's

strongest position. In the city itself Bolívar prepared to fight despite the fact he had few troops and scarcely any bullets. Early the next morning he pleaded for aid. To Miranda he wrote, "My General, an officer unworthy of his Venezuelan name has seized the prisoners at Fort San Felipe and is making a night attack upon the city. If Your Excellency does not attack at once from the rear, the city is lost. Meanwhile I shall hold it as long as I can."

Bolívar kept his promise. When the bombardment of July 1 reduced his force by 120 men, the future Liberator continued to fight. Even when only 40 men remained to him, Bolívar fought. On July 6, with Monteverde closing in from Valencia, Bolívar gave up. He and seven other men fled by sea to La Guaira.

It was a harsh defeat. In a letter to Miranda Bolívar explained, "If the soldiers deserted, that was not my fault. There was nothing which I could do to prevent this desertion and to compel them to save the country; but alas! the post has been lost in my hands. . . . With respect to myself, I have fulfilled my duty, and although I have lost Puerto Cabello, I am blameless, and I have saved my honor. I regret that I have saved my life and that I was not left dead under the ruins of a city which should have been the last asylum of the liberty and glory of Venezuela."

In La Victoria, Miranda reacted differently. To Bolívar's first appeal for aid Miranda replied, "From your report of the first instant I am informed of the extraordinary events that have taken place in San Felipe. Such things teach us to know men. I impatiently await more news from you." Wrote republican Pedro Gual of a visit to the Generalissimo's quarters after receipt of Bolívar's news,

"Filled with the presentiment of an unexpected calamity I approached the General. 'Well,' I said to him, 'what news is there?' Even to a second inquiry, he made no response, but to a third inquiry, made after an instant had elapsed, drawing a letter from his vest pocket, he said to me in French: *'Tenez, Venezuela est blessée au coeur!'* Never shall I forget the pathetic picture presented at that critical moment by those venerable patriarchs of American emancipation who were profoundly depressed by the intensity of actual misfortune and by a foreboding of other calamities that were about to afflict unfortunate Venezuela! . . . After

the first surprise was over, General Miranda broke silence to say:
'You see, gentlemen, how things happen in this world. A short
time ago all was safe:—now all is uncertain and ominous. Yester-
day Monteverde had neither powder nor lead nor muskets; today
he can count on forty thousand pounds of powder, lead in abundance, and three thousand muskets! Bolívar told me that the royalists were making an attack but by this time they should be in
possession of everything!' "

The difference between Miranda and Bolívar is revealed in their
respective attitudes to the Puerto Cabello disaster. Puerto Cabello
put them both in a hopeless position. Bolívar fought for six days
after the position became hopeless. Miranda threw up his hands
and called it quits. He might have attacked Monteverde from the
rear. Since all was lost, he had nothing to lose. Miranda knew when
he was beaten. Bolívar never did.

In the presence of high government officials Miranda verbally
surveyed the plight of Venezuela. The royalists were conquering
the country "less by force of arms than by the influence of perfidy,
fanaticism, and fraud which instead of diminishing, are increasing and offering new advantages to the enemy." Caracas and La
Guaira were the only republican cities left. Rebellious slaves from
Curiepe in the east were moving on the capital, strewing the
countryside with corpses and charred ruins. Miranda once said
that rather than lay Venezuela open to anarchy he would see it
bear the yoke of Spain for another hundred years. On July 12,
he sued for peace.

Two weeks later Miranda gave Venezuela to Monteverde on
the following terms: both sides would free all prisoners; all persons wishing to leave Venezuela would be furnished passports;
all persons in unconquered Venezuela would be protected; no
one would be persecuted because of his political conduct during
the First Republic; Venezuela would lose none of the prerogatives enjoyed by other Spanish provinces. Monteverde could do
as he pleased in all territories he controlled before the truce.

As his agents negotiated a treaty, Miranda behaved like a guilty
bank clerk planning to skip town before the inspector arrives.
He arranged for his books and papers to be shipped to Caracas
and tried to charter a ship for the use of himself and other Vene-

zuelan patriots. He kept the news of the treaty a secret. It is said that the first hint officials in Caracas received of the capitulation was the arrival of royalist troops at the capital. However, Miranda had given a sketchy report of the surrender to the Caracas city council on July 26.

Meanwhile he had also been carrying on a few financial transactions. Destitute as usual, he apparently accepted one thousand ounces in gold from a wealthy go-between, the Marqués de Casa León, who later deserted to the royalists and received a post in the new Spanish colonial regime. Miranda directed subordinates to turn over 22,000 pesos from the National Treasury to an English merchant, George Robertson, who was about to leave the country. On July 30, the Generalissimo arrived in La Guaira where his belongings and some gold had been packed aboard a British warship which had fortuitously arrived the day before.

During these final days, Miranda refused to discuss why he had surrendered Venezuela to an inferior force. Though he had arranged a treaty which guaranteed protection to everyone, he demonstrated an appalling lack of faith in it by trying to escape the country before it could take effect. His financial operations coupled with his reticence to explain his conduct left him open to accusations. Critics said that he had sold Venezuelan freedom for Spanish gold.

By placing the most benevolent construction on Miranda's flight, it can be argued that he was motivated by the purest patriotism. According to Gual, the Generalissimo said just before the final capitulation: "Let us direct our views toward Nueva Granada where I count upon Nariño who is my friend. With the resources that we can probably obtain in that viceroyalty, and with the officers and munitions that we can take from Venezuela, we shall again regain Caracas without risking the dangers by which we are menaced at the present moment. It is necessary to allow Venezuela to recover from the effect of the earthquake and the depredations of the royalists."

History proves his plan feasible. It is exactly what Bolívar did. Moreover, when Bolívar arrived in Curaçao, he immediately put in a claim for the money Miranda had packed aboard the British warship. For that matter, according to a British customs list, two of the chests which were filled with silver plate bore Bolívar's name.

Even Miranda's refusal to discuss his plans and his reasons for capitulating may be defended. Surrounded by critics and already completely convinced of the unreliability of many patriots, the General may have felt that explanations would be unnecessary for those who remained loyal to him while they would supply ammunition to potential traitors.

Ample evidence exists to prove he considered the safety of others. During the negotiations with Monteverde he placed an embargo on all shipping in La Guaira harbor. This insured that the maximum number of vessels would be available to carry emigrés from Venezuela when the time came.

On July 30, revolutionary soldiers and supporters of the new republic came tumbling over the hill from Caracas. Prevented from leaving by the embargo—which like everything else Miranda did during these last weeks was not explained—the patriots milled about, asking each other what had happened. They were worried, depressed, and frustrated. Rumors raced through the town concerning gold aboard the *Sapphire,* the British warship waiting for Miranda. Then, upon this maelstrom of confusion burst the final and the most perfidious piece of treachery to besmirch the memory of the First Republic.

Chief of La Guaira port was Manuel María Casas, who had been in communication with Monteverde for several days before the General arrived in the port. Monteverde had no intention of abiding by the armistice and may have given Casas orders to detain Miranda. In any event, when the General arrived in the port, Casas demanded four thousand pesos from him. As the money had to cover the needs of all patriots, Miranda offered him only eight hundred. Casas was angry. He schemed and intrigued among the patriot refugees in the port.

Miranda played into his hands. Instead of boarding the *Sapphire* on the evening of the 30th, the General joined other patriots for dinner in La Guaira. The impassioned young men, Bolívar among them, badgered the General for an explanation of the surrender. They treated the old man like a prisoner in the dock. The Dictator had taken action which not only affected their country but their personal safety as well. They wanted to know what he had done and why he had done it. They minced very few words. Miranda refused to justify himself. He resorted to fiery invective and insults. His performance was peculiarly in character. To vain and pompous Miranda, the accusations of his compatriots must have seemed presumptuously insulting. He had considered their welfare and now they repaid him with humiliation. The more they asked, the less he told them. Haughtily, he finished his dinner and went to bed.

The patriots were furious. Bolívar favored shooting Miranda on the spot. Casas, who knew what would please Monteverde, wanted the General alive. Before dawn on the 31st, the patriots went to Miranda's room and pounded on the door.

Appearing before them fully dressed and in complete control of himself, Miranda listened while excited Bolívar loudly announced his arrest. With the dignity that came naturally to him, Miranda took a lantern from his aide, Carlos Soublette, and held it up to the faces of the conspirators, one after another. "Uproars! Uproars! That's all these people are good for," he said. He gave them his sword and the patriots led him to the prison castle of San Carlos. Miranda was to spend the rest of his life in jail. He died at Cádiz on July 14, 1816.

The patriots planned to deal with Miranda themselves. It was the traitor Casas who delivered him to the Spaniards. With Miranda safely in prison Casas turned on the rest of the refugees. He slapped another embargo on La Guaira, trapping four hundred patriots. One small English ship which tried to leave was sunk. By August 1, Monteverde had already broken most of the agreements he had made with Miranda. He began to persecute the rebels. Eight of the most important, including Canon Madariaga, were shipped to Spain in chains.

As for Bolívar, he fled to Caracas. He hid in the home of the Marqués de Casa León and asked a neutral friend to petition Monteverde for a passport. The friend offered his own life as guarantee for Bolívar's, and Monteverde agreed to let the young colonel leave the country. With Bolívar before him, Monteverde ordered an aide to issue a pass "as reward for the service he rendered the King by the arrest of Miranda." Too proud to let this contemptuous remark go unanswered, Bolívar replied, "I had Miranda arrested to punish him for betraying his country, not to serve the King." The bravado nearly cost him his passport. Monteverde canceled but later revalidated it, a move he soon regretted. It is said that Monteverde, remembering how he let the most important figure of Latin-American independence slip through his fingers, used to blanch every time he heard Bolívar's name.

Bolívar maintained to the end of his life the rightness of his conduct at La Guaira. He was proud that he had risked his own safety to insure Miranda's punishment for betraying the First Republic.

But Miranda had not betrayed the First Republic. He was no more a traitor than Bolívar himself. To answer the charges against him Miranda might have used the words Bolívar wrote after the Puerto Cabello debacle: "If the soldiers deserted, that was not my fault. There was nothing which I could do to prevent this desertion and to compel them to save the country."

The First Republic had been built in the air. It was inevitable that it should have fallen as soon as the laws of gravity took effect. A peculiar set of circumstances allowed the republicans to guide the destiny of Venezuela for a few months. Napoleon helped. So did the incapacity of Spain to interfere. The republican oligarchy moved into a political vacuum caused by the confusion and apathy of the mass. Even so, the patriots never controlled the entire country. Pockets of resistance existed, and this opposition became significant when government misfortunes and the earthquake turned the populace against it. The patriots fought to save a country which only wanted to be rid of them.

It was not Miranda, but Venezuela, which betrayed the First Republic. Confused, divided Venezuela, too immature to know what it wanted, still had a long way to go before it could live up to the expectations of a Miranda or a Bolívar. To make into a sovereign nation a land area filled for the most part with people who didn't know what independence meant and didn't care to find out seemed a hopeless prospect. Clearly, Miranda was not the man to try. For this task Venezuela would need a dedicated zealot, courageous enough to defy nature and arrogant enough to think he could bend it to his will.

Chapter IX

THE LIBERATOR

To THE AVERAGE American school child, George Washington is a little boy who, by never telling any lies, got to be first president of the United States. Sugared by Venezuelan chauvinism Simón Bolívar becomes a gilded saint on horseback who spent his life chasing nasty Spaniards out of South America with a sword in one hand and a proclamation in the other. Both men deserved a better end.

The incense of fifth-grade minds has so obscured the real Bolívar that scholars have been trying to disperse the fog for at least one hundred years. It is a futile task. Hero worship is a more common human phenomenon than scholarship, and the truth has long since been suffocated by a cloud of hot air. What Bolívar really was and why will always remain tempting mysteries for the academic sleuth. Studies of his life have already yielded scores of different interpretations. Like God, Simón Bolívar is all things to all men.

"Every political creed cut the man to its measure," says Waldo Frank in *Birth of a World*. "Bolívar favored a life presidency, therefore he justified dictators; Bolívar was an authoritarian, therefore a school of 'democratic Caesarism' made him its model; Bolívar toward the close of his career leaned on the Church, therefore the Church reactionaries leaned on him."

In Venezuela the tiniest hamlet has a monument to Bolívar. His memory has become the purest expression of Venezuelan nationalism. In the National Pantheon, where he was buried, a ceiling fresco depicts Bolívar just "one step to the rear and one step to the right" of Jesus Christ. Yet this adulation is not for Bolívar, the man, but for Bolívar, the National Hero. There would have been a National Hero had Bolívar never been born. As for Bolívar, the man, contemporary Venezuelans not only did not worship him, they let him die a virtual exile from the country to which he devoted his life. When the news of Bolívar's death reached Maracaibo, the mayor immediately issued a proclamation announcing that "Bolívar, the evil genius, the anarchist, the enemy of the country, has ceased to exist."

Simón Bolívar was one of the most remarkable men who ever lived. As general, statesman, writer, and prophet, he possessed a combination of talents matched by very few figures in world history. Born into an extremely wealthy family, he spent his last peso trying to destroy the system which had produced his own financial and social pre-eminence. A sophisticated aristocrat whose endurance and horsemanship won him the respect of savage, city-hating llaneros, Bolívar used to cap days of rough riding or grueling administrative work by dancing until dawn. A man much addicted to pompous ceremonies, gold uniforms and formal wreath givings, he once received a British emissary while lying almost nude in a hammock. Torn between a natural inclination to wield supreme power and a revulsion for dictatorship, Bolívar constantly refused unlimited authority until the insistence of the public gave him no other choice but to accept. A sincere reformer who thought he was acting only for the welfare of his countrymen, he encouraged them to wage a war which left the nation in ruins and committed to tyranny.

Born on July 24, 1783, Simón Bolívar was the youngest of the four children produced by Don Juan Vicente Bolívar and Doña María de la Concepción de Palacios y Blanco, whose wealth and social position made their children heirs to an opulent tradition. When Juan Vicente died in 1786, he left 258,000 pesos, two cacao plantations, thirteen houses in Caracas and La Guaira, two country estates, a plantation at San Mateo, one indigo ranch and three cattle ranches, a valuable copper mine, and thousands of slaves.

Though his parents gave Bolívar riches and rank, they could give him little of themselves. Fatherless at three, orphaned at nine, Bolívar lost his grandfather through death and his sisters through marriage at the age of eleven. He and his brother, Juan Vicente, became the charges of an uncle, Carlos Palacios. By Bolívar's own admission, we know that his strongest emotional attachment in childhood was to his Negro nurse, Hippolita.

Simoncito was a dark child with a strong personality, given more to play than to study. Upon resigning his position as Bolívar's tutor, Miguel José Sanz reported that his pupil was "insupportable, restless, imperative, audacious, wilful, heedless to all counsel, intolerable before his own family and before strangers."

Bolívar had his first lessons in language, geography, and history at the family's enormous, patio-filled house on the Plaza San Jacinto in Caracas, where the boy was born. After Judge Sanz, Carlos Palacios tutored his ward. Later Bolívar became the pupil of Andrés Bello, gifted poet and scholar, who later wrote a book on Castillian grammar which is considered authoritative to this day.

The man who most profoundly influenced Simón Bolívar's intellectual life was a genius who straddled the hypothetical line between brilliance and madness. An ardent disciple of Rousseau, Simón Carreño or Rodríguez or Robinson, as he later called himself, loved original man and nature. He concentrated upon developing Bolívar's understanding, perception and judgment instead of grinding his student's nose into books. As a devotee of Rousseau Rodríguez must have warmed to the instruction of young Bolívar. The boy fitted the description of Rousseau's fictional pupil, Emile. He was wealthy, intelligent, and an orphan. Moreover, Rodríguez became almost the only adult with whom Bolívar came in contact. Taking up residence at rural San Mateo Bolívar and Rodríguez studied out of doors, swam, and rode horseback as Rousseau would have recommended. The Liberator himself described the effect of this unorthodox training; writing to Rodríguez later in his life, Bolívar said, "You have molded my heart for liberty and justice, for the great and the beautiful."

This relationship between Bolívar and Rodríguez ended abruptly in 1797. The capture of conspirators involved in the abortive España revolt induced the tutor to flee the country. An ardent liberal and a reformer, Rodríguez was suspected of complicity.

Bolívar had exhausted the intellectual potentialities of Venezuela by the time Rodríguez fled. He was old enough to go to Spain. After a year in the regiment his father had organized in Aragua, Simón Bolívar sailed for Europe in January 1799. A letter he wrote home during the trip reveals that while Rodríguez may have stimulated Bolívar's imagination he had left him practically illiterate. When he arrived in Madrid, Esteban Palacios, another maternal uncle, hired tutors to drill the boy in languages, mathematics, dancing, and fencing. Bolívar proved diligent, but disturbing to the tranquillity of Esteban's life. He was sent to live in the home of the Marqués de Ustariz, a noble and well-educated Caraqueño, under whose guidance Bolívar began to read history and philosophy. Equally educational was his contact with the Spanish court and the atmosphere of a great European capital. Bolívar began to take an interest in fine clothes, gambling, and women.

It was at the house of the Marqués de Ustariz that Bolívar met María Teresa de Toro y Alaysa, niece of Venezuela's Marqués del Toro. María Teresa lived nearby. Bolívar saw much of her and soon asked the girl—plain, serious, gentle, and twenty months his senior—to marry him. In June 1802, Simón Bolívar and his bride sailed for Venezuela. Six months later she was dead of yellow fever. Bolívar vowed never to remarry, a promise he technically kept, though his list of mistresses is long and impressive.

Once again bereft of family by death, the twenty-year-old widower left almost immediately for Europe. After a short stay in Madrid, he traveled to Paris where a distant relative, Fanny du Villars, introduced him to its pleasures. From cousin and friend, Fanny soon graduated to mistress.

This was the Paris which became before Bolívar's eyes the capital of an empire. Napoleon, who had deposed half the kings of Europe in the name of republicanism, threw pretense aside and crowned himself Emperor of France in 1804. Like other liberals, Bolívar recoiled from Napoleon's hypocrisy. He refused an invitation to the coronation in Notre Dame but could not ignore the magnificence of the accompanying ceremonies. He wrote:

I saw the coronation of Napoleon in Paris during the last month of 1804. The gigantic show thrilled me, less by its glamor than by the love accorded the hero by this great people. This universal expression of all hearts, this free and spontaneous mass demonstration aroused by Napoleon and his great deeds seemed to me, as he was being thus honored by more than a million men, to be the pinnacle of man's desires—the realization of man's highest ambition. I regarded the crown, which Napoleon placed on his own head, as a poor example of outmoded custom. What seemed great to me was the general acclaim and the interest which his person generated. This, I admit, made me think of my own country's enslavement, and the fame that would accrue to him who liberated it. But I was far indeed from imagining that I would be that man.

With him on this occasion was his old friend and tutor Simón Rodríguez. Troubled by Bolívar's reckless pursuit of pleasure in Paris and his fits of despondency, Rodríguez proposed a walking tour. The two tramped through Rousseau's favorite haunts and hiked to Italy. Atop Monte Sacro in Rome, Bolívar and Rodríguez mused upon the glories and cruelties of the Holy City's past. It was here that Bolívar, falling to his knees, declared: "I swear before you by the God of my fathers and the honor of my country I will not rest, not in body or soul, until I have broken the chains of Spain."

How long Bolívar had been harboring notions about Latin-American independence is unknown. The first verifiable reference to his interest in republicanism dates from his sojourn in Paris. In one of her letters to the Liberator, Fanny du Villars wrote, "Now everything has been realized of those great projects which you confided to me when you were twenty-three."

Bolívar returned to Venezuela in 1807 and at first showed no inclination to fight Spain. His belligerent impulses were vented rather in a prolonged verbal and legal battle with Antonio Nicolas Briceño, whose hacienda in Yare adjoined his. On the other hand, no one knows what Bolívar was thinking. One must remember that the *criollos* had learned how far the country was from supporting independence when Miranda tried to invade Venezuela in 1806. We do know that long before the coup of April 19, 1810,

Bolívar had been plotting with other bluebloods like the Marqués del Toro, his uncle José Félix Ribas and Andrés Bello.

When Napoleon monopolized Spain's attention in 1808, the patriots joined other Venezuelans in agitating for the recognition of Ferdinand and the establishment of local autonomy under his crown. Bolívar was one of those who plotted to kidnap Governor General Vicente Emparán. Since he was not a member of the Caracas cabildo, he took no part in the deposition of Emparán in 1810. However, he served as emissary to Great Britain for the new government (a post he obtained after offering to pay his own expenses). Together with Miranda, Bolívar agitated for complete separation from Spain, and when independence was declared, he fought to preserve it.

During the tumultuous life of the First Republic Bolívar was only one among many ardent youths who put their elementary military training at the service of the new country and who occupied posts whose responsibility was commensurate with their zeal, not their experience. But when the First Republic tumbled to the ground Simón Bolívar walked away from the ruins carrying free Venezuela within himself. A year later he had become the personification of Venezuelan liberty.

So rapid was Bolívar's transfiguration into the leader, the hero, the very soul of South American revolt, that it must have seemed incredible to the man himself, and impossible to those who had known him as a "petulant little colonel." Thirteen months after the fall of Puerto Cabello, Bolívar entered Caracas a victor and received the title of Liberator, the only one he ever deigned to accept. To do it, he had coaxed Nueva Granada into giving him some men, violated instructions, hacked his way through pestilential swamps, wandered across burning llanos, scaled Andean spurs and routed Monteverde's royalists in a series of ingeniously conducted battles. It was a thrilling performance. But to Bolívar it simply proved something he had known all along—that he was a great man.

Simón Bolívar had a disease common to famous men. He was an egotist, as any man who thinks he is capable of leading others must be. But egotism alone does not explain the ascendancy of Simón Bolívar. History had to be on his side as well. The paralyzation of Spain by France created a power vacuum into which colonial revolutionaries surged. There were hundreds of them— men like Miranda, San Martín, Nariño, Bermúdez, Bolívar, Arismendi, and Santander, all motivated by a desire to express their egos by leading their homelands to freedom. In their race for supreme command, Bolívar prevailed. He became the leader by virtue of his superior intelligence, persistence, dedication, and audacity. In egotism he transcended his rivals. Life for him was an avenue to immortality, little more. He wanted to be one of the greatest men who ever lived. And he was.

Like all little boys, Simón Bolívar must have dreamed great dreams. With neither parents nor close relatives to assure him of his importance, he had to take a special interest in himself. His material environment fed an illusion of greatness. He had splendid houses, fine clothes, and horses. He had slaves to do his bidding. He was a little prince, the heir to a tiny realm. Yet it might have been a ghost kingdom and he himself a ghost for all the attention anybody paid to him. Denied the affection which turns most children into domesticated human beings, Simón Bolívar continued to dream.

Then into this inadequate life plunged a weird personality to give the boy companionship and shape his mind. When a father might have been teaching him the value of tradition, Bolívar was exposed instead to criticism of that tradition. Rather than the Virgin Mary the orphan heard about Rousseau's God of nature. For want of a better model Bolívar had to identify himself with Simón Rodríguez, his erratic, brilliant, and unconventional tutor. Simón Bolívar's ideas of the good, the just, the noble, the beautiful and the true became inextricably confused with those of Simón Rodríguez. New concepts began to color Bolívar's dreams of greatness, whose heroes perhaps sought political and social change instead of the Golden Fleece or the Holy Grail.

When Bolívar was twelve, just such a hero captured the imagination of the Western world. Napoleon Bonaparte began his junket of liberation through Germany, Austria, and Italy in 1795. Napoleon indirectly produced Venezuelan liberty and also helped mold her liberator.

That Napoleon was an idol for young Bolívar became obvious

later on. Bolívar in Spain, however, behaved like any other young man of his class and time. It seemed as if he had shelved the notions of Simón Rodríguez in order to take his proper place in society. He decided to marry, raise a family, and tend his lands. But when his wife died, the rare contentment he had found in domesticity was snatched from him. Alone, aimless, bored, and without emotional roots, he drifted to Paris where he tried to conquer confusion and unhappiness with a round of sensual pleasures.

In this frame of mind he saw Paris turn out to crown Napoleon. What a comparison he must have drawn between himself—a lonely purposeless idler—and Napoleon, the man who had remade Europe and enjoyed the adoration of a nation! He admired Napoleon's greatness and detested him for not being greater.

A few months later Bolívar made his vow on Monte Sacro. Swearing to devote his life to the principles Napoleon had betrayed, the youth envisioned a glory as dazzling as the Emperor's—but purer. It was no coincidence that he made this vow in front of Simón Rodríguez. The direction which Bolívar had vowed to give to his life conformed exactly to the one Simón Rodríguez would think most admirable.

Still, Bolívar was young and inexperienced. He may have wanted to free South America at twenty-three, but he had yet to prove it to himself that he could. At home in Venezuela he bided his time and contributed his talents to subversive activities. He yearned to lead, but his confederates considered him too immature. To convince them and himself of his abilities, Bolívar needed a test. Francisco de Miranda gave it to him.

The incompetence of the famous general during the defense of the First Republic was profoundly reassuring to Bolívar. Miranda provided a basis of comparison, a singularly flattering one for the youth. In Miranda's defeat, he read a testimony to his own greatness. He knew he could have conducted the defense of the First Republic with more intelligence and courage than Miranda. Though he himself had suffered defeat at Puerto Cabello, Bolívar gained confidence when Miranda capitulated under far more favorable circumstances.

He fled from Venezuela in August 1812. In Curaçao, Bolívar looked about to find himself practically alone. There was no one to lead the Venezuelan revolution. In fact, there was no Venezuelan revolution to lead. In total disaster, Bolívar met his destiny. He became the leader. Like Napoleon, he became a monument to his own will. The road to glory passed through Cartagena and Bolívar took it.

Cartagena, the walled city, the supreme expression of Spanish power in the New World, dominated the coast of Nueva Granada. In 1812 Cartagena remained in the hands of Colombian revolutionaries who had declared their country free a few days after Venezuela. But the independence of Nueva Granada was dying of the same disease which killed free Venezuela—disunion and inexperience.

There were three independent governments in Nueva Granada. The patriots of the province had united only long enough to announce their opposition to the Junta Central of Spain in 1810. Then the revolutionaries had begun to bicker among themselves. A government at Bogotá under Antonio Nariño favored centralist rule while President Camilo Torres and his government at Tunja supported federalism. Proud Cartagena refused to recognize either party and formed a third state with Manuel Rodríguez Torices as President.

The fall of Venezuela frightened the centralists and federalists into signing a truce, but at the end of 1812 the three governments were still at odds, even though Spanish troops threatened them from royalist centers on the Magdalena River and along the Nueva Granada–Venezuela border.

This was the Nueva Granada to which Simón Bolívar traveled from Curaçao. He had already decided to erect his South America on its political quicksands. Practically penniless, a refugee, the young Venezuelan revolutionary entered Cartagena a changed man. He had matured since Puerto Cabello. Instead of racing out to fight the Spaniards threatening Cartagena from the Magdalena, he retired to his room and thought.

He drew comparisons. He considered Venezuela's fall and the lesson it provided for all South America. Then he wrote. The

result, his Manifesto de Cartagena, was a rare document. States-
man-like, clear, and persuasive, the Manifesto de Cartagena was
the voice of a leader talking to the people he intended to lead:

The first proofs our government gave of its insensate weakness
manifested themselves when the city of Coro refused to recognize
its legitimacy. The Supreme Junta, instead of subjugating that
defenseless city . . . permitted it to arm so that it later subjugated
the Republic as easily as the Confederation might originally have
subjugated it.

The codes which our magistrates consulted were not those which
could have taught them the practical science of government, but
those which good visionaries had written. Thus, we had philoso-
phers for leaders; philanthropy for legislation, dialectics for tactics
and sophists for soldiers.

But what weakened Venezuela more than anything was the
Federal system which she adopted. . . . The Federal system,
though it may be the most perfect and the best way to apportion
human happiness in society, is nevertheless the worst suited to
our infant states. Generally speaking our citizens are not capable
of exercising their own rights. Also . . . it is not possible to preserve such a system in the tumult of war and conflicting interests.
It is necessary for a government to modify itself to circumstances,
times, and the men who surround it.

Our division and not Spanish arms returned us to slavery. If
Caracas instead of a languid and insubstantial confederation had
established a simple government which the political and military
situation required, you would exist, Venezuela, and enjoy your
liberty today. . . .

Nueva Granada has seen Venezuela succumb and ought to avoid
the mistakes which destroyed her. To this effect, I submit as a
measure indispensable to the security of Nueva Granada the reconquest of Caracas. . . .

Applying the example of Venezuela to Nueva Granada and
forming a proportion, we find that Coro is to Caracas what Caracas
is to all America. . . . Possessing the territory of Venezuela, Spain
can easily . . . penetrate from the provinces of Barinas and
Maracaibo to the final confines of America. . . .

Let us take advantage then of moments so propitious; before
reinforcements arrive from Spain and absolutely change the aspect
and we lose perhaps forever the said opportunity to assure the
liberty of these states.

With his last funds Bolívar had this appeal to Colombians printed. Meanwhile he had begun to implement his plans on a military front. The government of Cartagena had given him a commission in its fighting forces but the French commander Pierre Labatut assigned him to an insignificant post on the lower Magdalena and ordered him to stay there.

Simón Bolívar had taken his last military order. From now on, he was to give them. A few days after he took command at Barrancas, Bolívar and his two hundred men started to move. In river craft they glided up the Magdalena and swept royalists from Tenerife and Mompox. Fifteen days after the action began the river was clear of Spaniards. His force swollen by three hundred recruits gathered along the way, Bolívar made camp at Ocaña and pondered what to do next. Royalists were threatening the three independent governments of Nueva Granada from Cúcuta, just across the Táchira River from Venezuela. When Colonel Manuel del Castillo, patriot commander near Cúcuta, appealed to Bolívar for help, the Venezuelan obtained permission from Cartagena to go to his aid.

Across the llanos of eastern Colombia and into the mountains marched Bolívar's little army. He reached the environs of Cúcuta on February 28. A Spanish force twice as large fled as Bolívar's untrained hordes stormed down the slopes with fixed bayonets. The threat of a Spanish invasion had been eliminated. What seemed more important to Bolívar, the way to Venezuela was now open.

From Cúcuta, Bolívar begged Nueva Granada's three governments to support his plan for the liberation of Venezuela. His campaign bore fruit. In May, 1813, Tunja reluctantly sanctioned the invasion, but specified that Bolívar should occupy only the two border provinces of Mérida and Trujillo.

Bolívar had been fighting dissension in his army. Colombians were jealous of the dashing Venezuelan. They plotted against him and told their governments that his projected invasion of Venezuela was risky and ill-advised. Castillo and other Colombian officers resigned rather than march with Bolívar. Francisco de Paula Santander, future vice-president of Gran Colombia, marched into Venezuela only after Bolívar threatened to shoot him if he didn't. On the face of it, Bolívar's plan appeared ridiculous. Against Monteverde's two armies of 2,000 men each, the patriots could throw only 650 ragged, ill-trained amateurs. The Colombians could not believe as Bolívar did that once in Venezuela he would gather thousands of recruits.

Bolívar knew that Monteverde had taught fickle Venezuelans a lesson. After a year of tyranny and persecution, many were ready to scuttle back to the standard of free Venezuela. In eastern Venezuela, an aristocrat named Santiago Mariño had been mauling the Spaniards with increasing success ever since he launched an invasion from Trinidad in 1813.

Bolívar could lead troops and fire them with blind loyalty. While some malcontents deserted, more men remained to serve. Rafael Urdaneta, a devoted friend and courageous officer, supported Bolívar as chief of staff. The Colombian, Girardot, was to give his life for Bolívar and independence. With Bolívar, too, was his uncle, José Félix Ribas, who became a symbol of Venezuelan resistance to tyranny even in death.

Bolívar and his band stepped across the Táchira River into Venezuela in the middle of May. After brief skirmishes Monteverde's forces quitted both Mérida and Trujillo. With a force doubled in size by Venezuelan enlistments, Bolívar entered Trujillo on June 14. Disregarding the limitations set upon his operations by the Colombian Congress, he prepared to march east.

At Trujillo he proclaimed the famous "War to the Death." The curiously-worded decree read, "Spaniards and Canary Islanders, count on death even though you be neutral, if you do not work actively for American liberty. Americans, count on life even though you be guilty." Prompted partly by Spanish atrocities in eastern Venezuela, partly by Monteverde's announcement in March that rebels should receive no quarter, Bolívar's wording of the proclamation aimed to produce a permanent cleavage between colonists and peninsulars. He wanted to arouse a sense of nationality in the Americans, who still thought of themselves as Spanish citizens.

Many have considered Bolívar's declaration a blot on his record. They say it encouraged terrorism and bloodshed. Yet both sides perpetrated atrocities before it was written as well as after. Bolívar chose to ignore his War to the Death more often than not. He must be judged by what he did, not by what he said he would do.

Late in June, Bolívar led his troops south over mountain passes and descended upon Barinas, where the second largest Spanish force in western Venezuela was gathered. Surprised by Bolívar's indirect approach, the commander at Barinas fled. Safe from attacks in the rear, the patriots began the trek to Caracas.

Bolívar's army swelled as it moved. The advantage of momentum was with the patriots, as it had been with Monteverde the previous year. Whole platoons of royalist prisoners switched their loyalty to Bolívar. At San Carlos, Bolívar found that his force had quadrupled since his arrival in Venezuela.

It was near San Carlos that the patriots fought the most important engagement of the 1813 campaign. Upon the approach of Bolívar's armies twelve hundred Spaniards quitted the city for Valencia where they planned to join other royalists for a last-ditch stand. Bolívar selected two hundred horses, mounted two men on each, and gave them orders to cut the Spaniards off. At night the force outdistanced the enemy and the following morning the royalists found the road ahead of them blocked. The patriot cavalry battled savagely, detaining an army three times larger, until Bolívar and the main contingent overtook and annihilated the twelve hundred Spaniards.

The Battle of Taguanes broke Spanish resistance in Venezuela, at least for a while. Monteverde fled and shut himself up in Puerto Cabello. Bolívar marched triumphantly into Caracas on August 7. On the 8th he declared the re-establishment of Venezuela as a free republic and became its absolute dictator under the aegis of the Tunja Congress in Nueva Granada.

Just eleven months had passed since Bolívar sailed in exile to Curaçao. August 1813 found him on the summit of glory just as August 1812 had found him at its foot. Even so, his position was far from secure. The Venezuelan War of Independence was a game of "King of the Mountain." Bolívar commanded the crest only so long as it took another contestant to push him off. Within a few weeks, the enemy had regrouped his shattered forces and, like an octopus, unleashed terror from as many directions as he had arms. Monteverde sat in Puerto Cabello waiting for the Spaniards to reinforce him by sea. In Coro, Governor Cevallos was preparing to strike east. The greatest threat to the republic, however, festered in the llanos. There, two Spanish leaders, Francisco Yáñes and Tomás Boves had mobilized armies of savages under the standard of Holy Spain.

The llanos of Venezuela sweep east from the Andes, consuming the heart of Venezuela. For thousands of square miles, nothing grows except tough grass as tall as a man and an occasional tree. Baked by tropical sun for six months and flooded by hundreds of rain-gorged streams for the rest of the year, the llanos seem hospitable only to the jaguars, crocodiles, snakes, and lethal insects who infest them. There lie Venezuela's cattle ranches, vast tracts of plain unbroken by churches or towns.

In response to these elements developed a breed of men whose thoughts, bodies, and lives reflected the land they lived on. The Venezuelan llanero is tough, savage, and suspicious. During the Wars of the Revolution he was human only in speech. He lived among the grasses, often in the open air. He felt rich if he owned a pair of pants. A naked demon who learned to ride and walk almost simultaneously, he herded cattle to eat, killed to stay alive, and tortured to amuse himself. The llaneros worked the ranches owned by great landowners like Simón Bolívar. They sublimated their destructive and aggressive instincts by breaking in wild horses and wrestling cattle. Strangely enough, it was not a Venezuelan but a Spaniard who first thought of using such natural talents in the War of Independence. An army of llaneros was just the kind of barbaric horde Tomás Boves had been born to lead.

While the men of the plains were indifferent to murder and destruction, Tomás Boves loved horror as a musician loves music. He liked to watch men die. To hear them scream in agony was a symphony. He indulged his sadism by wounding men and leaving them to die in the sun, by cutting off their noses and ears, by watching his dusky hordes spend their desire on the shivering bodies of well-born women. A favorite torture involved skinning the feet of captives and forcing them to walk on broken glass.

Boves came to Venezuela after a career aboard contraband ships. Soon he was smuggling on the plains and learning the ways of the llaneros. He understood these people. Spain was his country and

Spaniards his countrymen—but only by birth. The dark llaneros were brothers of his soul.

When the revolution broke out he tried to join the patriot forces, but landed in a republican jail for smuggling instead. Released in 1812, he became a monarchist fighter the instant his cell door swung open. He knew the llanos. Promising loot to the naked, freedom to the slaves, and vengeance to the oppressed, he raised an army that eventually numbered ten thousand, almost all cavalry. The llaneros swung their taut legs over the backs of their horses, grabbed knives, lances, or a club, and galloped after Boves—not for the King of Spain, but for a shirt, a swig of aguardiente, or a few minutes of relaxing lust astride a *criollo*'s daughter. Boves dreamed of leading the mestizos, the Negroes, the Indians, and the mulattos to domination of Venezuela. But for his own death he might have done it.

His army was incredibly effective. It needed nothing. Unlike the patriot forces who demanded pay, food, and weapons, the llaneros were self-sufficient. They ate what they plundered, considered loot their pay and fought with their bare hands if necessary.

Bolívar might have coped with the llaneros, Monteverde, and Cevallos if these had been the only threats. But Spain was menacing the Second Republic with renewed energy. The mother country began to prepare expeditions against revolutionists as soon as Napoleon lost his hold on Europe in 1813. Moreover, Bolívar had troubles in his own camp. Santiago Mariño, the patriot general, who had conquered eastern Venezuela, refused to co-operate with the Caracas government. He formed his own state in the east.

Bolívar commanded only the mountainous spine of Venezuela. The Andes separated royalists in the llanos from their allies in Coro, Puerto Cabello, and Maracaibo. It was imperative for the Spaniards to breach Bolívar's Andean realm and join forces, and it was just as important for the patriots to prevent it. The monarchists held the advantage. They could attack from a half-dozen different directions at once. Critically short of men, Bolívar fought a fire that encircled him. While he quelled the blaze in one sector, flames crept closer in another.

Bolívar had begun to lay siege to Puerto Cabello before he

entered Caracas. Monteverde refused to capitulate. He knew a sizable Spanish army was sailing to his aid. So did the republicans. When the Spanish fleet approached La Guaira under the impression that Monteverde still held the port, José Ribas attempted to lure the soldiers ashore by flying the royal flag. The Spanish commander sensed the ruse in time and sailed west to Puerto Cabello.

With these reinforcements of twelve hundred well-armed men, Monteverde took the offensive. He marched from Puerto Cabello toward Caracas, but patriot forces sent him running back to cover after a battle at Bárbula on September 30. It was Monteverde's last battle. Shot in the jaw by a rebel bullet, he soon relinquished his command.

Two weeks after the Bárbula victory the patriots had to rush forces to the defense of Caracas. Boves and his plague of centaurs were racing toward the mountains. At Mosquiteros on October 14, Campo Elías blasted them and averted the threat. Campo Elías was a fanatic. A Spaniard by birth, he detested his countrymen with the same unreasoning hatred that Boves directed toward his fellow whites. He had sworn to kill every Spaniard and then commit suicide in order to clear the world of his own kind.

Meanwhile a new menace was developing in the west. Governor Cevallos had advanced from Coro toward the center of the republic. After punishing patriot armies near Barquisimeto, he joined forces with a royalist army from the llanos in December. What the patriots dreaded most had occurred. Their mountain domain had been cut in half. Two powerful royalist armies had united. Against this combined force of 5,000 the republicans could throw barely 2,500 soldiers. To meet the challenge, Bolívar personally took command of his troops and led them to Araure.

Behind Bolívar's superb generalship and individual daring the patriots fought like men possessed. The Battle of Araure was a great republican victory. After routing the royalists, the patriots gave the llaneros instruction in their own art, putting every enemy soldier they could capture or overtake to the sword.

The Battle of Araure gave Bolívar a two-month respite, but late in January, Tomás Boves stood ready to test the defenses of Caracas a second time. On February 2, he slaughtered the patriot army resisting him at La Puerta. By the end of the month the llaneros were hurling themselves at the outer defenses of Caracas.

Bolívar decided to meet Boves at San Mateo, his own plantation. Boves besieged the point from late February to late March with mixed success. Though he succeeded in weakening the patriots, he could not breach their lines. On March 25, as word reached him that Mariño had finally decided to aid Bolívar's fight to preserve the Second Republic, Boves launched an all-out battle to dislodge the defenders before the forces from the east could reach San Mateo. Throughout the day he charged the patriot lines. Bolívar and his men held. At dusk, Boves retreated to the llanos.

The Battle of San Mateo was featured by a stirring act of individual heroism. A Colombian named Ricaurte commanded the patriot ammunition dump and when the llaneros overran the position early on March 25, he sealed himself in the sugar mill where the munitions were kept and blew himself up, rather than let the matériel fall into royalist hands.

Caracas had been stripped of available man power. Agriculture and business in the country had ground to a standstill. There was scarcely any ammunition. Foreign governments refused to sell weapons to Bolívar. Morale had slipped to a new low. Sick of Monteverde in 1813, Venezuelans had decided by 1814 that the royalists weren't so bad after all. They wanted peace. Bolívar gave them war. Many again switched sides, taking up arms with Boves or other Spanish generals to drive the patriots from the country.

For most, however, it was too late to change sides. Forces had been loosed which could not be quelled by laying down one's arms. Boves massacred innocent and guilty alike while Bolívar occasionally resorted to the same tactics. In the spring of 1814, Bolívar allowed eight hundred Spanish prisoners to be executed at La Guaira to liquidate a potential fifth-column threat. Both Bolívar and Boves had told Venezuelans: co-operate with me or die.

During the spring and early summer of 1814 Bolívar worked tirelessly to save his Second Republic. He led troops, planned strategy, and directed the government. Any one of these tasks would have driven a normal man past the point of exhaustion, but Bolívar could leave a dance floor after a night's revel to take his place behind a desk for a day of work. Action was the man's element.

His valiant efforts, only postponed the demise of the Second Republic. Though the patriots managed to win another resounding victory over the royalists on May 28, at the First Battle of Carabobo, Boves slaughtered Bolívar's troops at La Puerta on June 15 and was ruling in Caracas a month later.

The news of Boves' victory at La Puerta terrified free Venezuela. When Bolívar evacuated Caracas on July 6, twenty thousand people chose to go with him. It was a difficult decision for high-born *criollos* to make. Bolívar planned to strike out through the jungles to reach eastern Venezuela where Mariño still held the coast. Trekking through the steaming hell between Caracas and Barcelona meant indescribable privations, especially for people who considered it demeaning to carry a bundle. Now, they lugged what possessions they could lift into a dank and tepid labyrinth of vines and trees. When they could stand it no longer, they tossed their valuables aside in order to swat mosquitoes. Yellow fever and malaria began to course through their blood. Sloshing across fens, they fell exhausted into carpets of green scum, struggled panting to their aching feet and pushed on. Mothers drowned their children to save them from the rigors of the march. Twenty days and four hundred kilometers later, a little column of filthy men and women staggered into Barcelona. They found no rest. The city faced imminent attack by llaneros under a henchman of Boves named Morales. The patriots made their last stand near Aragua de Barcelona. Morales wiped them out. Bolívar and a few others fled to Cumaná.

The fate of the Second Republic had destroyed Bolívar's prestige. Mariño and his two brilliant but undependable allies, Manuel Piar and José Francisco Bermúdez, were reluctant to follow Bolívar's lead. He was to leave Venezuela a few weeks later, accused even by his uncle José Ribas of being a traitor.

Bolívar had carted some treasure from Caracas to finance the resistance. In Cumaná he entrusted the chests to one of Mariño's men, an Italian ship captain. One night Bolívar and Mariño learned that the Italian was putting out to sea. They dashed out and boarded the departing vessel. As it sailed away, they argued with the captain to turn about. They eventually convinced him, but this took a few days. By the time Bolívar returned to the coast with the money, Piar and even Ribas were convinced he had betrayed them. Refusing to accept Bolívar's explanation and the returned treasure as proof of his innocence, Ribas and Piar threw the Liberator in jail, just as he had disposed of Miranda under a similar delusion two years before. Released two days later, Bolívar prepared to go into exile a second time. With Mariño, he sailed for Cartagena on September 8.

Sporadic resistance to royalist rule continued throughout Venezuela. In this guerrilla warfare Boves was killed, but Venezuela lost one of her most noble defenders. The Spaniards captured and executed José Ribas.

In 1814, Venezuela seemed destroyed. Three years of almost continuous civil war had broken her economy, disrupted her social order, killed nearly a third of her citizens and reduced the survivors to misery. Most of those aristocrats who had dreamed of independence for Venezuela had died. So had most of their enemies, as well as many of those who had simply tried to stay neutral. Venezuela was nearly as dead as her Second Republic, but as that Second Republic rose from the ashes of the first, so would a new Venezuela rise from the ashes of the old. Before 1814, the revolution was a race war, a class war, a civil war. Afterwards, it became what its liberator had maintained it should be—a war of Venezuelans against Spaniards, a War of Independence.

Chapter X

A PROPHET IN HIS COUNTRY

As Simón Bolívar sailed to Colombia, a plan for the reconquest of his country was already forming in his mind. He would enlist the support of Nueva Granada as he had done two years before. This time he had more reason to expect success. In 1812 he was virtually unknown to the Colombians. It was as a famous general, a conqueror who had won the greatest battles in free Nueva Granada's short existence, that he landed in Cartagena on September 19, 1814. Colombians understood and accepted his defeat. Camilo Torres, the former president of the Tunja government, expressed the sentiments of many patriots when he said, "General, your country is not dead, so long as your sword lives. Parliament will give you protection, for it is satisfied with your conduct. You were unfortunate as a soldier but you are a great man."

Bolívar threw himself into the task of unifying divided Colombia. For the Tunja government he subdued rebellious Bogotá and then turned toward the coast, where he hoped to dislodge Spaniards in Santa Marta. By this time, however, his efforts on behalf of one Nueva Granada government had alienated partisans of the others. These dissident elements called him a would-be dictator. As Bolívar moved down the Magdalena toward Santa Marta, he learned that independent Cartagena would neither aid his campaign nor give him supplies.

Bolívar was reluctant to wage civil war. He had heard that General Morillo with fifteen hundred troops fresh from the Napoleonic Wars was sailing to the rebellious New World. Unity in the patriot camp became more necessary than ever before, but only Bolívar seemed to understand why. Cartagena proved deaf to all entreaties, all appeals to reason. Finally, the Liberator besieged it unsuccessfully for a month. Still Cartagena refused to co-operate in its own salvation. With the Spaniards pressing closer to South America daily, Bolívar made a drastic decision. Since his presence in Colombia only seemed to aggravate the disintegration of the country, he resigned his position and took ship for Jamaica on May 9, 1815. Cartagena might now join with the Colombian army at its gates, but Cartagena had delayed too long. The Spanish General Morillo soon brought his vaunted force to Cartagena's massive walls. After a 106-day siege, he took a city filled with rotting corpses and a handful of living skeletons.

In Jamaica, Bolívar continued to wage untiring war, this time with his pen. He turned from military to political speculations. In spontaneous, moving, and inspired phrases he set forth in his "Letter from Jamaica" the results of his musings on the future of a free South America; and in this remarkable document Bolívar foresaw the history of South America for the century after his death.

Everywhere Spain had gained the upper hand. In full control of its national sovereignty and fiercely loyal to a despotic king, the once-imprisoned Fernando, Spain was in a position to stamp out republicanism in the New World. Could free America survive in the face of these conditions? It was inevitable that it would, Bolívar declared: if not in 1815, in twenty years. "A people that loves freedom will in the end be free." The break had been made and could never again be healed.

After this statement of faith, Bolívar went on to list the internal and external changes which would follow the independence of Spanish America. Europe would find in South America profitable markets, a great new body of states to upset the old balance of power, and in the time of Europe's self-destruction, a refuge and sanctuary for its culture and learning.

The fate of the republics themselves seemed to him less predictable. What would a people unaccustomed to self-rule and responsibility make of freedom? "As long as our fellow citizens do not acquire the talents and virtues which distinguish our brothers to the north, a radical democratic system, far from being good for us, will bring ruin upon us. Unfortunately, we do not possess these traits. . . . We are ruled by corruption, which must be accepted under the rule of a country which has distinguished itself by inflexibility, ambition, vengefulness, and greed." For such infant nations Bolívar recommended a paternalistic democracy, an enlightened authoritarianism, a republic with a lifetime president —in sum, a monarchy without a king.

Reluctantly he set aside the feasibility of a union of South American states. His immediate aim was the formation of seventeen free republics. "It is a lofty idea to risk the attempt to make a single nation of the New World, with a single bond to hold all its parts together. Because they have one religion, one language, similar customs, they should logically have one government. . . . But this cannot be, for extremes of climate, differing conditions, opposing interests, and variations of characteristics divide America. . . . How ineffable it would be if the Isthmus of Panama became for America what the Straits of Corinth were for the Greeks. May God grant that we can someday enjoy the good fortune of opening a congress of representatives of the republics, kingdoms, and empires that will discuss peace and war with the rest of the nations of the world." Ten years later he opened just such a congress; it failed, as did most of his more farsighted projects, but the concept of Pan-American solidarity has never wavered since he first enunciated it.

The "Letter from Jamaica" reveals a most remarkable side to Bolívar's character. Though he clearly saw what independence would bring to Latin America, he did not flag in his efforts to produce it. Assurance of failure did not discourage him from trying to avert that failure. His job, as he saw it, was to liberate South America from Spain. The democracy and union which he also sought would have to wait upon a century of public enlightenment and experience. Nevertheless he strove constantly to stimulate union and democracy as well as independence. To him, the inevitable was just one more thing to fight.

The "Letter from Jamaica" was intended to influence English opinion in favor of independence, but as England did nothing, Bolívar sought a humbler ally. He went to Haiti, where President Pétion of the newly established republic sympathized with his aims. In return for Bolívar's promise to free all slaves in Venezuela, President Pétion provided him with 250 well-trained men and seven small ships.

Bolívar's strategy in this campaign would be inspired by a new concept. He foresaw that the province of Guayana with its control of the Orinoco would give him the key to all Venezuela. He might open from this base a two-pronged attack on the cordillera by sea and through the undefended southern plains. He had been making a thorough study of Napoleon's campaigns and was prepared to use his "war by surprise," striking the enemy where he least expected it.

The terrain on which he was to work, the resources of his army, his army itself, were to present him with inconceivable difficulties. According to Baralt and Diaz in *Resumen de la Historia de Venezuela,* he had to overcome "immense distances without bridges or roads . . . ; impassable deserts; scanty, ignorant population, part of it enemy; ambitious companions whom failure brought to his side as friends and who declared themselves enemies at the first gleam of triumph or hope; bitter, implacable, active opponents."

Bolívar's first attempt to take Guayana was a disastrous failure. After occupying Carúpano on June 1, 1815, he found that Mariño and Piar would not help him. The Spaniards were closing in by land and sea. Reluctantly he abandoned the port. With one thousand recruits he sailed west to Ocumare, a port near Maracay. He planned to take Caracas in eight days and then return to the east. From Ocumare part of his army marched inland. Some distance from town royalist forces met and defeated the advancing patriots. Though they retired in good order, false news that the Spaniards were only a few miles from Ocumare itself panicked the patriot rear guard holding the port. The city was evacuated. All the rifles and supplies Bolívar had so arduously gathered in Haiti were left behind. So were the men who had lost the inland battle to the Spaniards. Bolívar, believing all was lost, embarked for the east. He landed in Güiria where Mariño and Piar accused him of desertion. He had no recourse but to sail for Haiti to raise more men and another squadron.

During his absence the troops near Ocumare whom Bolívar had thought dead fought their way across Venezuela to join guerrillas in the llanos. There they performed the brilliant feat of taking Barcelona, which put them in touch with independent strongholds in Margarita and Cumaná. At the same time an illiterate youth named José Antonio Páez who headed a force of llaneros was threatening the Spanish along the Apure River. These were the same llaneros with whom Boves had destroyed the Second Republic. However, when Morillo arrived in Venezuela with his fifteen hundred men, he disdained llanero aid. A European educated in the fine art of Napoleonic warfare, he could not visualize the effectiveness of this force of savages in Venezuela. Leaderless, the llaneros responded to the call of Páez.

Early in 1817 Bolívar rejoined his men in Barcelona. Piar came to the city as did Urdaneta, Santander and others of the Liberator's old guard. This corps of revolutionary leaders marched with Bolívar toward Guayana where Piar had previously begun the siege of Angostura.

General Morillo, alarmed at the situation, returned from his conquest of Nueva Granada, declaring: "This is not the Venezuela I left with sufficient forces to maintain its integrity!" Margarita had expelled the Spaniards; the provinces of Cumaná, Barcelona, and the plains south of Caracas were largely lost; Páez controlled the land between the Apure and the Arauca; and Piar was hammering at Guayana. The patriots now commanded the second most important part of the country and occupied precisely the positions which Boves, Morales, and Yáñez had held three years before.

On the other hand, all was not well in the patriot camp. Bolívar had to contend with the disloyalty of Mariño, who had organized a private congress to declare him, and not Bolívar, supreme army commander. Shortly afterward Piar, too, involved himself in a conspiracy to take control, but was imprisoned, tried, and shot. His execution discouraged treason among other minor caudillos and when Mariño's army was destroyed in an unsuccessful campaign Bolívar became undisputed master and could concentrate once again on conquest.

With the help of a Haitian-supplied fleet under the command of Admiral Brion, a Curaçao merchant who bankrupted himself to aid South American independence, Bolívar cleared the Orinoco of Spaniards. Immediately he moved to join Páez, planning to hurl a combined force at Caracas. Páez insisted on attacking San Fernando de Apure instead. When the Liberator was caught between two Spanish armies near Valencia, he had to retire. At Rastro, where his men were encamped, a party of Spaniards succeeded in slipping through the lines in the guise of patriots. They made an attempt on Bolívar's life and completely demoralized his troops, who fled thinking their leader had been assassinated. Bolívar had left his hammock only a few moments before the Spaniards riddled it with bullets. In the confusion he lost touch with his scattered army and wandered for hours, on foot, in the llanos. It was typical of the man's soaring faith in himself that he should have emerged from this psychological nadir to tell the first group of patriot soldiers he saw: "I shall liberate Nueva Granada and create Gran Colombia. I shall carry the banner of liberty to Lima and Potosí."

His best infantry destroyed, Bolívar returned to Angostura. There in 1819 he called a congress to formulate a new constitution. The Congress of Angostura laid the political foundation for Venezuela's Third Republic. The constitution it adopted conformed generally to Bolívar's ideas. To no one's surprise he was named president.

Concurrently, Bolívar was incorporating a batch of new recruits into his army. In 1818 and 1819 a steady stream of Irish, British, German, and French soldiers, lured to Venezuela by fantastic and largely specious promises, trickled into the patriot quarters at Angostura. After the Napoleonic Wars, economic conditions in Europe were bad. Ex-soldiers, who had learned only the art of war in their short lives, could not find work. Many succumbed to the outlandish offers of Venezuelan emissaries, who promised good pay, bonuses, gaudy uniforms, and free transportation to veterans willing to fight a few skirmishes for a glorious cause in an exotic country where any fool might expect to make a fortune.

When European soldiers arrived in unexciting Angostura and discovered that the tropical paradise they had anticipated was green hell, their enthusiasm for Venezuelan independence naturally flagged somewhat. Nevertheless the British Legion, as it was called, made a significant contribution to the cause.

Bolívar went west again to meet Páez in March 1819. Their armies sallied forth from the llanos, attracted Morillo's attention, enticed him further and further into the plains, and ran rings around him, completely destroying his cavalry at Queseras del Medio. Bolívar was contemplating new diversions in the llanos when messengers from Santander, who commanded a force in the Colombian plains south of Bogotá, convinced him that the liberation of Nueva Granada should be the next step. From the Andean heights of Colombia he could sweep back the Spaniards to the west and the east and penetrate south to Ecuador and Peru—his ultimate goal.

If Morillo did not learn of his intentions—if Páez remained loyal—if dissensions did not break out again in Guayana—if the mountains could be crossed by an army; it would be a master stroke. Hazarding all on the throw, Bolívar made his decision. With three thousand of his men and his most able lieutenants—Soublette, Anzoátegui, and Colonel Rooke of the British Legion—he went to meet Santander. The plains were flooded; day after day the army waded forward, with inadequate clothing, harassed by mosquitoes, on minimal rations. Then came the crossing of the Andes south of Bogotá, heretofore considered impassable. The llaneros from the torrid prairies suffered agonies of cold; horses dropped on steep mountain slopes; corpses of the cattle on which the army was to feed littered the route of march.

Bolívar led his men over Pisba Pass, which the Spaniards had left unguarded because they did not believe any human being, much less an army, could cross it. Troops froze; officers abandoned their units; hundreds died of exhaustion. At last the descent began. The army found rest, warmth, and food at Socha. The survivors of Bolívar's army, far from being discouraged by what they had endured, were convinced that beside such a superhuman feat the conquest of the Spanish army was nothing. A wave of optimism swept them along.

By two flanking marches Bolívar slipped past Spanish troops in the area and took Tunja. He stood between the main Spanish army and the capital. The outflanked royalists headed for Bogotá to defend it, but Bolívar cut them off at Boyacá where, in a two-hour battle, their army was utterly destroyed. The republicans lost thirteen men. On August 10, the Liberator entered Bogotá.

Bolívar had no sooner completed this triumphal march than he had to retrace his steps. In Venezuela a revolt against his authority was in full swing and profiting by his absence. Hurrying to Angostura the Liberator squelched the opposition by reassuming power. He improved his time by prompting Congress to declare the twin provinces of Venezuela and Nueva Granada united under the name of Colombia on December 17.

During the year 1820 patriots cleared out some remaining pockets of resistance in Nueva Granada—at Rio de La Hacha and Santa Marta. A siege of Cartagena, this time by the patriots, was successful the following year. In Venezuela, nevertheless, large areas remained under Spanish control. Morillo maintained an army of twelve thousand men. Militarily, the two sides had fought to a stalemate. On the psychological front, however, the patriots were winning. The year 1817, with the formation of the Guayana fortress, was the strategic turning point of the war; 1820 marked its psychological turn. Thereafter, not only the republicans of South America, but Europe and the United States were convinced that Spain's relinquishment of her colonies was inevitable. For Spain had consented to negotiate a truce with the patriots.

Since 1813 Ferdinand VII had been sitting on the Spanish throne. He had been in power scarcely a year when he destroyed all political progress and returned to the absolutist principles of his forebears. All liberal tendencies were severely suppressed; press censorship was established, advanced thinkers imprisoned. In 1820 Spain had a liberal revolution. With strong army support the dissidents cornered Ferdinand and made him agree to all their demands. As less doctrinaire minds began shaping policy at home, Morillo was ordered to seek a reconciliation with Venezuelan rebels.

In Trujillo, Venezuela on November 25, 1820, an armistice was arranged. When its stipulations had been signed Morillo expressed a wish to meet the brilliant opponent who had so often undone his plans. Bolívar entertained the Spanish captain-general at a sumptuous banquet; toasts were drunk and compliments exchanged. Morillo, like so many men and women before him, fell victim to Bolívar's genius and charm. He was so impressed that he proposed some monument be erected to mark their meeting place. He, his host, and soldiers of both sides promptly went out and rolled up a cairn of stones. Once in Caracas Morillo resigned and returned to Spain, depriving royalist Venezuela of its most competent general.

The truce did not last long. Early in 1821 Maracaibo declared for the republicans, thus upsetting the lines of occupation laid down in the armistice. To keep the territory Bolívar notified the royalists he had renounced the truce. He said he would recommence hostilities on April 28. His goal would be Caracas and final domination of Venezuela. While Bermúdez held down one royalist detachment in the Aragua valley, Bolívar joined Páez at San Carlos and confronted the main Spanish army on the fields of Carabobo outside Valencia. In this second battle on the site, the Spaniards held strong positions commanding the only debouchement onto the battlefield. Judging this army invulnerable to frontal attack, Bolívar sent Páez and the British Legion to attack the royalist rear. Through an almost impassable but unguarded ravine the patriots crept. They forged a breach in the Spanish rear. The enemy, thrown into confusion by this unexpected assault, put up little resistance as Bolívar's main force attacked across the plain. The Spaniards met complete defeat. In all Venezuela, only Coro, Puerto Cabello, and Cumaná remained in their hands, and even the latter fell to Bermúdez in September.

The Second Battle of Carabobo ended the Venezuelan War of Independence. Resistance to republican rule remained, of course. Puerto Cabello was not wrested from the Spaniards until 1823 when Páez raised the Venezuelan tricolor over Fort San Felipe for all time. Nevertheless Spanish power in Venezuela was broken on the fields of Carabobo. Bolívar never had to fight in Venezuela again.

Venezuela suffered in the War of Independence more than any other South American nation. Eleven years of continual warfare left her prostrate. Her economy was broken. The most stable force in her society—the *criollo* class—was all but wiped out. She now enjoyed de facto independence which became more secure as the United States enunciated the Monroe Doctrine and Britain recognized the new states later in the decade. Venezuelans yearned for an end to sacrifice. Yet Bolívar demanded more. Convinced that independent South American states were threatened by provinces still in Spanish hands, he goaded his countrymen to help liberate Ecuador and Peru.

Bolívar thought in terms of continental unity, a concept far beyond the imaginative powers of his contemporaries. He saw that a divided South America would be poor, weak, and insignificant, while united as a political entity stretching across most of the Western Hemisphere it could become the most important nation in the world. Out of Ecuador, Nueva Granada, and Venezuela he forged Gran Colombia, the core of the greater, mightier federation he hoped to make. This aim baffled Venezuelans. They had struggled, bled, and impoverished themselves in the fight for independence. Now they saw that independence being submerged in a regional arrangement which seemed to leave their country as much a satellite as before. Instead of the sun in a minor solar system, Caracas promised to be just another planet in a constellation.

Regionalism worked against Bolívar. Many of his old associates became enemies, fomenting popular reaction to suit their own ends. Reaction to Bolívar, more than Bolívar himself, shaped the course of history between 1821 and 1830.

But reaction took a while to develop. In 1821 Bolívar still commanded tremendous prestige. Spain continued to menace the New World and his point about routing the royalists from Peru made sense. No one was sufficiently well known as yet to challenge him anyway. So temporarily Bolívar had his way. When the Congress of Cúcuta, which established a government for Gran Colombia in 1821, named Bolívar president of the country, he accepted on the condition that he be permitted to wage the war and leave administrative details to a vice-president. Congress agreed. Santander, the somber, twenty-nine-year-old Colombian law student and guerrilla fighter whom Bolívar had once threatened to shoot, was made vice-president at the Liberator's suggestion. Capable, ambitious, and shrewd, Santander probably had more to do with Bolívar's ruin than any other man except himself.

In Venezuela, Carlos Soublette was named administrative head. He was responsible to the Colombian Congress, Bolívar, and Santander when Santander was acting for Bolívar. Under Soublette came the commanders of the Venezuelan provinces. Among them were some familiar names—Páez, Mariño, and Bermúdez, caudillos in the making or already made. Each controlled a section of Venezuela as his reward for fighting the war. Prominent veterans were also given grants of land, the vacant haciendas whose original owners had perished during the war. A new aristocracy arose from them. Páez became one of Venezuela's richest men.

Leaving his Gran Colombia to the dubious loyalties of Santander, Páez, Mariño, and Bermúdez, Bolívar marched south to Ecuador in December 1821. In effect he no longer controlled the nation. The caudillos did. As he became liberator of Ecuador, dictator of Peru and founder of Bolivia, Santander was busily undermining his hold on Colombia while Páez bent an interested ear to the seditious suggestions of unscrupulous advisers.

Affairs in the south occupied Bolívar from December 1821 until September 1826. His career during this period was magnificent. He received jeweled tributes, directed nations, and liquidated the last Spanish armies on American soil. Even a nation was formed to perpetuate his name. But the campaign in Ecuador and Peru was as much the work of another Venezuelan—Marshal Antonio José Sucre, the most selfless and sympathetic of all the fiery youths who fought for South American liberty. Bolívar saw in this man a greatness which exceeded his own.

Antonio José Sucre came from one of the best families in eastern Venezuela. He joined the independence movement early, fighting under Miranda in 1812, and contributed his talents to Mariño's liberation of the east the following year. His preeminence in the fight for independence was always marked. Devotion to duty, loyalty, personal charm, modesty and courage made him Bolívar's most trusted officer and valuable friend. An idealist, ten years his junior, Mariscal Sucre was Bolívar's chosen successor.

It was Sucre who initiated the conquest of Ecuador in November 1820. As Bolívar suffered his first bouts with the disease which eventually killed him, Sucre directed the Colombian armies in the conquest of Peru. The Battle of Ayacucho in 1824, which destroyed the last Spanish army of any size in South America, was Sucre's victory. He also conducted the conquest of Alta Peru and first declared it an independent nation. Its name became Bolivia.

In a time of jealousy, disloyalty, and intrigue, Sucre remained Bolívar's staunchest advocate and friend. The other central figure of the Liberator's declining years was a woman. Manuela Sáenz Thorne left husband and home to follow her lover around South America. She captured Bolívar's emotions as no other woman before her, with the possible exception of his wife.

The illegitimate daughter of a Spanish nobleman and an Ecuadorian, Manuela Sáenz learned to affront society early. In a region where illegitimacy is a grave social crime, despite its appalling frequency, she cared little for what people thought since they had considered her demeaned to begin with. Being of violent and passionate temperament, she reacted against this stigma with all the violence and passion at her command. She learned to shoot and ride like a man and to flirt and make love like the beautiful and captivating hellion she was. She obeyed her whims and fancies. While attending a convent school for the good of her soul, she ran away to have an affair with a soldier. As a woman of twenty-five married to an English physician nearly twice her age, Manuela Sáenz accepted the attentions of Bolívar as a call to personal duty. The two met at a dance following the liberation of Quito, where she lived. Manuela set her sights on Bolívar and a few months later he gratefully succumbed. Manuela followed him to Peru and later to Colombia, serving him with fanatical devotion. She never regretted her affair with him, not when notoriety produced slander and disgrace, nor even when the connection induced Bolívar's enemies to exile her from Gran Colombia after his death. She died in virtual poverty.

Manuela Sáenz succored Bolívar at the time of his life he perhaps needed such support most. Physically and spiritually, Bolívar was dying as he pushed Peru and Bolivia into the patriot ranks. Tuberculosis began to eat his slim frame, destroying energy he might have directed toward curing the political diseases which had begun to afflict his South America. From 1826 to 1830, Bolívar's star steadily waned. With the elimination of Spanish threats to national sovereignty, caudillos threw off their wraps and showed themselves for what they really were. Their personal ambition helped tear South America apart. Bolívar himself most eloquently described the dilemma their machinations created for him when he said: "If I go north, the south will disintegrate; if I go south, the north will revolt."

Yet, when everything promised disunion, Bolívar continued to plan for larger and larger unions of South American nations. Just as Venezuela, Nueva Granada, and Ecuador had become parts of Gran Colombia so should Gran Colombia, Peru, and Bolivia join together in a Federation of the Andes. Perhaps the adulation the Bolivians accorded him when he visited that country in 1825 convinced him that he was popular enough to effect this. Not only did the Bolivians insist on naming their country after him, but they commissioned him to write the constitution for the new state as well. The result—the Bolivian Constitution—was the distillation of Bolívar's political ideas. He thought to make it the rock base for his Federation of the Andes. Instead it helped destroy the only supranational authority which existed—Gran Colombia.

In almost everything he wrote on politics, Bolívar openly advocated strong, central government in immature South America. His Bolivian Constitution reflected this studied judgment. He wanted a president who would serve for life and have the privilege of choosing his successor. It was a sensible suggestion, in view of conditions, but it fed his enemies damaging material. When he had the Peruvian Parliament adopt the constitution and sent a copy to Bogotá for study, he laid himself open to unflattering accusations. It seemed obvious to many that Bolívar was trying to crown himself king of northern South America.

The same year that Bolívar drafted his master constitution, reaction against him began to have a profound effect on the countries he had liberated. In 1826, Venezuelans under José Antonio Páez revolted against the government of Gran Colombia.

Santander called for Bolívar. In September 1826, the Liberator left Lima on the long trip to Caracas. As his army marched he learned that the part of Venezuela under Páez' control had declared its independence from Gran Colombia.

Bolívar wished to avoid fighting fellow Venezuelans. He aimed to conciliate rather than reprimand Páez. In the end, he avoided war by confirming the llanero as supreme leader in Venezuela. Páez reciprocated by recognizing Bolívar as the ultimate authority over him. In effect, Bolívar had sanctioned the revolt, and Santander was justly enraged. "The Pacification," as this agreement is termed, opened the door to anarchy and the eventual disintegration of Gran Colombia.

On the other hand, Gran Colombia would have disintegrated anyway. Peru abrogated Bolívar's beloved constitution in 1827. The Colombian army in Peru mutinied and sailed home the same year. Peru, left to her own devices, menaced Ecuador and demanded the annexation of Guayaquil. In a few months Bolívar's enemies in the south destroyed the results of four years' work.

The Liberator struggled to preserve what remained. He cited the Páez revolt as proof that Colombia needed a stronger constitution. A Congress was invoked at Ocaña, and when the delegates scrapped the old constitution without voting for a new one Bolívar had himself proclaimed dictator in Bogotá.

Throughout this period he was fighting the influence of Santander, who favored sovereignty for Nueva Granada and a representative government with limited authority. The brilliant Colombian had many partisans among his countrymen and opposition to Bolívar's dictatorship frequently took the form of support for him. His cause was liberal while Bolívar's was conservative. To many the Liberator, who had reluctantly established absolute rule as a check against anarchy, had become a tyrant. Secretly they planned to overthrow him, and on the night of September 25, 1828, some of them tried to assassinate him.

Bolívar was in the presidential palace with Manuela when the noisy cluster of Colombian revolutionaries besieged it. The insurgents overcame the guards, wounded an aide, and began pounding on the Liberator's door. Inside Manuela dissuaded Bolívar from fighting the lot of them and urged him to slip out of the window. By stalling the assassins while he made his getaway she saved his life. From then on Bolívar called her *"La Libertadora del Libertador."*

The revolt which was supposed to follow the assassination never developed. The army remained loyal to Bolívar and crushed the dissidents utterly. Among those prosecuted was Francisco Santander, an accessory before the fact. Though not one of the conspirators, Santander knew about the plot and might have warned Bolívar if he had cared to. He was exiled after a death sentence had been commuted, and lived to become independent Nueva Granada's first strong man.

This 1828 uprising was a symptom. Reaction kept cropping up along the northern shoulder of South America until every one of the old Spanish provinces had rejected Bolivarism and made itself a nation. A revolt broke out in southern Nueva Granada; Peru invaded Ecuador; citizens of Venezuela and Nueva Granada talked ominously of secession. To preserve the union, loyal Colombians began to consider some drastic proposals. The Colombian cabinet argued for the establishment of a monarchy.

This talk of monarchy was all Páez and Venezuela needed. Bolívar had invited them to express their wishes concerning the kind of government they wanted, as a preliminary to a National Assembly which was to be held in Bogotá early in 1830. Venezuelans were supposed to submit their thoughts upon a new Gran Colombian constitution. Instead, goaded by seditionists and rumors of monarchy, they supported independence from Gran Colombia. At meetings across the land citizens anathematized Bolívar as a dictator and a traitor. They plastered their cities with signs. Municipal councils voted to ignore Bolívar's orders. At the end of the year 1829 Páez gladly bowed to what seemed to be universal public sentiment and declared Venezuela a free nation.

Nueva Granada waited only a few weeks before traveling the same path. At the constitutional convention Bolívar had called to strengthen the Gran Colombian federation, Nueva Granada separatists urged that their country follow Venezuela's example. Everyone conceded that Bolívar was through. Legislators and Colombian officials ignored his offers to continue as president and were horrified by his suggestion that he lead an army against Venezuela. They established an anti-Bolívar government. Fearing the Liberator's influence, they gave him a pension and politely invited him to leave the country. On May 8, 1830, Bolívar left Bogotá forever.

Prematurely old, chronically sick and thoroughly discouraged, the Liberator trekked toward the lowlands and exile. It was a humiliating experience for the proud man who loved to appear before cheering crowds and deliver ringing predictions about South America's coming glory. He had dedicated his fortune, his health, and his being to a grand idea—personal liberty, political democracy in South America and international government. The idea was still grand, but Bolívar knew that for centuries it would remain a hope rather than an actuality.

Even today Bolívar is decades ahead of his compatriots. If George Washington could now revisit the country he helped establish, his astonishment and delight would be instantaneous and profound. "My God!" he might say. "Look what happened!" Given the same opportunity to survey his countries in 1952, Bolívar would find military governments in Peru and Venezuela, civil war in Colombia, and a bloody revolution in Bolivia. He could only shake his head and remark, "Just as I feared."

Bolívar was to learn more about South America's perfidious instability before his death. In July 1830, he heard that Marshal Sucre had been assassinated by a band of thugs, probably at the instigation of ambitious politicos who dreaded his popularity and influence. Word arrived from Venezuela that a National Assembly had declared the Liberator an outlaw.

During the summer and fall of 1830 Bolívar's strength ebbed. His death was clearly imminent. When he was transported from Barranquilla to his last sanctuary in Santa Marta, Colombia, he was too weak to walk off the ship. Ironically, it was a Spaniard, a former royalist, who took Bolívar into his home when most of his countrymen had turned him out. Those last few days were pathetic rather than tragic. The tragedies in Bolívar's life had already taken place.

"We have plowed the seas," was the way he now described his career. Yet from his deathbed he beseeched Colombians to unite.

On December 17, 1830, he died—not knowing whether his valiant efforts had contributed to the happiness of one single American. That was his cross. His last words were uttered in delirium.

"Let's go. Let's go," he said. "These people don't want us in this country. Let's go, boys. Take my luggage aboard the ship."

Chapter XI

DEFENDER OF THE FAITH

CALDERÓN DE LA BARCA, last great artist of Spain's Golden Age, deals with free will in *La Vida es Sueño,* a verse drama about a young prince who after spending his entire life in a prison is suddenly placed upon a throne to rule a nation. The prince, Segismundo, is both man and monster. Inexperienced, half-educated, crude, and passionate, he swings from generosity to brutality in the exercise of his powers. He grants bountiful gifts and insults his court, shifting like a weathercock in a hurricane. In one scene he kills a servant by tossing him from a balcony, simply because the lackey contradicts him.

Venezuela in 1824 was Segismundo—newly liberated by a group of discontented courtiers from a three-hundred-year imprisonment and flung raw into her stormy career as a self-governing republic. Her destinies for the first twenty years were guided by a man like herself: untrained and violent, but with remarkable native potentialities: José Antonio Páez.

Born in 1790 near Acarigua, Páez came from no such aristocratic stock as Bolívar or even Miranda. His father was a clerk in the service of the royal tobacco monopoly in Guanare. Páez received scant education. He studied reading and writing under a teacher almost as ignorant as her pupils, and promptly forgot what he had learned when one relative and then a second took over his care and set him to work tending store and planting cacao.

It was to a limbo of perpetual insignificance that José Antonio Páez had been born, and it was only by committing murder and becoming a fugitive from justice that he escaped into a field of action where his peculiar talents could assert themselves. When he was seventeen his mother sent him on business to a town some distance away and while returning young Páez was imprudent enough to flash his moderate funds in a village store. Some miles out of town he was attacked by four men. In self-defense, Páez says in his autobiography, he drew a pistol and shot the leader of the bandits. The others fled and so did the murderer, terrified by what he had done.

Páez sought sanctuary in the vastness of the llanos. He became a wild man of the plains. As a peon in the service of wealthy ranchers, he roamed the scorched prairie on horseback from three in the morning until nightfall. He guided cattle across wide rivers, though he had never learned to swim. His foreman, a Negro slave named Manuelote, disliked him and saved the roughest tasks for the novice. Páez rode until his buttocks and hands were raw. He ate fresh unsalted beef and slept on the ground. His stocky frame hardened like tempering steel. Dry winds, rough and hot as a sandblast, cured his light skin. He became a llanero, a strong, hardy, fierce, lusty, and unpredictable creature who measured a man by his ability to outwit a bull.

With the outbreak of war in 1810, Páez joined a regiment of patriot cavalry and fought with it until Monteverde overran Venezuela in 1813. The royalist victory sent Páez back to civilian life in Barinas, but when the Spaniards arrived and insisted he accept a commission in their cavalry, he fled to join a revolutionary band. The years from 1810 to 1815 saw Páez mature into a seasoned fighter. He also experienced a psychological revelation. He changed from a youth content to follow others into a man who sensed he was born to lead. In 1815 he began to emerge as the second most important figure in the fight for Venezuelan independence. By that year, he had conceived a plan for wresting Venezuela from the Spaniards, who had just reconquered the province for a second time. While Bolívar and Urdaneta were still thinking in terms of another invasion from Colombia, Páez implemented the strategy which eventually won the war. He sought control over the lands that had given the Spaniards their victory in 1814—the llanos.

On the surface, it was a mad scheme. The llaneros were royalists. Under Boves and Yáñez they had been the scourge of the patriots in the preceding campaign. But Páez, who knew them, recognized that the plainsmen had no political creed. They fought for plunder and for the love of fighting. Now that the Spaniards instead of the patriots owned Venezuela, *they* became the natural prey of the have-not llaneros. Despite his later declarations that he roused in his people an awareness of independence and a feeling for their own country, Páez won the llaneros by appealing to the same base instincts Boves had manipulated.

When Bolívar later asked Páez' chief bodyguard, El Negro Primero, why he had fought with the royalists before passing to the revolutionaries, the man replied, "Greed."

"How was that?" inquired Bolívar.

"I had noted," the Negro went on, "that everybody went to war without a shirt and without a peseta and came back afterward dressed in a fine uniform and with money in his purse. So I wanted to go and seek my fortune and more than anything to get—silver. The first battle we had against the patriots was Araure: they had more than a thousand men . . . we had many more men and I cried that they should give me a weapon to fight with, because I was sure that we were going to win. When I thought the battle was over, I got down from my mule and went to take a very nice coat from a white who was lying dead on the ground. At this moment the commander came along yelling, 'To horse!' How can this be, I said, hasn't the war ended? Ended, by no means; so many people appeared that they looked like a flock of vultures."

"Then what did you say?" said Bolívar.

"I wished we would make peace. There was nothing to do but run away, and I began to run after my mule, but the cursed animal had gotten tired of me and I had to catch a mount on foot. The next day I and my buddy José Félix went to a herd to see if they would give us something to eat; but its owner, when he knew that I was from the troops of Nana (Yáñez) looked at me so unpleasantly that it seemed better to flee and go to the Apure."

"They say," Bolívar interrupted, "that there you killed cows which didn't belong to you."

"Of course," he replied, "otherwise what was I to eat? Finally the boss (Páez) came to the Apure, and taught us what the fatherland was and that 'devilocracy' wasn't such a bad thing, and since then I have served with the patriots."

In both temperament and training Páez made an excellent commander. Toward his men he felt an almost paternal tenderness and pride. They in turn adored him, and referred to him as "Uncle." Discipline in what became the Páez battalion was not a matter of rules, but of mingled love and respect. Because their leader understood their backgrounds, their longings, and their needs, because he talked to them like younger brothers, because his wrath was immediate, just, and terrible, and because in strength, agility and daring he equalled or excelled them, his followers gave him a fervent loyalty. Their respect was mingled, too, with a breath of superstitious awe, for Páez was an epileptic and frequently, under the stress of excitement, rode into battle with reckless audacity, foaming at the mouth.

The measure of Páez as a man, however, did not rest in his ability to match or surpass his followers in their animalistic pursuits. Beyond his strength, his audacity, and his crudeness lay a rare capacity for intellectual and spiritual growth. When he first led the llaneros, he could not remember how to read or write. He had never used a knife and fork. In his lifetime, he not only mastered these rudimentary skills, he took up the violincello, wrote an autobiography, developed manners acceptable in Caracas society, and studied the classics. He brought the first symphony orchestra to Venezuela. Gil Fortoul in his *Historia Constitucional de Venezuela* describes Páez' conquest of his own brutal nature by comparing him with his royalist predecessor, Tomás Boves. "Both began with clouded minds. But Boves' mind remained clouded, while Páez' became gradually enlightened. The former stays the same until he dies; the other is transformed. The one was born to hate and revenge; from his mother's womb he came with the instincts of an uncivilizable barbarian. From his mother's womb the other brought a propensity to become civilized, to serve his fellow men, and finally becomes convinced that above instinct is idea, above base passion noble conscience, above momentary self-interest the permanent ideal."

Under Páez, consequently, the llaneros were not the marauding monsters they had been before. They fought like savages, to be sure, but when the battle was over, Páez did not egg them on, like Boves, to gory pastimes and wanton slaughter. He restrained them; punished despoilers of the innocent with bare fists. He spared prisoners when he could and intelligently tried to incorporate them into his own forces. This was not a man who lusted for blood, especially the blood of Venezuelans. Páez, for all his shortcomings, possessed a primitive sense of "la patria."

Páez was undisputed master of warfare in the llanos. Even from Bolívar he accepted no advice on how and where his men should fight. In the Apure, his tactics were extraordinarily successful. As a military strategist, he made the most of the two things he really knew: the terrain on which he operated and the men with whom he fought. He was ferocious, swift, and unorthodox. He had never read a book on tactics, but for that very reason he trampled continental soldiers who had. While they relied upon an efficient firing line and orderly formations, Páez looked to the wind, the rivers, and the expanse of the llanos for inspiration.

His genius for improvisation gave rise to some highly original maneuvers. Among his more spectacular feats is one that has become a legend. Bolívar, Páez, and their armies wanted to cross the Apure River. The sole ford was well-guarded by the enemy; the patriots had no ships and on the other side of the river Spanish gunboats made royalist control of the situation complete. Bolívar, pacing up and down, bemoaned the absence of water transport. The reaction of Páez was typical. He approached the Liberator and promised that if Bolívar would order an advance he would provide the ships.

"But man, where are they?" Bolívar demanded.

"In the river," replied Páez laconically.

"And how can we take them?"

"With cavalry."

"Where is this water cavalry?" inquired Bolívar. "I know land cavalry can't perform any such miracle."

"Here," said Páez, pointing to his llaneros; and he won Bolívar's permission to make the attempt.

When they reached the river bank, Páez and fifty men from his Guard of Honor flung themselves and their horses into the stream. They swam it and hurled themselves upon the gunboat crews who, aghast at this unconventional advance, fired a few shots and jumped into the water, leaving their ships in patriot hands.

On another occasion, when Páez had no craft to operate on the Apure and the Spaniards did, he and his men planted themselves on sandbars, water to their shoulders, in the middle of the river, and assaulted the gunboats as they went by. During the Battle of Mucuritas, Páez aligned his force upwind from the royalists. Then he set fire to the prairie grass. As the flames swept down on them Spaniards dropped arms, abandoned positions and fled for a nearby water hole where yelling llaneros completed the rout.

In the nature of José Antonio Páez, Bolívar found the elements of both his victory and his defeat. It was Páez who delivered the Apure region to the patriots. It served as a redoubt for patriot formations and as a catapult for attacks against the mountain strongholds of Spain. Using the llanos as a base, Bolívar conquered Nueva Granada, cleared the cordillera from Bogotá to Caracas and prepared the way for his march south. José Antonio Páez gave him that opportunity.

In 1816, the most powerful man in Venezuela was Páez, not Bolívar. When Bolívar arrived at Barcelona to begin the nine-year campaign which ended in total victory for the republicans, he had his name, a handful of soldiers recruited in Haiti, a squadron of ships, and a fanatical belief in his own capacities. Páez commanded the most formidable army in Venezuela and his command over that army was absolute. The Liberator, on the other hand, was forced to contend with the antagonism of Mariño and Piar.

When the Tiger of the Apure might have used his power to undermine Bolívar's leadership, he accepted a satellite role against the apparent interests of his own ascendancy and in defiance of his men, who claimed he did not have the right to transfer the authority they had given him to Bolívar. In his autobiography, Páez explains, "Consulting only the good of the motherland, taking into account the military gifts of Bolívar, the prestige of his name already known even abroad, and understanding above all the advantage of having a supreme authority and center to direct the different caudillos operating in various regions, I decided to submit my authority to that of General Bolívar."

General Páez' high-flown explanations of his own behavior does him more credit than he deserves. If he had possessed Bolívar's self-confidence the llanero might have usurped the Liberator's place. Unlike Piar, Bermúdez, and Mariño, however, Páez seemed to recognize his limitations. For the first of many times in his life, he is revealed as a man who bowed to competence when he moved in unfamiliar realms. He knew the Apure. He knew the llanos. He was sure of his military ability. But of governments, constitutions, and international federations, Páez comprehended next to nothing, and because he did not presume to understand them, he had the healthy humility to accept the advice of others more sophisticated than himself. He enjoyed his power, but except as a soldier, he needed someone else to show him how to use it. Sometimes, unfortunately, he could not tell a good suggestion from a bad one, especially if it involved a warmer place in the sun for himself. It was this trait which made him swear allegiance to Bolívar in 1817 and which laid him open, later on, to the seditious advice of his political tutors.

Bolívar and Páez met for the first time on January 30, 1818, south of San Fernando de Apure. As the two figures, the one bull-like, the other lithe, dismounted and embraced, they symbolically tied the entire southern tier of Venezuela to a common cause. Yet the meeting symbolized more than that. Páez, the man of the people, the defiant child of neglect, and Bolívar, a conceit of Venezuelan culture, a near relative to Plato's philosopher king, were violent expressions of a diverse society. They had two things in common: both believed in independence and both were Venezuelans. In their mutual devotion to these two concepts, the Venezuelan nation was born.

Páez grew with the revolution. At war's end, he enjoyed a popularity in Venezuela second only to Bolívar's. It was natural that the fledgling republic should fortify itself by naming its strongest military leaders to govern the three provinces into which the country was divided and it was not only natural, but inevitable, that José Antonio Páez should have been named governor of the choicest part, including Caracas, the valleys of Aragua and Valencia.

Páez was a man who could improve his time in peace as well as in war. He had the instincts of a peasant and his mind became riveted on the land. The infant nation had no gold with which to thank its liberators. She gave them credit slips instead. Since the men preferred money, Páez obliged many veterans by buying their slips at a cut rate. With the proceeds he purchased an estate, a personal economic empire. He loved to ride across his holdings on a white horse and the sight of his lands stretching across the horizon filled his primitive soul with exultant pride. A few years before he had suffered the torments and degradations of a peon's existence; now he had more wealth and power than his limited imagination could grasp. For a time he was satisfied.

There was still work for Páez the general. The remnants of Morillo's once mighty army now languished in Puerto Cabello, where they waited for Spain to reinforce or relieve them. They constituted a major menace to the existence of free Venezuela. Puerto Cabello could be the bow which might once again send a shaft through the heart of Gran Colombia. Páez besieged the point for two years before he broke Spanish resistance by subterfuge. Capturing a Negro slave who was being sent by his Spanish masters through an apparently impenetrable mangrove swamp to spy on the patriots, Páez won the man's devotion and induced him to divulge his secret route. A few nights later Páez' army emerged from the swamp, naked except for their weapons, to overwhelm the surprised defenders.

The fall of Puerto Cabello destroyed the last Spanish contingents in Venezuela, but roving bandits still harassed the countryside, brandishing a fealty to Spain to glorify their lust for pillage. The depredations of these ruffian crews demanded the constant vigil of republican military authorities. It was 1846 before Páez dispatched the last royalist chief.

The incursions of these bands, plus the rumor that the Holy Alliance might move against the New World, had induced the Colombian Congress in 1824 to pass a law providing for a militia in each state of the Gran Colombian federation. To fulfill Venezuela's obligation under this law Páez had shanghaied some of his fellow citizens after public meetings had produced only a handful of recruits. Out of this indiscretion arose the charge that Páez had violated civil rights under the Colombian Constitution. Congress removed him from his command and ordered him to Bogotá for trial. The reaction of Páez produced the schism of 1826.

Páez felt the accusation was unfair. He had only tried to implement the laws of the Colombian Congress. His removal from command appeared a calculated insult. Legal redress was open to him, but its nature did not appeal to the temperament of a man like Páez, to whom laws were as yet an argle-bargle of confusing nonsense, a trial an indignity and submission to criticism by a higher authority unbearable. Though Santander wrote persuasive letters, assuring him the Congress would acquit him, Páez morosely suspected the Gran Colombian vice-president of inciting the legislators to do just the opposite. It was Francisco Santander, whom Páez had supplanted as military chief of the llanos after an army-wide election in 1816. Santander might be harboring a grudge. If the Senate condemned Páez his future was ruined, and primarily through what appeared to him the intrigues of jealous enemies.

Nevertheless he surrendered his office and might have continued to obey Congress had it not been for the influence of his confidant, Dr. Miguel Peña, himself a fugitive from Colombian justice. Behind Peña were other forces which seized the opportunity to take advantage of Páez' surly humor—the parties favoring a revised constitution and more independence for Venezuela. So, under Peña's prompting, the Valencia cabildo declared for Páez in April 1826, insisting that the General return to power. Shortly afterward the Caracas cabildo followed suit. Mariño and other high authorities swore obedience to the llanero. The country lay in a state of open, if passive revolt.

In his autobiography, Páez bitterly denounces himself for cooperating with Venezuelan malcontents. "In an unlucky hour," he says, "I reassumed the command from which I had been so unjustly suspended, and the first step taken, it was necessary to continue in the error I had committed." Be that as it may, Páez tripped willingly enough down the primrose path to power in 1826. He called a public meeting in Caracas on November 7, to decide the political future of Venezuela. There, in the San Francisco convent, the secession of Venezuela from the Gran Colombian federation was officially proposed for the first time. Prominent Venezuelans who were opposed to this extreme step argued persuasively. Páez was presiding, and when he saw that their opinions might prevail, he guillotined the discussion and called for a vote. All those in favor of secession were asked to raise their hands. A few arms waved above the assembled mob. Without counting them or comparing the number with those which remained folded in their owners' laps, Páez announced the question had been resolved affirmatively. The act embodying the decision was signed by 43 citizens and 15 soldiers. After being publicly displayed in the Concejo Municipal for a week, this rump declaration attracted a grand total of 260 signatures. Thus, "democratically," Páez made Venezuela a sovereign state. He commanded a loyal army. He had the power and no one could stop him, not even Bolívar, who to preserve an influence over Páez and avert civil war had to rubberstamp his theft of Venezuela. After the "Pacification" of 1826, Páez was the supreme commander in Venezuela, responsible only to Bolívar. Technically, Venezuela remained a part of Gran Colombia. But in fact, Páez could do as he pleased.

The defection of Páez could not have surprised Bolívar. It was he who had said, "My friend General Páez is the most vainglorious and ambitious man in the world. He knows only his own nothingness, and the pride of ignorance makes him blind. He will always be a tool in the hands of advisers."

As supreme commander of Venezuela, Páez had to grope his way through the complications and responsibilities of his new eminence with the maleficent Dr. Peña to guide him. A personal loyalty to Bolívar manifested itself for a while. In the Pacification the Liberator had not reprimanded him, but, as Páez saw it, had taken his part against the "villain" Santander. Consequently he supported Bolívar's dictatorship in 1827, depended upon Bolívar's advice to a certain extent, and attempted to mitigate growing anti-Bolívar feeling in Venezuela. At the same time, he was enjoying his new power and since he wanted to keep control of a country whose strongest political party was opposed to

Bolívar's superstate notions, he learned to steer an independent course, one calculated above everything to preserve his personal popularity in Venezuela.

To stay popular in 1829 Páez had to help Venezuela secede. This is not to say that General Páez demonstrated any implacable aversion to independence from Bogotá; but this time his acts were really supported, even dictated, by the discontent of the country's leaders with Venezuela's status in the Gran Colombian federation. Two of the major political factions in the country vociferously urged the step. Bolívar had been dictator in Bogotá since 1827. His Bolivian Constitution and discussions by his cabinet of the possibility of installing a king to help unite Venezuela, Ecuador, and Nueva Granada gave rise to ugly rumors that Bolívar wished to perpetuate his hold on power forever. Venezuelans argued that one congress could not pass laws which would benefit the divergent economic and social systems of three distinct areas. More than anything, Venezuelans wanted to rule Venezuela without interference from any outsider, Bolívar included.

As in 1826, Valencia was the first Venezuelan city to insist upon separation in 1829. A citizens' assembly, dominated by Dr. Peña and other Páez disciples, introduced the motion. The Caracas assembly, mouthpiece of wealthy landowners and businessmen, followed suit. This time there was no need to juggle a count of hands. On January 13, 1830, Páez issued instructions for the election of a purely Venezuelan congress which met at Valencia in April.

This constitutional congress inaugurated a conspicuously successful regime. For the next eighteen years, Venezuelans had a strong, honest, fairly enlightened, and practical government which dragged the country from an economic mire and set its shaky feet on solid ground. It cajoled or coerced its unruly citizens into respect for law and allegiance to constitutional procedure; checked the power of the army on which its existence depended; and established the principle of civilian administration. This made it unique in Venezuelan history, and the man who made it unique was José Antonio Páez.

Páez [says Gil Fortoul in *Historia Constitucional de Venezuela*] revealed no little political talent, gathering into his own orbit the most influential men of the oligarchy, civilians and military men alike. He succeeded in making them respect unreservedly his authority and dissipated the fear they often felt of seeing the warrior's prestige overshadow the effectiveness of the law. Instinctively rather than deliberately he tended to fulfill the function of certain constitutional monarchs, preferring to exercise only a decorative role when no great national conflict arose and leaving to his ministers the daily administrative tasks. He freed the administration of government funds from dishonest maneuvers, and thus inspired the working classes, commerce, and industry with blind confidence. And thanks to his expansive open manner, courteous without affectation, he attached to his person the sympathies of all social classes, even the highest, to such a point that the censure which some aspects of his private life [women] merited, changed to affectionate tolerance. And yet this was the man who had passed his boyhood in the humble condition of peon of a herd and his youth in the battlefield, a life whose intimate impulses ran unchecked like the horse of the llanos.

Much of the credit for Páez exemplary behavior goes to Carlos Soublette, who ousted Peña and became the General's brains. Carlos Soublette deserves a more prominent place in Venezuelan history than he is usually accorded. He was the military aide who held the lantern so that Francisco de Miranda might contemptuously scan the faces of the young patriots who came to arrest him in 1812. For the rest of his life, he continued to hold a lantern for other spectacular Venezuelans while he illuminated their councils with sober insight and subdued brilliance.

Carlos Soublette was half Venezuelan, a condition Francisco de Miranda claimed was his only defect. Born in La Guaira, the son of a French father and a Venezuelan mother, Soublette joined the patriot movement in 1810 at the age of 31. His tact, intelligence, and French ancestry endeared him to Miranda, whose secretary and aide-de-camp he became. Miranda gone, he distinguished himself in the battles of 1813, the siege of Cartagena in 1815, and, as a staunch supporter of Bolívar, during the campaigns from 1816 to 1822. The designation of Soublette as Venezuela's constitutional chief after the war attests to Bolívar's faith in his abilities.

In this role he did his best to direct Páez, Mariño, and Bermúdez, his technical subordinates, and keep them loyal to the Gran Colombian ideal. He frequently quarreled with Páez, whom he accused of neglecting "la patria grande" in favor of his "patriecita," the Apure, and hazarded the llanero's enmity by meddling in military affairs which Páez considered nobody's business but his own. When Bolívar confirmed Páez' usurpation of Venezuela in 1826, Soublette was kicked upstairs to a post in Nueva Granada, where he served faithfully until it became clear to him that the future of his country lay with Páez rather than ailing Bolívar. He returned to Venezuela and helped Páez engineer the final separation of 1829.

Soublette married Páez to the oligarchy of prominent landowners and intellectuals which actually ruled Venezuela during the Páez period. They made a perfect couple. Páez was the head of the household and the oligarchy managed it. Unlike other dictators who feel their military prowess qualifies them to do anything from running the public treasury to reforming the law code, Páez stuck to his army. The result was a stable and relatively intelligent regime.

The oligarchy counted in its ranks the finest talents Venezuela could offer in 1830—men like Soublette, Martín Tovar, Santos Michelena, and Diego Bautista Urbaneja. Some were the survivors of the *criollo* aristocracy which had pushed Venezuela into the revolution in 1810. Others like Páez himself achieved wealth and position during the war. The members of the oligarchy had benefited from a peculiar experience in government. They had helped write three constitutions for their country. They had seen Venezuela as a colonial minion, a dictatorship, and part of a federation. These experiments had taught the legislators who gathered at Valencia in April 1830 that Venezuela should be the ward of the educated and propertied classes, which meant themselves. Military or popular rule would result in dictatorship or anarchy, they said. So they wrote a constitution restricting suffrage to property owners.

The constitution reserved a measure of autonomy for provinces and municipalities; each province had its own legislature and its own governor to deal with purely local problems. Freedom of the press, freedom of speech, and freedom of religion were guaranteed.

What is more, the oligarchs, or the Conservatives as they were later called, upheld these principles stoutly.

It was government by law. The Conservatives respected the law and Páez made the country uphold it. As long as the man who held military power respected the will of Congress, Venezuela could have orderly government. Unfortunately for the political maturation of the country, Páez was the only caudillo who ever did.

The period of Páez' supremacy presented numerous tests of his loyalty to principle and his respect for law. His first year as president of Venezuela was disrupted by a revolt not against him, but against the constitution. In 1830 certain army generals, upset by constitutional restrictions of army privileges, twice induced Venezuelan cities to denounce the government and proclaim a superficial allegiance to Bolívar and Gran Colombia. The militarists expected to have General Páez' sympathies. They offered to recognize his authority. But Páez threatened to lead superior forces against them unless they came to terms—which they did.

Páez even remained loyal to the constitution at the cost of his personal supremacy. The law forbade Páez to succeed himself and in the elections of 1835 he supported his deputy Soublette. The other important candidates were General Mariño and Dr. José Vargas, a professor at the University of Caracas. Vargas won. Páez, assuring the new president of his loyalty, promptly retired to his ranch at San Pablo. Not so the militarists. Contemptuous of Vargas who had spent the revolution studying abroad, and whose election had been intended to check their power further, the little colonels and generals organized a coup d'état on July 8, 1835. In the name of Páez and Mariño, they kidnaped Vargas and shipped him off to the Virgin Islands.

Páez heard the news a week later. Gathering a handful of peons from his ranch, he advanced on Caracas to proclaim the Constitution and Vargas. Recruits swelled his army along the way. Two weeks later the revolutionaries were defeated everywhere in Venezuela except in Puerto Cabello, which surrendered in February 1836. Good as his word, Páez reinstalled Vargas, who resigned the next year after a misunderstanding with Congress.

Vice-President Soublette succeeded Vargas as chief executive and served until Páez was elected to the presidency for the period 1839 to 1843. When Páez finished his second administration, propertied Venezuelans elected Soublette to a full term.

The Conservative oligarchy was a misnomer. Though its members demonstrated the usual reluctance of the rich to change, their administration was more liberal in many respects than any government Venezuela had until 1935. Their successors for the most part were dishonest, corrupt, totalitarian, and repressive. They called themselves Liberals, but reserved their liberality exclusively for raids on the public treasury.

In eighteen years, the Conservatives amortized one-third of the national debt, established foreign credit, stimulated road construction, doubled the number of municipal schools, revised the complex Spanish legal code, established pensions and guaranteed job security for civil servants, endeavored to free all the slaves and did free some of them, negotiated a peace treaty with Spain in 1845 (twenty-two years after the fighting stopped), and above all gave their countrymen a rare glimpse at political integrity and legal government. They may be criticized for never carrying good ideas far enough. Grave problems still faced the republic. For example, 416 out of 537 parishes in the country still lacked public schools even after the Conservatives built 119 new facilities. They instinctively mistrusted all radical steps or expansive projects. Dissatisfaction with the shortcomings of the government inevitably led to the formation of an opposition party.

The founders of the Liberal Party had been members of the Conservative oligarchy. Tomás Lander, Francisco Rodríguez (the former Marqués del Toro), Juan Bautista Mijares, Diego Bautista Urbaneja, and Manuel Felipe de Tovar, along with others, objected to the monopoly of the presidency by Soublette and Páez. Since the two worked hand in glove, they tended to surround themselves with the same faces. The dissidents favored a two-party system and true alternative government. In 1840, they established a newspaper called *El Venezolano* to express their points of view. Its editor was Antonio Leocadio Guzmán, a political opportunist, who fathered genuine democracy in Venezuela and a son who utterly destroyed it.

Antonio Leocadio Guzmán was a grasping little parvenu, who,

chameleon-like, changed colors to suit the political cloth. His father was a Spanish officer who fought the patriots and young Antonio was educated in Spain. Born in 1801 or 1802, eight years before his parents were married, Antonio Leocadio Guzmán was too young to take a political part in the Venezuelan Revolution, but in defiance of his father, he returned to Venezuela in 1822 and identified himself with the victorious revolutionaries at a time when Spain still planned to reinvade her rebellious province. He started a newspaper, *El Argos,* whose audacious articles gave its editor some notoriety. He wormed his way into Páez' circle and was sent by Páez to Bolívar in 1825 with a suggestion that the Liberator come home to Venezuela and make himself king.

When Páez and Peña espoused separatism Antonio naturally did the same. His devotion to Páez won him the post of Minister of the Interior in 1831. Eight years later intrigue brought about his removal from the administration. With the advent of *El Vene-zolano,* Guzmán spied a new avenue to power. In its pages he made himself the chief propagandist of the Liberal Party. A decade of rule by a wealthy oligarchy gave him juicy material.

He demanded universal suffrage, immediate emancipation of the slaves, and the abolition of capital punishment for political crimes. He ranted about a Conservative law which discriminated against debtors. Venezuela needed a legal maximum for interest rates. The "godos" (Goths), as he called the Conservatives, were grinding the lower classes, he said.

It was an attractive program. It appealed to the downtrodden, the economically oppressed, every segment of the disenfranchised mass. Antonio Leocadio Guzmán had a winning platform. He pushed it for all it was worth. Such was the violence of his views that within a few months of his newspaper's founding his "liberal" backers decided they weren't so liberal after all and withdrew their support. But Guzmán did not need them. It was his movement now. The common man wheeled into formation behind him.

If this program had become an actuality, Antonio Leocadio Guzmán, scoundrel though he was, would have been a democratic hero. Every charge he brought against the Conservatives had a basis in fact. But caudillos of the Liberal party did to Antonio what the Russians have done to Marx. They proclaimed liberal principles to mask despotic practices. Universal suffrage was guaranteed in the constitution but for the next one hundred years there was only one party to vote for. Central government was denounced —so Venezuela became an absolute dictatorship.

In February 1844, Antonio Leocadio discovered just how popular he was. He had been cited for libel after a newspaper printed in a shop he owned slandered a minor government official. Guzmán claimed the editor of the newspaper rather than he was responsible. He defended himself with great eloquence. A crowd of his partisans filled the courtroom drowning out the judge's voice with cheers for Antonio and cries of "Death to the government!" When the terrified jury returned a verdict of not guilty, the mob carried Guzmán through the streets in triumph, hailing him as a second Liberator.

Thus encouraged, Antonio Leocadio Guzmán ran for president, which was what he had been planning to do all along. This frightened the Conservatives. The Caracas Municipal Council deprived Guzmán of his voting privileges on the grounds that he had failed to pay court costs arising from a lawsuit. Guzmán's supporters feared the same excuse would be used to block his candidacy. Feeling ran high on both sides. Páez and Guzmán arranged a meeting to talk over the situation. On his way to La Victoria, where the two were to meet, Guzmán heard that some of his partisans had started a revolt without his authorization. Instead of leading the rebellion or disavowing it, the Liberal leader disappeared. When government officers later found him crouching in a newly-dug hole under the floor of a friend's house, his complicity in a plot to overthrow the Conservative regime seemed clear. The Liberal candidate rotted in jail while the election was being settled.

The Conservatives had also lost their candidate. Páez flatly refused to run, and the proposed substitute, Rafael Urdaneta, the aged half-blind veteran of independence who had served Bolívar in a dozen different capacities, died in Paris while floating a loan with which the Conservatives planned to finance the emancipation of all slaves. A thoroughly honorable man, Urdaneta was an eminently acceptable candidate. On his deathbed, he insisted that his sons return the funds which the government had advanced to him for the mission, despite the fact he was leaving his widow and eleven children destitute. "This one gesture," comments César Humberto Soto in *Personajes Célebres de Venezuela,* "so unusual in our country and among our political leaders, alone would suffice to elevate the hero to the pinnacle of human glory."

For want of a better man (and as it turned out almost any other man would have been better) Páez and the Conservatives threw their support to General José Tadeo Monagas, a rebel of 1831 and 1835. With this support Monagas swept into power.

José Tadeo Monagas hailed from the llanos. He had served the patriots throughout the War of Independence. Like so many other revolutionary leaders, he had long coveted control of his country. Once president of Venezuela, he was quick to see that as long as he governed with the Conservatives Páez would overshadow him. A few weeks after his election he dismissed his Conservative ministers and replaced them with Liberals. Meanwhile, he strengthened the army and appointed his personal henchmen to critical posts. In effect, he had declared war on the Conservative majority in Congress which had elected him. He would be the law in Venezuela, not they.

Monagas' treachery infuriated and frightened Congress. At the end of 1847 when the Provincial Deputation of Caracas presented a formal accusation against the President for infringement of the Constitution, the Conservatives pounced on it as a possible solution to their problem. If the charge could be proved Monagas faced impeachment. At a meeting on January 23, 1848, congressmen voted to examine the charges against Monagas. Afraid of retaliation should the President learn of its intention before the time was ripe, Congress kept the meeting secret. But Monagas was warned.

Next day Congress formally convened in San Francisco convent and stationed a civilian guard of thirty young men at the convent gates. Inside, congressmen took their seats to hear the Liberal minister Sanabria read the President's annual message. Outside a detachment of government militia and a pro-Monagas mob ominously appeared. Sanabria finished his message and looked about uneasily for his fellow ministers, also scheduled to arrive. Warned of impending trouble, his colleagues had stayed home. Sanabria waited. So did Congress. A rumor that the Conservatives had detained Sanabria by force swept the crowd in the street. Shots rang out. A captain of the militia fell dead. The thirty young defenders of Congress tried to slam the convent gate shut. In the uproar there were four other deaths.

Within the chamber some of the delegates, their worst fears confirmed, threatened to kill Sanabria. Shots continued to echo in the streets. Congressmen prayed or sought to escape. Some climbed out the windows. Others dropped over the walls. Seized by panic, those congressmen remaining in the building rushed out. In their passage through the excited crowd, José A. Salas, Juan and Julián García, Manuel María Alemán, Francisco Argote and the irreproachable ex-minister Santos Michelena fell. The first five died on the spot. Michelena staggered to refuge in the British Embassy where he later died of his wounds.

Whether Monagas directed this assault upon a congress about to impeach him or merely tolerated it has never been proved. Certainly he approved of it. Throughout his regime the 24th of January was celebrated as a national holiday.

Monagas wanted the trappings of a constitutional regime. The rape of Congress had sent most of the legislators scurrying for cover. His most outspoken opponents prepared to leave the country. So Monagas dispatched his henchmen to round up the quaking congressmen and force them to continue their sessions. They met again the next day. Impeachment proceedings were no longer on the agenda. Fearing for their safety and that of their families, congressmen had learned to agree with anything Monagas said. That evening a friend congratulated Monagas on the sagacity of his move. *"La Constitución,"* observed the General, *"sirve para todo."* (The constitution can be used for anything.)

Only one threat to Monagas' domination remained—José Antonio Páez. The St. George of the Venezuelan Constitution had sallied forth once more from San Pablo to battle with the dragon. He tried to raise an army. But Venezuelans were apathetic. The impending war seemed a personal duel for power and it didn't seem to matter who won. Páez was captured and imprisoned in Cumaná. There he stifled in a cramped dungeon, the air so foul he had to lie on the floor with his lips to the door in order to breathe. In 1850 he was exiled and took ship for New York where city officials received him with full honors. Páez was called back to Venezuela by his partisans in 1861 and he became dictator the same year. When the Federalists won the Federal Wars and signed a treaty with his government in 1863, Páez left the country. He died in New York on May 7, 1873, at the age of eighty-three.

It is difficult to appraise Páez' place in Venezuelan history because, like Calderón's Segismundo, he played both hero and villain. Yet, like Segismundo, Páez is an inspiring figure. He conquered himself.

This was a man inured to brutality and lust. He claimed he had killed seventy men with his own hand. In one battle, he bragged, he had slaughtered so many that his arm was nearly paralyzed. He was renowned for his affairs with women. As leader of his country he deserted his wife and family for a mulatto beauty named Barbarita Nieves, by whom he had several children. His intrigues against Bolívar put him in a class with all the other budding dictators. He apparently bilked his soldiers to enrich himself. All of this was normal behavior for an ignorant young savage. The amazing thing about José Antonio Páez was not that he abused his power occasionally, but that he sometimes employed it wisely. José Antonio Páez was the only Venezuelan strong man who has ever allowed the opposition to win an election; the only dictator who did not rob the public treasury. He was the best president Venezuela would have for a long, long time.

Chapter XII

EL GRAN ESTAFADOR

HELD IN CHECK for a score of years by the overwhelming prestige of Páez, Venezuela began to disintegrate under Monagas. The spirit of Spanish individualism which in the sixteenth century had made every man his own conquistador still breathed in hundreds of little generals and local chiefs; the instant Monagas weakened a dozen were ready to march to fame in his footsteps by leading the opposition or, a few weeks later, the opposition to the opposition. Rebellious caudillos—Castro, Falcón, Zamora—even the ancient Páez himself, helped tear the nation to tatters. The way was open for a man stronger and cleverer than the others—he needed no other qualification. Guzmán Blanco was that man.

Antonio Guzmán Blanco was his father's son, vain, dishonest, hypocritical and crazy for power. The father taught the son, but young Antonio graduated to the status of rival and eventually master.

Antonio Leocadio Guzmán and his son were working together even before Antonio Guzmán Blanco was born. Antonio Leocadio had social as well as political pretensions. So he contrived to fall in love with Carlota Blanco, a wellborn prize. She was related on both sides of her family to the Bolívars, and María Antonia Bolívar, sister of the Liberator, was her godmother. María Antonia recognized Guzmán as a social climber and violently opposed the match. Always equal to a situation, Guzmán melted María Antonia's opposition to the point where she could not get the couple to the altar fast enough. They were married on September 30, 1828. Five months later Antonio Guzmán Blanco was born.

Little Antonio heard talk of politics before he could read. When he was two, his father began an eight-year tenure in the Ministry of Interior. At eleven he was reading his father's fiery editorials in *El Venezolano* and at seventeen listening to the eloquent speeches Antonio Leocadio Guzmán delivered in his campaign for president. With his mother, Antonio Guzmán Blanco begged Monagas to save his father's life after the courts had sentenced Antonio Leocadio to death for his alleged connection with the revolt of his supporters in 1846. It was a touching scene. Monagas listened to the distraught Señora and her anxious son. He was moved. "Get up!" the General said, helping the woman to her feet. "Calm yourself! I haven't become president to be the instrument of anybody's passions." Behaving like a minor saint, Monagas commuted Antonio Leocadio's sentence to exile. The move suited his purposes. By saving Guzmán he annoyed the Conservatives and pleased the Liberals. Thus he prepared for his own elevation to absolute power. The next year, with Liberal support, he routed the Conservatives in Congress and in the army, making himself master of Venezuela. In 1849 he brought Antonio Leocadio Guzmán back to Venezuela and made him his Minister of the Interior and Vice-President.

That was the kind of political life Antonio Leocadio Guzmán led. In 1846 he was the spokesman of democracy; in 1849 the tool of autocracy—hardly the example best calculated to produce a son loyal to stable political principles and devoted to the cause of the people.

From his father, Antonio Guzmán Blanco also received valuable lessons on how to turn a dishonest dollar. In 1852, the elder Guzmán had himself named Ambassador to Peru. He remembered that Simón Bolívar had once been offered a million pesos by the city of Lima. It was a gift Bolívar had spurned. Representing the Bolívar family as destitute and ruined, Antonio Leocadio Guzmán beseeched the Peruvians to save them. Lima paid him the million pesos in government bonds worth 20 per cent of their face value. Its gesture of gratitude to the Liberator netted Guzmán a tidy fortune. He had previously made an agreement with Bolívar's heirs that he should collect 50 per cent of any amount he might recover.

As the son of an "in," Antonio Guzmán Blanco enjoyed many advantages. When he completed his law course at the Central University in Caracas, he entered the foreign service of his country. He went to Washington and New York. He liked what he saw and developed a taste for living abroad that colored his entire career. As a Monagas appointee, he lost his post through the revolution which deposed his patron in 1848 and returned to Venezuela. He was twenty-nine years old, handsome, agreeable, and polished. He was also ambitious. In the political confusion toward which his country was plunging in 1858, Antonio Guzmán Blanco began a laborious ascent to power.

Monagas had been a cynical tyrant and his autocratic methods produced a strong reaction. His rule had begun under the aegis of the Conservatives. When he exchanged Conservative ministers for Liberals and cowed the Conservative Party by his raid on Congress, he delighted Antonio Leocadio Guzmán and his supporters. They thought they could co-operate with him as the Conservatives had co-operated with Páez, but they soon discovered that co-operation was not what José Tadeo Monagas had in mind. He kept the Liberals around to fill the offices and vote him money. José Tadeo wouldn't listen to their progressive schemes. They cost money, and Monagas needed all the money for himself. By the boards went proposals for the simplification of judicial procedure, prison reform, educational expansion, and free trade.

Monagas had a program of his own. He increased customs duties, helped himself and his friends to the National Treasury, removed university professors he did not like and tried to perpetuate his hold on power. In 1851 he had Congress elect his brother, José Gregorio, president of Venezuela. In 1855, he allowed himself a second term.

The only tangible benefit Venezuela reaped from the Monagas administrations was the emancipation of the slaves. This belated fulfillment of Bolívar's pledge to President Pétion of Haiti occurred during José Gregorio's presidency in 1854. José Gregorio had been conspicuously insignificant while in office and was reluctant to leave without making his mark on Venezuelan history. His astute minister grabbed a chance to implement at least one of the liberal campaign promises. Though an intention of Venezuelan governments since Bolívar first proposed it to the Congress of Angostura in 1819, emancipation had never been proclaimed because previous governments said they were too poor to buy the slaves from their masters.

The second term of José Tadeo Monagas was a repetition of the first. As president, José Tadeo enjoyed himself immensely. He bullied Congress and the legislators relied on him for everything, including their pay. Said one senator, reporting on the disposition of a measure guaranteeing congressmen their salaries, "Our commission fixed its eyes on the face of the chief of the Supreme Administration, and as he appeared amiable, it judged he would act amiably; and so it seems to me, Mr. President, that the hopes of all the honorable Senators and Representatives will be fulfilled." José Tadeo liked his position so well that in 1857 he became violently opposed to the Venezuelan Constitution, which still barred successive terms. Needless to say, a new constitution was written and ratified. José Tadeo Monagas became the first president to win two elections in a row. But he never took office. This time he had gone too far.

Everybody was mad at him. The old line Conservatives and Liberals, including Antonio Leocadio Guzmán, realized their power had vanished. Even José Gregorio Monagas, who had thought his brother was going to hand the presidency back to him, was a bit piqued. The result was revolution.

The Conservatives headed by Manuel Felipe de Tovar and Fermín Toro and the Liberals under Wenceslao Urrutia and Joaquin Herrera combined forces, raised arms, and proposed to oust Monagas. All they lacked was a leader in whom everybody could have faith. The Liberals threatened to desert the movement if Páez were recalled to head it, as some Conservatives proposed. Two or three compromise candidates declined to serve. Eventually the rebels had to pick an obscure officer named Julián Castro, governor of Carabobo. Castro was incompetent and colorless. But he had an army.

The revolution ended in thirteen days. Castro marched on Caracas without encountering any resistance whatsoever. In the capital, José Tadeo Monagas, noble to the last gasp, prepared a resignation. "I could fight and win," Monagas told Congress on March 15, 1858, "but it would mean the shedding of Venezuelan blood in torrents." This thought he could not endure. As he well knew, the only Venezuelan blood in danger was his own. He raced for sanctuary in the French Embassy.

The revolutionary army took Caracas on March 18. Under Julián Castro as provisional president, a Conservative-Liberal coalition began to govern. The odds were against their governing well. The only thing the Liberals and Conservatives had in common was their opposition to Monagas. With his overthrow, the two factions of the governing alliance jockeyed for Castro's favor. The Conservatives pushed a bill through the new Congress making government employees responsible for past embezzlements, thus alienating many prorevolution Liberals who had at one time or another filched from the public till. Moreover, the government was handicapped by two legacies from the previous regime: an empty treasury, and Monagas himself, still hiding in the French Embassy.

The former president had become something of an international issue. When the revolutionaries took Caracas a mob besieged the French Embassy demanding that Monagas be turned over to the Venezuelan authorities for trial. The French ambassador refused. The mob insisted. Fearing for Monagas' safety, the Frenchman appealed to his colleagues in the diplomatic corps, asking them to support his stand. They sent their national flags which were flown above the French Embassy as a warning to the Venezuelan revolutionaries that an attack against Monagas would be considered an affront to most of the civilized world. The Ministers of the United States, Great Britain, France, Brazil, Spain, and the Netherlands then secured a written agreement from Wenceslao Urrutia, Venezuelan Foreign Minister, guaranteeing Monagas' safe passage out of the country. Since the signing of a diplomatic protocol to cover a purely internal matter was an insult to national sovereignty, Venezuelans were furious with Urrutia, who had signed the document without consulting anybody.

The government was further discredited when the French and British sent warships to blockade Venezuelan ports because they did not believe the protocol was being obeyed fast enough. Aging Carlos Soublette, tactful as ever, smoothed over the incident, but the Castro government's prestige had dropped below zero.

A weak and unpopular government constituted an open invitation to all the backwoods generals. They strutted about in their dirty uniforms and looked for bandits to make into armies. The two strongest men looked like Ezequiel Zamora, who had battled for the Liberal cause since 1844, and Juan Crisóstomo Falcón, the governor of Coro. To these leaders flocked discontented Liberals like Antonio Leocadio Guzmán and Antonio Guzmán Blanco. It was obvious that Castro could not last. A new strong man would send him the way of Monagas, and the Guzmáns, father and son, wanted to be that man's friend. They chose different generals. Antonio Leocadio went to join Ezequiel Zamora while Antonio Guzmán Blanco picked the eventual winner, Juan Crisóstomo Falcón.

They were ready now, the little generals and their civilian allies. All they needed was a cause. Antonio Leocadio Guzmán, a practiced causemaker, reached into the air and produced a slogan. Federation was the motto over which thousands of Venezuelans would die. Boasted Antonio Leocadio Guzmán to Congress in 1867, "I do not know where the people of Venezuela got their love for the Federation when they do not even know what the word means; this idea came from myself and others who said to ourselves, since the revolution needs a slogan, and the Constitutional Congress of Valencia did not care to baptize the constitution (of 1859) with the name of Federal, let us invoke that idea; for if our opponents had said Federation we would have said Centralism."

Yet the factor which made the Federal War a five-year slaughter was the Venezuelan people for whom Antonio Leocadio evinced such contempt. To the mass, the word Federation became imbued with every kind of democratic concept—universal suffrage, redistribution of wealth, and a classless society. Ironically enough, the Federal leaders feared these ideals as much as the Centralists.

The War of Federation consisted of only two proper battles. At Santa Inés the Federalists triumphed and at Coplé the government swept the field. These victories ought to have been decisive, but in each case the winner failed to press his advantage by destroying the retreating army. As a result citizens assassinated one another for three more years.

In both camps the civil war was signalized by acts of savagery and rapine; the Federalists sinned more gravely than the Centralists because so many of their troops came from the oppressed classes whose motives for revenge against landowners and officials goaded them to frequent outrages. There was a Federalist mulatto captain who punished enemy towns by butchering all "goths" with a machete and forcing the priest to marry him to all the women he fancied. On the other hand, the government commander Pedro Aranguren was so bad-tempered his own soldiers shot him without trial.

The Centralists, as the government forces were called, proved to be their own worst enemies. Julián Castro, Venezuela's president, secretly favored the Federalists. So government troops imprisoned him to forestall any treasonable act. Manuel Felipe de Tovar, the Vice-President, acted in his stead. Tovar was a good man. Aristocratic, honest, and enlightened, he refused to play dictator, even though a lot of people thought a dictator was what the Centralists needed to crush their enemies. This faction under Pedro José Rojas brought Páez back to Venezuela in 1861. When Tovar found he could not cope with the coercion of Páez and his friends, he resigned. On August 29, 1861, a coup d'état unseated his successor, Vice-President Gual, who was thrown into jail. José Antonio Páez became dictator.

Páez had aged. He was seventy-one years old and depended more than ever on outside advice. Unfortunately, Pedro José Rojas was not Carlos Soublette. As Páez' only minister, he devoted himself to the national treasury and made a private fortune through negotiating a foreign loan for Venezuela. By their armed coup, Páez and Rojas had robbed the Centralist government of its last legal justification. Loyal army officers, disgusted and disillusioned, deserted to the Federalists. In 1863 Páez had to make peace with the rebels.

Divided leadership also plagued the Federalists. During the first year of the Federal War, Ezequiel Zamora and Juan Falcón had

waged separate revolutions. Although Zamora had recognized
Falcón's over-all leadership from the beginning, he behaved like
an independent ally rather than a subordinate. The men were
brothers-in-law, but they had little else in common. A better general, Zamora was ardent, impetuous, and a sincere revolutionary,
while Falcón was placid, cautious, and malleable. It was a situation made for the talents of amiable Antonio Guzmán Blanco.

Young Antonio cultivated the friendship of both men. He
fawned, flattered, and said tactful things. He soon convinced the
rivals that they did not understand each other but that he, Antonio, understood them both. By serving as go-between he helped
everyone, particularly himself. He acted as Falcón's secretary and
accompanied Zamora to his death. Antonio and Zamora were
strolling behind the lines at the Battle of San Carlos when a bullet
interrupted their conversation. The General uttered his last sound
—the first syllable of an obscene exclamation—and fell dead in
Antonio's arms.

The death of Zamora simplified Guzmán Blanco's problem. No
longer were there two stars to tempt his wagon. He concentrated
upon Falcón and made himself indispensable—so indispensable,
in fact, that in August 1862, Falcón gave this young man of thirty-
three, who had no military experience or political prestige, a
crucial assignment. Falcón wanted to unite the scattered guerrilla
chiefs of the central provinces. These minor caudillos, many of
them little more than bandits, were a tough lot for a young Caracas
lawyer to handle, and Guzmán Blanco's acceptance of the job
attests to considerable courage as well as calculated ambition.
Countering their scorn with compliments and their jealousy by
a reminder that he was only Falcón's shadow, Antonio won them
over one by one and with the aid of General Linares Alcántara,
he unified military operations in the sector. As a soldier Antonio
was a good supply sergeant, but his organizational abilities proved
a valuable asset in Federal campaigns. He even managed to direct
a minor skirmish against government troops, later to be known as
"the glorious battle of Quebrada Seca."

At this point in his career, Antonio's ambitions transcended
military fame, and even political power. He wanted to live in Europe for the rest of his life, but he estimated that he needed several

hundred thousand pesos to do it properly. Government was, and still is, the most lucrative of all professions in Venezuela. His success as Falcón's Secretary General assured him a choice of posts in the first Federalist cabinet. What he needed now was peace. In 1863, Antonio Guzmán Blanco proposed a cessation of hostilities.

He met with Pedro José Rojas, the government minister, at a hacienda called Coche just outside Caracas. They discussed terms and drew up a draft treaty. The Treaty of Coche provided for the termination of hostilities and for the appointment of an assembly, chosen half by Páez and half by Falcón. The two negotiators agreed that Falcón would be the new president and that Páez would leave the country.

Their meeting was secret. And a good thing, too. For the principal topic of discussion, after terms had been drawn up, was new techniques in government graft. During his two years with Páez, Rojas had made significant contributions to this study. He had acquired a great deal of money through contracting a foreign loan for the Páez government. In exchange for Antonio's promise that a Federalist government would honor Venezuela's obligations under this loan, Rojas taught him all he knew. Which explains why, only a few days after Falcón settled in the capital, Guzmán Blanco sailed for London with authorization to contract a foreign loan of £1,500,000.

With the help of Giacomo Servadio, an associate of Rojas in London, Guzmán Blanco succeeded in floating the bond issue. Less than 25 per cent of the loan ever reached Venezuela; nobody has yet decided just how much Guzmán Blanco absorbed.

The financial chicanery by which he made the largest part of £1,500,000 disappear is fascinating, if confusing. The cash value of the loan was about £900,000 for the bonds were sold at 60 per cent of their face value (on account of Venezuela's low credit standing abroad). The issuing company also withheld 6 per cent interest and 2 per cent amortization to cover payments which would be due to bond buyers during the first year. This meant that even if all the bonds were sold Venezuela could not receive more than £780,000 for bonds she promised to redeem later at £1,500,000. Despite the favorable terms, only one-third of the bonds were purchased on the market. The remaining two-thirds were divided by Servadio and Guzmán Blanco. Servadio bought bonds worth £500,000 for £5,188, claiming the Venezuelan government owed him the difference. (He had acted as agent for the Páez loan.) Guzmán Blanco pawned his £400,000 worth of bonds for £108,000. The following year he sent his father to redeem them. Antonio Leocadio then sold the redeemed bonds at 35—he told Congress. The market price was 41⅞. Presumably he pocketed the difference.

In cash the loan actually produced:

£222,820 from English subscribers (£428,500 at 60 per cent less 6 per cent interest and 2 per cent amortization)

£5,188 from Servadio

£140,000 (estimated) from the bonds Antonio Leocadio redeemed and sold at 35

Total: £368,008

But Venezuela didn't even get this much.

In commissions alone, Guzmán Blanco collected £75,000. The company which floated the loan made the same amount. £20,000 went to members of Boulton & Co., a Venezuelan firm, "for their assistance in the loan." W. H. Morgan, with whom Guzmán Blanco had pawned his £400,000 worth of bonds, took £20,000 commission and £12,000 interest. Antonio meticulously listed lawyers' fees, press costs, and travel expenses as unavoidable deductions. When all of his bills were in, Venezuela found that out of the £368,008 which the bond sale had actually netted only about £200,000 remained. It is estimated that Guzmán Blanco, all things considered, made a profit of £176,000 on the deal. But, in all fairness to Antonio, it must be admitted that he may have had to spend a part of his loot persuading congressmen to approve it.

Guzmán Blanco pushed this disadvantageous transaction to earn a commission. In this respect alone, his behavior was triply irregular. Government ministers do not take commissions on negotiations which are part of their job. If they did, they would not ask 5 per cent, as he did. Even presuming there could be such a swindler in office, it is dubious whether anybody but Guzmán Blanco would have had the consummate gall to take his 5 per cent on the *total value* of a loan being sold at half-price.

Once back in Venezuela Antonio Guzmán Blanco restrained himself for a while. His financial talents found useful expression in a reorganization of the Treasury and the Customs, the establishment of the Banco de Londres and the formation of a Junta de Hacienda to foment agriculture. He had a free hand, as Falcón preferred to live away from Caracas and left the authority to his vice-president, Antonio Guzmán Blanco. But while contributing, very efficiently, to the country's financial solvency, he still could not resist the temptation to improve his own. In 1864 a dispute arose between the creditors of the external loan and those of a previous internal loan, both of whose holdings were guaranteed by customs revenues. The courts declared that internal creditors should have prior claim. But Guzmán Blanco, who had impounded customs revenues to the tune of 1,574,000 pesos while the decision was pending, told internal creditors the Englishmen had to be paid to maintain Venezuela's foreign credit, and the foreign bondholders that the court had ordered him to pay Venezuelans first. When the Venezuelan creditors got wind of the English story, they sent the Vice-President a furious petition demanding their rights—and got thrown in jail for their pains, while the impounded customs duties vanished like the London loan.

Having accumulated much more than the several hundred thousand pesos he had planned to acquire, Guzmán Blanco decided to realize the second stage of his dream. He had himself sent to London on government business, then in 1867 appointed Ambassador Extraordinary and Minister Plenipotentiary to several European countries. There was a dual reason for the 1867 appointments—he guessed Falcón would be ousted before long and he did not want to be involved.

The Falcón administration had begun with several flourishes —universal suffrage, increased political autonomy for states, freedom of the press, and the abolition of capital punishment. Pure icing, as Venezuelans soon found out. The right to vote meant little with only one party to vote for. The relative independence of the provinces gave free rein to hundreds of local caudillos, former leaders of Federalist guerrilla bands, who now considered themselves kings of miniature kingdoms. They imposed duties on goods entering their district, displaced one another by coups d'état, and sometimes waged open war. One such chief used to exact a toll from everyone who walked in front of his house.

Instead of combating political and fiscal disorder, administration officials abetted it. Less refined than Antonio Guzmán Blanco, Falcón's friends attacked the treasury frontally. Much too nice ever to say no, Falcón liked to give his admirers drafts on the treasury, scrawled on pieces of scrap paper. Outside of this, the President took little interest in government. He was always in Coro—or at any rate not in Caracas. In his absence, he surrendered his powers to men who had no qualifications for office except that they also came from Coro. Indeed, Falcón's vacations were so frequent he once proposed that Congress declare whatever land he trod the Federal District. In sum, confusion had become so confounded by 1868 that one group of exasperated Venezuelans wanted to give the country in trust to England.

The inevitable revolution erupted in 1868. Under José Tadeo Monagas, insurgents raised a blue flag and captured Caracas. This Blue Revolution, as it came to be called, illustrates the peculiar adaptability of Latin-American politicians. A coalition of Liberals and Conservatives, the same kind of alliance which had ousted Monagas ten years before, now supported him. As strong man, Monagas filled the power vacuum for only a few months. His death in November 1868 left vacant a seat in a perennial game of musical chairs. It was a seat which Antonio Guzmán Blanco determined to grab.

Guzmán Blanco had returned to Caracas shortly after the death of Monagas. He did so at considerable risk to himself, for anti-Falcón feeling still ran high. The Liberal-Conservative coalition had chosen Ruperto Monagas to succeed his father. Nevertheless, some Liberals who feared Conservative influence with Ruperto rallied around Guzmán Blanco when he arrived. Antonio figured that a judicious display of wealth and a modicum of tact might win more discontented Liberals to his side. On August 14, 1869, he gave a luxurious ball to which he invited everyone in Caracas who mattered.

Scarcely had the musicians tuned up when a mob paid by the Conservatives appeared outside his mansion. They insulted the arriving guests and barred their entry to the house. Stones broke windows and mirrors in the lighted ballroom. One of the rioters even penetrated the house, where a resolute guest knocked him down. Terrified señoras hid their jewels, the musicians fled, late-arriving dignitaries took refuge in nearby homes. Distinguished guests inside the house attempted to calm the rabble, but "vain were the benevolent and generous exhortations of the honorable diplomatic ministers of the U.S., France, and Spain, and the severe observations of the Belgian Consul. . . . So high rose the fury and blindness of the invaders that when the Spanish minister, Dr. Alvarez de Peralta, got up on a chair to make his authoritative voice heard, they threw an enormous rock at him, which passed between the orator's head and that of the American minister Mr. Patridge, and if it had hit the victim it would have killed him on the spot. Before such insolence the consular and diplomatic corps desisted from any attempt to bring to their senses the criminals who had so brutally replied to their illustrious observations." [1]

The ruin of Guzmán Blanco's ball benefited him much more than its success could ever have. The Liberals, outraged by an act they believed the Conservatives had provoked, and full of sympathy for its martyr, thronged to Guzmán Blanco and put themselves at his orders. Because of additional mob attacks on other important figures, Guzmán Blanco thought it safer to retire temporarily to Curaçao. Generals Pulido, Crespo, Salazar and Colina rose in revolt and called him back to lead them. On April 27, 1870, the forces of the Regeneration, as they called themselves, took Caracas. It was the last successful revolution for twenty years.

For the next eighteen of those twenty years Venezuela was Guzmán Blanco's fief. There was no political party but the Gran Partido Liberal which Antonio Leocadio Guzmán had headed twenty-five years before, and of which his son was now the epitome. One would expect the old man to be happy, but he was not. He had nothing in common with "los liberales de Antonio," as he jeeringly called them. He was surrounded by respect and adulation, but nobody really listened to him, least of all Antonio, who had since the moment he chose Falcón instead of Zamora, been a rival and not a disciple. Antonio, who half-despised the old man

[1] Aldrey, Fausto Teodoro de, and Rafael Hernández Gutiérrez (editors): *Rasgos Biográficos*, Caracas, 1876.

for his hypocrisy and opportunism and had outdone him in both, used him when it was convenient and ignored him when it was not. Antonio Leocadio died in 1884 and they buried him in the Pantheon.

The new age was to Venezuela what the Victorian was to England and the Second Empire to France, a time of peace, relative prosperity, and material progress. Intensely bourgeois, though on a vast scale, Guzmán Blanco loved riches, comfort, and display. His conquest of Venezuela meant to him a swelling bank account, ease for the rest of his life, and the opportunity to marry off his daughter to the Duc de Morny. Because he liked the amenities of civilization, and had to live in Venezuela now and then, he made sure that Venezuela possessed some of these amenities; because his income depended on Venezuelan investments, it was in his interest to keep Venezuela prosperous.

Guzmán Blanco's actual presidencies cover three periods, the Septenio from 1870–77, the Quinquenio, 1879–84, and the Bienio or Aclamación, 1886–88. In the interims he left the presidency to chosen lieutenants and retired to Europe.

For the period 1877–79 he chose General Linares Alcántara, whose aid in uniting Federal troops in 1862 had started Guzmán Blanco on his rise to power. Alcántara had a sense of humor. When an acquaintance asked him to go into business with him, Alcántara is said to have replied, "Why should I go into business? I have the best business in the world—the National Treasury." He said his political program would be "to climb the cathedral tower and throw gold pieces to everyone who passes." Alcántara made a habit of couching his thoughts in ambiguous phrases and his reflections on the National Treasury may have been spoken in jest. At any rate, the record shows that he proved to be a pretty good man. With his boss, Guzmán Blanco, in Europe as Minister to Germany, France, Italy, Switzerland, Spain, and the Vatican, President Alcántara accepted advice from progressive elements, relaxed press control, allowed the people to demonstrate against Guzmán Blanco and was on the verge of repudiating the Guzmancistas when he died. The anti-Guzmán Blanco forces destroyed all of Guzmán Blanco's statues and named Alcántara's illegitimate brother, Gregorio Valera, to succeed him. Valera's rule was short. In 1879 General Cedeño rebelled and urged Guzmán Blanco to return home.

From 1879 to 1884, Guzmán Blanco personally presided over his dominion. During this period he manipulated his re-election in direct violation of a constitution he had originally proposed, but in 1884 he decided he could not discreetly succeed himself again. So he handed the presidency to General Joaquín Crespo and sailed for Europe. This time his substitute was loyal.

Guzmán Blanco's last term lasted from 1886 to 1888. This period was called the "Aclamación," after the *Libro de la Aclamación Nacional,* which contained fifteen hundred pages of exaggerated prose, verse, and speeches, from municipalities, states, and individuals, begging Guzmán Blanco to stand for election again. When he obliged, *all* the states of Venezuela named him their representative on the Federal Council, the constitutional entity which chose the chief executive.

Despite his unanimous election, signs of dissension appeared during Guzmán's last term. There were risings in the Andes, where many old-line Conservatives and former Alcantarists, as well as Colombian refugees, had their stronghold. Resentment was also widespread over what Andeans considered their exclusion from national affairs, and over Guzmán Blanco's interference with Mérida University, which during most of his regime continued to function only because professors taught without salaries.

The question of who would succeed Guzmán Blanco was also a disrupting issue. Crespo confidently expected to receive the presidency once more, but Guzmán Blanco supported the candidacy of Dr. Rojas Paúl, president of the Senate, long-time Guzmancist, and a civilian. Crespo was annoyed; and rather than precipitate open conflict both he and the dictator left the country, preferring to rig the elections from Curaçao and London. Guzmán outmaneuvered Crespo, of course, and Dr. Rojas Paúl was elected.

If Guzmán Blanco expected his candidate to keep Venezuela intact for yet another return, he was mistaken. Like Alcántara, Rojas Paúl developed his own policies, and with no open break retreated slowly from the absent dictator's influence. First Congress refused to approve a Guzmán contract to give Caracas sewers —not that Caracas didn't need sewers, but Guzmán Blanco had a share in the firm which was to do the work. Then Rojas Paúl consolidated his popularity with all parties by announcing a general amnesty for all political prisoners. When through tact and generosity he won over Crespo, who had attempted an armed uprising against him, he felt secure. While Guzmán Blanco kept sending him draft contracts from Paris for one thing and another, Rojas Paúl deftly pigeonholed them or passed them from one committee to another until they got lost. Encouraged by Rojas Paúl's neutrality, Guzmán opponents demonstrated against him on April 27, 1889—the anniversary of his conquest of Caracas—attacked him in the press, and finally for the second time mobs destroyed the statues of the Dictator. This time they were not put up again. Guzmán Blanco faded from the Venezuelan political scene in 1889. Old and more fond of luxury than ever, he may have been just as glad. With his millions he lounged in Paris until he died in July, 1899.

Guzmán Blanco was ahead of his time. He ruled like a modern dictator. He had absolute power. He demanded deification. He suppressed civil liberties. He identified public welfare with his own. He maintained a superficial respect for constitutional forms. He sought justification by public works. All of these characteristics have signalized the administrations of Hitler, Mussolini, Stalin, Huey Long, Perón, Trujillo, and a host of minor Latin tyrants. The modern world is familiar with this phenomenon, but to his contemporaries, Antonio Guzmán Blanco came as a surprise. His interest in public welfare seemed a peculiar form for overwhelming egoism to take. But in the case of Guzmán Blanco it was logical.

Guzmán Blanco had lived in the United States and had traveled through France and England. All three countries had been thoroughly exposed to the liberal notion that power must be justified by benevolence, not simply strength or divine right. Napoleon III and Guzmán Blanco, as well as most contemporary dictators, were affected by this ethic. It made Guzmán Blanco react to power in a different way from the traditional caudillo, who instinctively assumed that "might made right."

For a modern dictator, it is not enough to be powerful. To justify his omnipotence in the face of public opinion, he must appear infallibly good, a philosopher king, a god. Often, he believes he is. To bolster this belief in himself and others, he flaunts his virtue. He gives gifts to his friends. He builds theaters, roads, museums and waterworks. He helps the poor. From him all blessings flow. A grateful people must hang his picture in every public place, erect statues to him, honor streets with his name, and unanimously re-elect him.

Subconsciously, he tends to confuse his personal preferences with the universal good, as almost everybody does. It is his duty to impose this good on others. If they object, they are obviously evil, and to jail with them. And so the oppressive side of dictatorship is sanctified too.

Guzmán Blanco thought he was divinely fitted to rule. "Only led by the will of Providence," he said to Congress in 1873, "could I believe myself capable of assuming the immensity of the duties which are imposed upon me by the past, the present, and the future of my country." He claimed infallibility. "For my successor," he bragged in another speech, "there are only two choices: the way of Guzmán Blanco who, finding nothing, had to create everything . . . or the way of Alcántara who, having everything, lost everything through his personal plans and rapacious ambitions and his disloyal behavior. There will be two horizons open to the elected: one which will blazon the dishonor and shame of Alcántara and another of glory through the gratitude and love of the people."

Once, wishing to do the future son-in-law of a friend a favor, Guzmán Blanco offered the boy a post as engineer in the Ministry of Public Works. Since he knew nothing about engineering, the youth protested. "How dare you!" Guzmán Blanco said. "You are an engineer. You have to be an engineer, and don't argue with me."

"Yes, General, if you order it."

"It is not a question of orders; I have already made you an engineer, and now I'm going to make you the Director of the Ministry of Public Works."

Guzmán Blanco's regimes were absolute and autocratic. He took every opportunity to make this fact clear. "I don't need, nor do I want, ministers who can think. They only have to write. I am the only one who can think and the only one who does think."

Commenting on the resignation of a government minister, the Dictator said, "As it is I who govern and govern with my brains, I think you did well to resign, since you cannot sacrifice your personal interest to what I esteem to be the public good."

His appetite for worship was insatiable and it grew with the years until his conceit bordered on insanity. In fact, when he learned in Paris that a Caracas mob had destroyed his beloved statues, Guzmán Blanco reacted so violently that doctors feared he had lost his mind. He published a testament of hate, enjoining his sons to wreak eternal vengeance on the heretics who had defamed his effigy.

In 1883 he dared to equate himself officially with Simón Bolívar. It was the centenary of Bolívar's birth. For two years Venezuelans prepared to celebrate the sacred date. An equestrian statue of the Liberator was purchased. Bands were hired; special poems and essays composed. The government sponsored a National Exposition. In the middle of the festivities Guzmán Blanco inaugurated his pet project, the Caracas-La Guaira railway. The slogan for the centenary was "Viva Bolívar, Gloria a Guzmán." The commemorative medal showed Guzmán Blanco in the foreground and Bolívar behind. Newspapers gave both men an equal play. The many foreign delegates present must have had a hard time telling which man they were supposed to honor.

Antonio Guzmán Blanco sported the absurd title of "Ilustre Americano y Regenerador de Venezuela." It accompanied his name everywhere—on statues, in newspapers, and at Paris balls. He was pathetically proud of it. Chile won his displeasure when she suggested it might be more seemly if he called himself "The Illustrious Venezuelan" instead of "The Illustrious American," since he had never done anything for the rest of America. He never forgave Chile. When that country went to war with Peru and Bolivia he sympathized with her enemies, apparently for no other reason.

Antonio could absorb the most outrageous flattery without the trace of a blush. The banner which waved above him as he inaugurated the Caracas-Petare telegraph line read:

"You are greater than Napoleon Bonaparte because he was conquered at Waterloo and you have never been conquered;

"You are superior to Moses because Moses made water gush from a single rock and you have made it spring forth everywhere;

"Your work is more excellent than that of Jesus because Jesus called children to him only to love them, and you call them to feed and educate them."

To sustain his megalomania Guzmán Blanco went to ridiculous lengths. Since he had no sense of humor—another trait of the modern dictator—he took unbrage at the merest bagatelles. Dr. Jesús Morales Marcano was jailed for having said, intentionally or inadvertently, that the president of Colombia was "a really illustrious American." Guzmán Blanco suspended two newspapers for having published the obituary of a political opponent. He jailed Dr. Laureano Villanueva for writing a history on the abuse of public power. He retracted a prize awarded to a young poet in a contest because the winning ode did not mention him.

Guzmán Blanco wiped out all opposition, armed or parliamentary, and made the Liberal Party the only party in Venezuela. His suppression of the Conservatives was ferocious. In 1870–71 terrorism reigned; Conservative lands were confiscated, political prisoners rotted for years in the dungeons of the Rotunda, and men were shot without trial simply as a lesson to other rebels. Informed of one political murder, he said, "Perhaps the death of Carrillo will have a salutary effect on the furor of the prisoners. In any case, he represents just one more corpse in this struggle." "We ought," he added in the same memorandum, "to forget everything but putting down the oligarchy by repression, carrying it as far as terrorism if necessary."

Yet Guzmán Blanco's conscience, tinted as it was with a faint shade of liberalism, insisted that he pay lip service to democracy and representative government. He always posed as the champion of the Liberal Party and talked of it as of a sacred thing. Congresses ostensibly initiated legislation. Elections were held. Constitutions were altered or completely rewritten to legalize Guzmán Blanco's monopoly of power. Some of his manipulations were so crass it makes one wonder why he took the trouble to mask the truth. In the elections of October 1872 for president the official tally read as follows: Guzmán Blanco, 239,691 votes; General Pulido, 9; General Colina, 6; and all others, 3.

In one important respect, Guzmán Blanco was more caudillo than modern dictator. He loved money more than power. The extent of his embezzlements is astounding. His greedy fingers reached everywhere. Ostensibly to pay the expenses of the 1869 revolution which put him in power, he began his rule by collecting 1,044,000 pesos. Of this amount 80,000 paid the debts and 964,000 went into his pocket. The next year he filched 84,000 pesos from the funds allotted for the upkeep of his private-guard regiment. While mopping up rebels in the Apure region in 1871 he seized cattle for army supplies and sold them for a personal profit of 180,000 pesos. In 1874, on the pretext that enemies in Curaçao were smuggling arms to Venezuela, he closed the ports of Maracaibo and La Vela de Coro and awarded a navigation monopoly to Francisco Fossi and Antonio Aranguren—partners of his. From this business he cleared an estimated 1,118,280 pesos. He collected 347,000 pesos by calling in foreign coins and paying 33 per cent of their worth in Venezuelan pesos, and then recirculating them at full value. Expropriation of church property netted him 400,000 pesos.

After the Septenio most of his graft came through association with businessmen and construction firms. He owned part interests in bakeries, millinery shops, and even a cemetery. A slice of every public works contract went to him. His son-in-law Morny got the contract to build the Caracas aqueducts. Other big projects were granted to General Juan Francisco Pérez, Luis Oduber, and H. L. Boulton and Company, all of whom served as fronts for Guzmán Blanco's capital. H. L. Boulton and Company received a contract to mint nickel coins for Venezuela, and was accused by anti-Guzmanists of having cheated on the weight and purity of the metal used. Guzmán Blanco, replying to charges of complicity, exclaimed, "Nickel! Oh what infamy! Would a man who has millions prostitute himself to the point of stealing cents from the public treasury?" The answer, apparently, was yes.

The public works which lined his pocket fed the popularity of the Dictator as well. Under his stimulus the Plaza Bolívar was beautified, the Capitolio, the Teatro Nacional, Santa Teresa church, the Santa Capilla, and the Masonic Temple erected; Macuto was transformed into a resort town; La Guaira received a breakwater; Caracas, Valencia, La Victoria, Chacao and Petare got aqueducts. Transportation was vastly improved. Caracas and La Guaira, Puerto Cabello and Valencia, were linked by railways and better roads. Telegraph lines were extended to the Colombian frontier. Caracas, La Guaira, and Valencia got telephone connections. A submarine cable to Europe was laid.

Immigration and education attracted Guzmán's interest, too. Government statistics, though they may be unreliable, indicate that 12,083 immigrants entered the country during the Septenio. Guzmán Blanco's first act on coming to power was to promulgate the principle of universal free education. He allotted large sums from the budget for this purpose. By 1887 there were five normal schools, 28 secondary colleges, and at least 1949 elementary schools in Venezuela. Many of these elementary schools, of course, consisted of one poorly-paid teacher in a hut, but Guzmán Blanco's program was still the most ambitious effort to combat ignorance that Venezuela had yet seen.

As a conservative stronghold, the Church sustained frequent attacks during Guzmán's regime. Ostensibly to finance education, Guzmán Blanco seized convent property in 1874. Civil registration of birth, marriage, and death took the place of parish records; religious seminaries were banned; cemeteries secularized. By drastically reducing the Church's hold on the country's economic and social life, Guzmán Blanco spared Venezuela the church intervention in politics from which Colombia still suffers.

Perhaps Guzmán's greatest gift to Venezuela was his final abdication in favor of a progressive civilian president, and there is some evidence to prove that he may have done it believing Venezuela was ready for democratic rule. Rojas Paúl made an excellent president, but in 1890 he relinquished office to Dr. Raimundo Andueza Palacio, who attempted to succeed himself unconstitutionally. Chaos engulfed Venezuela until Cipriano Castro and Juan Vicente Gómez united the nation under an absolutist government in 1899.

Guzmán Blanco imposed a trace of modernity upon his country, but because it was imposed, it was short-lived. The autocrat had awed and browbeaten the local caudillos into submission; when he abused them to their faces as blockheads and dolts, they merely bowed their heads, meek before the magic of his mental agility and political achievements. But he had suppressed, not destroyed, the spirit of disorder and barbarism, and once his iron hand was removed it sprang up all over Venezuela until cruder and heavier fists rammed it down again. The inevitable cycle ran its course as it had since Venezuelan independence—anarchy to autocracy to anarchy once more—and the rise of the modern age made scarcely an impression on it. Once more, and in a more dreadful form, brute force was to triumph in Venezuela.

Chapter XIII

DESCENT FROM THE ANDES

WHEN A COUNTRY submits to the rule of one man, its institutions tend to become reflections of the tyrant. Seldom is his influence benevolent. The man who fights his way to absolute power can't allow himself the luxuries of honor, sentiment, kindness, faith, or tolerance. These are "weaknesses" which make him vulnerable to treachery and destruction, in a country full of contenders for absolute power. "Weaknesses" of one kind or another had toppled Miranda, Bolívar, Páez, Julián Castro, Falcón, and Guzmán Blanco. Juan Vicente Gómez, on the other hand, had no weaknesses. So he ruled Venezuela for twenty-seven years and died in his bed, still president. During his reign, from 1908 to 1935, Venezuela's political system reached its logical nadir.

He was an expression of the worst in Venezuela just as Simón Bolívar, Francisco de Miranda, Antonio José Sucre, and Andrés Bello personified Venezuela at her best. He burst from the soil, an emanation of nature, a creature of pure instinct, incapable of distinguishing good from evil, trusting only fundamental stimuli like thirst, hunger, sex, discomfort, and desire. Yet he was shrewd enough to conquer Venezuela and keep her his slave for a quarter of a century. A peasant who spent the first forty-two years of his life mastering an Andean farm, he plowed Venezuela until he died, uprooting every man, every moral, intellectual, or natural obstacle that stood in his way.

Juan Vicente Gómez was born on a farm near San Antonio, Venezuela, the son of Pedro Cornelio Gómez and Hermenegilda Chacón. The date was July 24, 1859—anniversary of Simón Bolívar's birth.[1]

From both his parents, Juan Vicente inherited Indian blood. He grew up on his father's mountain ranch—"La Mulera"—high above San Antonio and learned the ways of a Venezuelan mountaineer. At the age of fourteen, when his father died, young Gómez became the head of the household and boss of the hacienda.

The semitropical valley embracing both Cúcuta, Colombia, and San Antonio, Venezuela is a tremendous cup formed by mountain walls. In Juan Vicente's youth, the valley was lost among the folds of the Andes. It was connected with the outside world by a network of burro trails. Life in the valley was rugged. Houses were adobe shacks with hard-packed dirt for floors. Around the shanty structures grew maize, coffee, and if the farm was on the valley floor, bananas. Cattle grazed on the slopes.

The people were Indians, mostly. The Spaniards had passed through the valley leaving their architecture, their religion, their language, and their sperm. Still, Indian ways and characteristics persisted, and in some respects dominated the enclosed society. The people were stolid, independent, suspicious, and inured to hardships and cruelty. As a respite from branding and castrating cattle during the week, they watched cockfights on Sundays. Hombría—manliness—meant brute strength and sexual virility.

---

[1] While Juan Vicente Gómez tyrannized the country, both his propagandists and his enemies invented absurd lies about him to substantiate their opinions. Many of these assertions gained wide circulation through the publication of Thomas Rourke's *Gómez, Tyrant of the Andes*. In this book Rourke says that Juan Vicente was born in Colombia, the bastard son of a man named García; that the birth record which proved he had been born in Venezuela was forged; that his mother had thirteen children by three different men. There is absolutely no evidence to support this view. It is generally accepted that Dr. José Rosario García, his counselor for many years, was his uncle, but that Dr. García was a half-brother of Juan Vicente's father, Pedro Cornelio Gómez. As for the birth record, which is actually a baptismal record, no one has ever proved any forgery, and it would appear extremely difficult for a man to change his birth date—presumably widely known—at the age of fifty.

The man who could use his fists and his machete survived. The weaklings often lost their cattle; occasionally their lives.

In this atmosphere, Juan Vicente Gómez learned to rule. He discovered several local facts which seemed universal truths. The dishonest, the strong, the wary, and the ruthless ones succeeded. Docility, courtesy, education, sentimentality, and religious faith were useless, and therefore contemptible. This was a law of nature—and nature, its way with animals and men, was one thing Juan Vicente thought he understood. When he dominated Venezuela, the people called him "brujo"—witchdoctor—because he seemed to read men's minds. In a sense, he did. He imagined what he would do in the place of another and acted accordingly. He was immune to every wile—flattery, deceit, or treachery. He himself had used them all. His knowledge of evil made him suspect everyone and his suspicions made him invulnerable in power. He sensed every conspiracy and prepared for them even when they didn't exist. As president, he had the army build a bridge on one of his haciendas. At the inauguration, he refused to drive over it first. Instead, he made the foreman stand under the span and ordered the engineer who planned the bridge to drive the first vehicle across.

This was a man who never went to school. When the death of his father dumped the responsibility of running "La Mulera" on his shoulders, he taught himself to read and write. Even so, he was scarcely literate. He had a peasant's acquisitiveness and wealth seemed the only thing worthy of a persistent interest. He worked from morning to night, tending his cattle and coffee. In little books, he scrawled crude figures of income and expense.

"La Mulera" flourished. By now, the household embraced a small community. There was Hermenegilda, her eleven children, and a natural son of Pedro Gómez by a woman named Matute. In addition, two children of Pedro Gómez' brother by a woman named Prato had been incorporated. As the boys matured, more anonymous children appeared. The Gómez clan sowed its seed throughout the valley. When the neighbor girls yielded an authentic Gómez, the child was admitted to "La Mulera." Some worked as servants; favorites became part of the family. Thus the tribe achieved formidable proportions.

It was a good system. Juan Vicente's growing herd required

extra hands. An addition to the clan might mean another mouth to feed, but it also meant another back for the chores. To the swelling crowd Juan Vicente added his own contributions. No one knows how many children he fathered during his life. Probably he didn't either. One estimate puts the figure at ninety-seven. In the mountains they begin procreating early, and Juan Vicente was still begetting children at the age of seventy. None of them were legitimate. Juan Vicente Gómez was a lifelong bachelor.

In Venezuela, illegitimacy was not unusual, nor is it today. The Venezuelan government estimated that 51.9 per cent of the babies born in the country in 1949 were illegitimate. According to law a father may recognize a child if he chooses. This gives the child the right to inheritance. Of all his children Gómez recognized only fourteen. As for the others, he usually contributed to their care.

Seven of the fourteen were the fruit of Dionisia Bello, the wife of an Italian merchant, whom Gómez carried off to "La Mulera" when he was twenty-eight. How the Italian reacted has never been reported. Presumably he did nothing. Few dared to quibble with the Gómez men, who had become the bullies of the region.

They made a well-organized mob. Juan Vicente was tougher and smarter than the others. He gave the orders. Juan Crisóstomo, his brother, and Eustoquio Gómez (really Prato), his cousin, were his triggermen, dense but reliable. They and the rest of the tribe did what they were told.

Gómez had one outstanding talent. He knew how to make money. In 1892, "La Mulera" was one of the most prosperous farms in the state of Táchira. Juan Vicente had a good herd. He also had a bank account. Through cattle rustling, shrewd business deals, and hard work, Gómez had made himself as rich as an Andean farmer could expect to get. To make more money his ambition had to range in a new direction. There was only one: politics. To join a caudillo meant gravy when the caudillo won. In 1892 Juan Vicente Gómez went to war and supported General María González, commander of government troops in Táchira.

This was the year Andueza Palacio tried to succeed himself as president unconstitutionally. He had been elected chief executive when Rojas Paúl, the excellent administrator who followed Guzmán Blanco, retired to private life in 1890. Though a civilian, Andueza Palacio behaved like a military caudillo. He neglected his duties and spent his time amusing himself. A heavy gambler, he drank to excess and liked to do it in public places. He tolerated scandals and graft in his administration. When the end of his term drew near, he followed the example of José Tadeo Monagas and tried to ram constitutional reform through Congress. It was an incomparably stupid attempt. Without military or popular support, he was all alone. When friends told him he was courting revolution, Andueza Palacio scoffed. "In Venezuela," he observed, "even the cocks won't fight. They have to be imported from Puerto Rico."

He apparently didn't know much about Venezuelan history. Joaquín Crespo, who had rattled his saber only three years before, gathered his army and declared war. Crespo was the man who had served as second interim president under Guzmán Blanco. He had tried for the presidency again in 1888. Upon losing to Rojas Paúl, he staged an unsuccessful revolution and landed in jail. Able Rojas Paúl won him over by shows of generosity, and for a promise to support the government, Crespo was released. He kept his word as long as the government was legal. He began his campaign against Andueza Palacio in February, 1892, and entered Caracas seven months later. Needless to say, he became president.

This state of affairs proved disastrous to Juan Vicente Gómez, who had wagered his future on Andueza Palacio's success. Instead of receiving riches and privileges for serving government forces in Táchira as supply officer, he lost practically everything he had. He had invested ten thousand bolivars in the campaign. "La Mulera" had to be abandoned, and the Gómez family together with other Andueza Palacio supporters crossed the Rio Táchira into Colombia.

He had learned his first lesson in Venezuelan politics. It mattered whether you were a friend or an enemy of the man ruling in Caracas.

This was his only exile, his only international experience, a matter of fifteen kilometers. In Colombia, within sight of the mountains around "La Mulera," he established a new hacienda with the cattle he had managed to drive across the border. His genius for making money was unimpaired, and the new location afforded first-rate facilities for an experienced rustler. By night he sent his relatives across the Táchira to snatch cattle from his old neighbors. He grew richer than ever. In a few years, he had thirty thousand bolivars in the bank.

It was his prosperity and his family army which attracted the interest of another refugee, who was to give Gómez the greatest opportunity of his life. Juan Vicente had met Cipriano Castro in Venezuela when they were both fighting for the maintenance of the Andueza Palacio regime. Cipriano Castro, small, nervous, and authoritarian, yearned to be president of Venezuela. Not so much for the power nor for the prestige. One gets the impression he wanted to be chief executive simply for the fun of it. An Andino from Táchira who reveled in civilization's pleasurable excesses, he could appreciate the drowsy opulence of Caracas. He wanted the capital. Bawdy parties, sprawling mansions, girls, liquor, and the money to buy them. Perhaps from this ambition sprang his interest in politics. He had no program, only a plan. He would invade Venezuela when Crespo's government weakened, in other words, when he had a chance to win.

As a fighter he was clever and audacious. He had directed winning battles for the Andueza Palacio government even as it crumbled. In exile from Crespo's Venezuela, he bided his time, waiting for a propitious moment to strike. Meanwhile, he cultivated the friendship of Juan Vicente Gómez. Not only did Juan Vicente have lots of male relatives and money, but he knew where a large store of weapons and supplies was located, on the Venezuelan side of the Rio Táchira. As supply officer for fleeing troops, Gómez had hidden his stores before he left San Antonio.

Juan Vicente was slow, methodical, and self-contained—exuberant Cipriano Castro's opposite. Yet they made a natural team. Castro needed the supplies and men Gómez could give him. For his part, Gómez saw in Castro's military talents and ambitions a way to regain his lands in Venezuela—forfeit as long as Crespo remained in power. As Castro talked of revolution, Juan Vicente's horizon spread from "La Mulera" to Caracas. He heard about richer haciendas in the valleys of Aragua and Chacao. Since he rarely spoke, he probably listened to Castro with a minimum of comment. There was time to make up his mind. Crespo's regime remained strong enough to resist rebellion until 1899.

Joaquín Crespo is an ambiguous figure in Venezuelan history. While in power he allowed freedom of the press and tolerated political enemies to a point. On the other hand, he knew nothing about government or administration and, as a consequence, ruled ineptly. Though basically honest himself, he harbored a host of embezzlers who quietly milked the public treasury and advised him to contract a ruinous loan for fifty million bolivars from a German firm. The loan benefited Venezuela in no way, since the largest part of it was stolen by administration officials.

Perhaps through no fault of his own, Crespo became involved in an international dispute. The English and Venezuelan governments had been bickering about the border between Venezuela and British Guiana for decades. In April 1895, the Venezuelan authorities briefly imprisoned some British Guiana policemen on the grounds that they had illegally exercised the functions of British officials on Venezuelan territory. The British government, which held that the territory in question was theirs, broke off relations with Venezuela and prepared to dispatch warships. At this point, President Grover Cleveland of the United States declared in a message to Congress that any armed attempt by the British to enforce claims against Venezuela should be considered a violation of the Monroe Doctrine. The First Venezuelan Incident, as it is called in American history, ended peacefully when the two contending governments agreed to arbitrate their differences. Around the conference table, Venezuela lost most of the disputed territory and consented to pay an indemnity for the jailing of the policemen.

Crespo served as constitutionally elected president from 1894 to 1898. For a while, it looked as if he would permit an absolutely free election to choose his successor. In 1897, several hopefuls beat the backwoods for votes, when Crespo made it clear he would not interfere with the popular mandate. Thus Venezuelans got their first look at a real election campaign as the candidates wooed the common man's vote by making speeches and purchasing space in newspapers. The most enthusiastic campaigner was José Manuel Hernández, an idealist and perennial revolutionary. Tremendously popular with the mass, Hernández was called "El Mocho" —the mutilated one—because he had lost a finger in battle. True to his word, Crespo did not interfere in any way with the electioneering. The government saved its tricks for election day when the inexperienced electorate was pressured into voting for General Ignacio Andrade, the man Joaquín Crespo had decided to support. Charging fraud, El Mocho Hernández traveled to the llanos and started a revolution.

Crespo favored Andrade because he could control him. One account has it that when a friend asked Crespo why he was supporting Andrade, the President said, "Look. Andrade is a Colombian and the Venezuelans can't forgive him for that; and as he has become a Venezuelan, the Colombians can't forgive him for that; he was a Conservative and the Liberals can't forgive him; now that he is a Liberal the Conservatives can't forgive him. Thus, not having a country, nor a political party, he can count on no support except mine. Moreover, this man has never commanded; he has never done anything but obey and he is already too old to learn how to command: he needs someone to command him." (Actually Andrade was born in Maracaibo, though many of his contemporaries believed him to be Colombian.)

Be that as it may, Crespo didn't live to command Andrade long. He was killed in his first battle with the rebel El Mocho Hernández, Andrade, however, stayed in power for eighteen months without him. They were eighteen months of continual revolution. General Ramón Guerra defeated and imprisoned Hernández for the government. Then he himself turned around and revolted against Andrade. Government troops liquidated this threat, but by now the civil strife in Venezuela had convinced an exile in Colombia that his hour had arrived. Cipriano Castro rode out to the hacienda of Juan Vicente Gómez and invited his silent friend to help him invade Venezuela. All Gómez said was "You command and I obey." No explanations were necessary. Gómez attached no conditions.

Juan Vicente called his clan. They took to their horses and followed Cipriano Castro into Táchira State on May 23, 1899. There were sixty in all—brothers, friends, and retainers of Juan Vicente Gómez. First, they located the hidden cache of arms Gómez had sequestered seven years before and then they gathered reinforcements. The beady-eyed caudillos were looking for a winner. With their bands of cutthroats they fell in behind Cipriano Castro. In a few weeks he had two thousand men.

Gómez had never been a warrior. Nevertheless he occupied an important place in the hierarchy of Castro's invasionary force. He had the money, so he managed supplies and provisions. He found the meat, the rice, and the guns. When the expedition arrived at Valera, Castro named him his second in command, ignoring all the experienced officers who were climbing on his bandwagon. He felt he could trust Juan Vicente.

Castro's goal was Caracas and he never forgot it, not for a moment. He by-passed government forces when he could, risking the danger to his rear. He knew that the further he advanced into the country the more men his army would attract. Thus he took Tovar, Mérida, Trujillo, and Nirgua—fighting minor skirmishes, always on the move, leaving his enemies intact but far behind him.

He was now in a vise. Ahead lay the most populous cities of Venezuela, the bulk of government strength. Behind him the by-passed generals hurried to catch up. At Tocuyito, south of Valencia, Castro made his stand. There he pulverized the enemy. Valencia, second largest city in Venezuela, was his.

To all intents and purposes the campaign was over. After the Battle of Tocuyito, Andrade began to lose control of his supporters. The government generals could see only two choices: to fight on their own account or join Castro. In the end, everybody declared for Castro—the Liberal Party, the Nationalists (El Mocho's party), businessmen, officials of the Andrade government. A phenomenon typical of Venezuelan history had asserted itself once again.

This was a phenomenon which had been apparent in the wars of independence when landowners became royalists or republicans depending on which wind was blowing what force toward Caracas. Most spectacularly successful at this technique had been the Marqués de Casa León. Casa León, a rich proprietor with vast tracts in the valley of Aragua, served Francisco de Miranda, Monteverde, Simón Bolívar, Boves, and Morillo. As soon as one occupying army began to desert Caracas, he quietly moved to the enemy

camp, offering to help the victor. His lands grew and he prospered while more dedicated souls sacrificed everything, including
their lives. Many of the early oligarchs were like him—from Conservatives they became Liberals, and as Liberals supported Monagas, Castro, Falcón, as it suited their interests. The same class,
from generation to generation, had only one principle—their own
salvation; they simply wanted to be close to a government, any
government which happened to be in power. Antonio Leocadio
Guzmán and Antonio Guzmán Blanco personified the zenith of
this kind of mercenary opportunism.

During stable periods in the nation's history, like the Páez and
Guzmán Blanco eras, such political parasites had no problem.
They could remain a member of one party for a respectable length
of time. But with the confusion following Guzmán Blanco, when
administrations shuttled in and out of power with disquieting
frequency, it became necessary to jump from one camp to another
in imitation of the Marqués de Casa León. Thus the groups around
Guzmán Blanco, Andueza Palacio, Joaquín Crespo and Ignacio
Andrade bore remarkable resemblances to one another. In effect,
the administration of the country throughout this period was mis-
handled by the same cultured thieves. They passed from one government to another, still with their hands in the treasury. Always
the same faces, the same pandering smiles, surrounded the man
in power. When the president went into exile, they rushed as fast
as they could to insinuate themselves into the confidence of the
presidential contender who looked most likely to succeed. That
was why they sent an emissary to Valencia in 1899 to greet Cipriano
Castro.

The officials of the Andrade government feared the Nationalists
of El Mocho Hernández, whom they had put in jail after his revolt. The Nationalists thought Castro could help them into power.
Businessmen and generals were looking for lucrative and influential posts. Everybody had his reason. They all planned to use
Castro, each against the other. Instead, Castro used them. Juan
Vicente Gómez was the man who used Castro.

Cipriano Castro entered Caracas in triumph on October 22,
1899. Andrade had fled the day before, taking a path over the
Avila to La Guaira and leaving the presidency to General Víctor

Rodríguez, who surrendered it to Castro the moment the victor arrived in the city. Through the streets Castro rode in a coach. Crowds of Caraqueños, curious to know what the new dictator looked like, lined the streets. That evening the little man appeared at one of the balconies in the Casa Amarilla and announced his program. "New Men, New Ideas and New Procedures" would signalize his regime, he said. New men! Around him on the balcony stood these men—the generals and ministers of Linares Alcántara, Andueza Palacio, Joaquín Crespo, and Ignacio Andrade, smiling blandly at the multitude below them in the Plaza Bolívar.

Troops of the Restauración, as Castro called his crusade, camped in the Plaza Bolívar and the corridors of the Casa Amarilla. Fires were built. Between the trees around Bolívar's statue, rough Andinos slung their hammocks. The next day Juan Vicente Gómez arrived with the bulk of Castro's army. This was the last successful revolution for forty-six years.

In 1899 Gómez was forty-two years old. Before he marched east with Castro, he had never been more than twenty miles from the place where he had been born. Tall, well-built and muscular, Gómez had slant eyes and heavy lids. He sported a luxuriant mustache. (In his later years, he looked so much like Joseph Stalin that one Venezuelan has used the resemblance in an effort to prove Stalin a Gómez bastard by a Russian ballerina who visited Colombia.) He had no emotions. Though he enjoyed women, he didn't love them; he simply relieved himself with their help. He neither drank nor smoked. Even when he owned Venezuela, he continued to sleep in a barely furnished room and eat the monotonous food of mountain folk. Nothing outside of himself ever moved him. It is said that his mother asked him on her deathbed to release some political prisoners. Juan Vicente agreed, but when she died he reneged on the promise. "She died happy," he explained. "But now she's dead and there's nothing to be gained by doing it."

Gómez had a rare capacity to see where his own interests lay and to adjust his perspectives to new horizons. After a week as governor of the Federal District, his reward for service to Castro, this highland peasant who had only a few months before seen his first city felt perfectly at home in his job. He didn't understand the Caraqueños and never would, but that didn't bother him. They had to do as he said.

In 1900, Gómez moved up one notch in the Castro hierarchy. He was named governor of Táchira, which five months after the entrance of Castro into Caracas, still belonged to the defeated regime. The Restoration hadn't conquered the Andes. It had only passed through the region.

Gómez established Castro's hold over his homeland and did it so competently that his boss had Congress elect him First Vice-President of Venezuela in February 1901. Castro needed all the good men he could find in Caracas. One by one the generals and businessmen who had joined him at Valencia in 1899 had become dissatisfied and had turned against him.

The keynote for Castro's regime had been sounded in 1899 by an adviser who laid down the qualification Castro should set for Minister of Hacienda (Treasury). "He should be," the counselor said, "a man from whom you would not feel ashamed to ask one hundred thousand pesos." Castro's cabinet for the most part was composed of dishonest incompetents, and Castro proved to be the greatest incompetent of them all.

He neglected many of his old comrades in favor of the new allies he had made at Valencia, thus weakening his administration before it ever began to rule. From Andrade he inherited a country racked by two years of civil war. Saddled with foreign debts for which she had nothing to show, Venezuela was an economic mess. Instead of succoring Venezuela, Castro contributed to her ruin. He forced Caracas bankers to lend him money and then he and his thieves pocketed the funds.

In exchange for his depredations, Venezuela received a box seat at a burlesque show. Castro maintained twenty-three establishments. He acquired a mansion for his wife and twenty-two mistresses for himself. He loved to dance and drink. To him the presidency of Venezuela and the national treasury seemed vehicles for his own amusement. Once he bathed nude in the fountain of the Casa Amarilla, one of the main government buildings.

In 1900 one government supporter painted the following dismal picture of Venezuela's condition under Castro:

Six years of fiscal disorder, two more of incessant war, the price of coffee falling in the world market, many haciendas abandoned as a consequence, the sugar industry burning cane because of a drop in the value of the product, work interrupted throughout the Republic for lack of peace, confidence, and specie; the interest on the outstanding debt repudiated, which besides producing grave concern in the country has sunk the credit of the nation abroad; and the disastrous consequences of all the foregoing has created a situation in which commerce, capitalists, and professional and small businessmen are reduced to such penury that we can expect no help from them except that which may be compatible with their straitened circumstances.

The man who wrote this was Manuel Matos, the emissary who went to Valencia in 1899 and engineered the alliance of Castro and the oligarchs of the Andrade government. He was the banker of the Restoration and had arranged a one million bolivar loan which Castro had squandered on his little games. Matos included this summary of conditions in a note, explaining why bankers wouldn't lend Castro any more money. And for this, Castro threw him into jail together with the bankers. When Matos was released a few weeks later, he went to Trinidad and planned a revolution. Disillusioned officials and caudillos were eager for a blow at Castro. With Matos, they staged a revolution called "La Libertadora," which lasted for two years and initiated the most humiliating episode in Venezuelan history.

In Trinidad Matos procured a ship of British registry, which he rechristened *El Libertador*. While the caudillos revolted in the interior of Venezuela Matos raided the coast with his ship late in 1901. The Venezuelan government protested to the British, who ignored the issue of the ship and requested instead that Venezuela reimburse British residents for losses incurred during the civil wars. Germany had previously made a similar request.

To its credit, the Castro regime did make some efforts to pay the claims, despite a barren treasury. It established an office to examine them and several were paid. In addition, the government promised to reimburse all claimants who could submit "sufficient supporting documentation." This provision seemed like a subterfuge to the Germans and the English, exasperated as they were by the habitual bankruptcy of the Venezuelan government. They recalled their ministers and Italy, another creditor, followed suit. These governments imposed an armed blockade in December 1902. They sank three Venezuelan gunboats, and to avenge the sacking of an English merchant ship by an enraged mob of Venezuelans, they bombarded Puerto Cabello on December 13. The island of San Carlos off the Maracaibo bar was shelled on January 17, 1903. Such acts of outright aggression finally proved too much for the United States, which waved the Monroe Doctrine at the European nations and proposed that everybody arbitrate peacefully. The International Tribunal at the Hague rendered a decision in 1906, obligating Venezuela to pay foreigners a total of £1,571,160.

The Castro government had a knack for getting into trouble with foreigners. In 1905, Venezuela and the United States tangled over the Venezuelan government's treatment of an American company. The next year France ruptured relations because Castro had refused to let the French minister, M. Taigny, land in Venezuela on the grounds that he had violated quarantine regulations. Venezuela repudiated her debt to Belgium in 1907 and expelled the Dutch minister in 1908.

The revolution led by Manuel Matos had a special significance in the career of Juan Vicente Gómez. Through it, he changed from a subaltern to a power behind Castro. During the two years the rebellion lasted Gómez, the Vice-President, battled the insurgents. Except for one brief campaign when Gómez was incapacitated by a wound in the leg, Castro remained in Caracas and left the prosecution of the war to others. It was a peculiar disposition of responsibilities. Castro had years of military experience while Gómez knew nothing about war. True, he had served as a supply officer in two campaigns, but that did not qualify him to lead troops. Yet he did lead troops against Manuel Matos' rebels, and what is more, he fought exceedingly well. Following instructions telegraphed him by Castro, he crushed rebellion everywhere —at La Puerta, in the llanos, near Coro and throughout the east. In six campaigns he emerged triumphant. By July 1903, the revolution was squelched.

With each new success Gómez lifted his sights. Perhaps he had been content to remain Castro's vice-president before the Matos revolution. Afterward, he definitely wasn't. Of his victory at La Puerta, Gómez later said, "It was then I knew I would be president of Venezuela."

He did not hurry. He might have tried to grab the presidency any time after 1903. On the other hand, he might have lost all his recently won perquisites and emoluments in the attempt. To risk his haciendas and political post on a mere possibility did not appeal to Juan Vicente Gómez. So he waited for five years until he could seize power with the odds stacked mountain-high in his favor. During those five years, he constructed a political organization loyal to him. He tried to wheedle jobs for friends, relatives, and supporters. He lent a sympathetic ear to those whom Castro had annoyed and when he made a convert, he warned, "If you see me at the Palace, don't let on that you know me." To cast-offs from Castro's victorious army of 1899 he gave jobs on his haciendas. Gómez never forgot a friend. They all received their reward.

These maneuvers, of course, roused the suspicions of the oligarchs who surrounded Castro. Men like Ramón Tello Mendoza, Linares Alcántara, Eduardo Celis, Carnevali Monreal, Torres Cárdenas, and Román Delgado Chalbaud realized that any menace to Castro constituted an equal threat to their positions and plunder. They plotted against Gómez and whispered lies, misrepresentations, and rumors, as well as the truth, into Castro's receptive ears.

Castro was an ailing man, thanks to his dissipations. At times he seemed seriously ill. It was thought he might have to go to Europe for treatment. If he died or left the country, Gómez, the vice-president, would succeed him—a prospect which filled the black little hearts of Castro's friends with horror. Juan Vicente had to counteract their propaganda by an utter show of loyalty, a difficult task in view of his behind-the-scenes maneuvers. He did it by unequaled duplicity. The following account of Gómez' deception of Castro is by Pedro María Morantes (quoted in *Juan Vicente Gómez, Un Fenómeno Telúrico*, page 14):

When he won a battle, Gómez modestly wrote, "I don't know anything about these things. I attribute my triumph to having followed to the letter the brilliant instructions of The Greatest Man of Modern Times." And when he lost he wrote: "I had to retreat: I attribute this defeat to having neglected some precept of The Greatest Man of Modern Times."

Never did Gómez, not once in his life as a subaltern, oppose Castro: he obeyed and applauded all the orders Castro gave him. To each command Gómez would invariably respond with one of these phrases: "Very well thought out, General." "A master stroke, Chief." "Good, good. Excellent." "That'll suit us to a *T*." If Castro had ordered Gómez to kill one of his dearest friends, Gómez without an instant's hesitation would have answered, "Excellent, General. That'll suit us to a *T*."

Castro had vexed Gómez and had made him seem ridiculous. It was logical to suspect Gómez of plotting against him in revenge: but there was no proof. Castro put a spy in whom he had absolute confidence in Gómez' house. Someone denounced the spy, but Gómez answered imperturbably,

"I already know about him."

"But, General, we ought to oust this spy."

"To the contrary," Gómez responded. "We have to treat him very well and remove all obstacles in his way: but we mustn't make it too easy for him or else Castro will suspect something."

The spy made a hole in a door which separated one room from the study where Gómez used to receive his intimate friends: then he put a screen in front of the door. Gómez spotted the hole, but he let no one repair it. When the spy, who had been masquerading as a servant, suggested Gómez keep the screen in front of the door, Gómez affected to consider the request normal and reasonable. "Fine," he said. "Excellent."

Upon receiving those who counseled him to revolt against Castro, Gómez didn't answer until he knew the spy had entered the adjoining room. Then Gómez, tears standing in his eyes, would say:

"I will never take arms against Don Cipriano: without him I would have been nothing; with him I shall be much better off in future; I don't want anybody to misunderstand. I shall always be loyal to my chief."

The spy heard all this and told Castro. The spy was above Castro's suspicion and Gómez used him for his own ends. It was a war of tricks and treachery. Gómez had suffered an infinite number of humiliations from Castro, but these humiliations only sweetened Gómez' smile. Castro offended Gómez, but Gómez absorbed offenses in his impassivity. Castro ridiculed Gómez, but

Gómez' plans surpassed ridicule. What no man tolerates nor pardons is ingratitude. Gómez did not pardon it, but he did tolerate it. His prudence exceeded his love of himself. The jibes of Castro bounced inoffensively off his dry skin. . . .

Gómez knew that Castro's tumors were going to get worse. The end would be his death or a trip to Europe. It was urgent for Gómez to inspire in the Dictator a belief in his loyalty so that in the event Castro should die or leave the country he would give the presidency to him. . . . Because of this, Gómez knew he must submit to everything—jokes, offenses, and ridicule. He destroyed Castro's suspicions with unchanging meekness: he disoriented Castro's tricks with measureless hypocrisy. Castro's disease and Gómez' dissimulation continued to parallel one another. When El Restaurador decided to go to Europe, the spies had submitted their reports, which corresponded perfectly with Gómez' public manifestations. Castro then began to treat Gómez cordially. He called him "Don Juan Vicente" and told his intimate friends: "Don Juan is the same healthy and stupid man of La Mulera."

This trial period was called "La Conjura"—the conjuration. From 1906 to 1908 Gómez subordinated every interest to his deception of Castro. He performed his duties faithfully—as vice-president, provisional president and even, briefly in 1906, as actual president. He made daily visits to Castro's house and asked for his orders. When Castro subjected Gómez to the supreme test of giving him the presidency and retiring to La Victoria for his health, Gómez begged the baffled Dictator to reconsider his decision. "Look, my friend," he said. "I wasn't born for this. You're the one who knows how to command." In 1907 Juan Vicente's cousin, Eustoquio, got drunk and murdered the governor of the Federal District in a Caracas bar. Eustoquio had been noisily shouting his loyalty to Juan Vicente just before the murder. Despite this fact—or perhaps because of it—Gómez did absolutely nothing to save him. He played the honest citizen. Eustoquio went to jail like any other criminal. Of course, one of the things Juan Vicente did when he came to power was secure Eustoquio's release. Displaying a morbid sense of humor, Gómez then named the assassin commandant of the prison from which he had just been freed.

The patient intrigues of Juan Vicente Gómez continued until November 1908, when Castro sailed for Europe to undergo an operation. Castro still didn't trust Gómez completely. He favored leaving the presidency to an oligarch, Linares Alcántara. It was Zoila Castro who persuaded her husband to name Gómez acting president. During those years of "La Conjura," while the rest of the politicians exclusively sought to influence Castro, crafty Juan Vicente used to visit Zoila and talk to her for hours. Now, in the decisive moment, this stratagem gave him the final advantage over his enemies.

The Vice-President continued to fawn until Castro had sailed far out in the ocean. He accompanied Cipriano and Zoila Castro halfway down the hill to La Guaira. Then he returned to Caracas and waited another month before he supplied the last master detail in his intricate plan. He was still somewhat unsure of himself. He wanted to be absolutely certain of success.

Gómez contacted old enemies of Castro, wooing their support. Meanwhile, he amicably arranged a settlement to a dispute with Holland so that the opprobrium for the foreign entanglement might fall on Castro's administration instead of his own. He lined up support in the barracks of Caracas. On December 13, the people, angered by the menacing appearance of a Dutch cruiser off La Guaira, staged an anti-Castro demonstration. Even then, Juan Vicente Gómez had doubts. He delayed another week. Finally on December 19, 1908, after eight years of cautious preparation, he delivered the coup de grâce.

He rose early, as was his custom. He ate breakfast and left his villa. It was a cold morning, but Gómez, a bit terrified by his own temerity, began to sweat profusely. Surrounded by an armed band, he visited the one barracks in the city of which he was not sure. "Do you recognize Juan Vicente Gómez as president?" he asked the commandant. Only at the Casa Amarilla did anyone dare to protest. There the governor of the Federal District, one of the oligarchs, ordered Gómez arrested for treason. He was arrested instead. As the governor was conducted down a flight of stairs at the Casa Amarilla, Gómez lifted his cane and smashed it across the man's back. The humble inclination of the head, the agreeable smile, the obsequious gestures, and even the perspiration had disappeared.

He was dictator of Venezuela.

Chapter XIV

NADIR

J̲ᴜᴀɴ V̲ɪᴄᴇɴᴛᴇ G̲óᴍᴇᴢ remained tyrant for twenty-seven years, a feat unequaled in Venezuelan history. During that period, the only benefits Venezuela received from the dictator were those which happened to coincide with his personal welfare.

In 1908, however, no one imagined that the nation had submitted to the most brutal dictatorship of her history. Gómez was popular for the moment. He had ended the nine years of Castro's offensive personalism. Venezuelans remembered how he had let his brother, Eustoquio, go to jail. Perhaps this simple peasant from the interior, they told each other, would continue to behave himself in office.

From New York, Trinidad, and Colombia, the enemies of Castro trooped back to Venezuela. Many of them were generals whom Gómez had defeated in the two-year revolution of Manuel Matos. Now, suddenly, they were "friends." For that matter, everybody was Gómez' friend. The oligarchs—the conniving clique of men around Castro who had gleefully tried to slit Juan Vicente's throat —circled about the sleepy-eyed Andino, protesting admiration, offering to help. Their object was the same: to preserve their influence by a connection with The New Man, to use him as a steppingstone to power.

They didn't fool Gómez for a second. With the cynicism that

came naturally to him, he referred to them as "Los Amigos Caudillos" and "Los Amigos Doctores." These men were superior to Gómez in almost every way. They were cultured and understood the problems of government. They counted on these advantages to help them destroy Gómez and seize power themselves. Said Linares Alcántara, a former Castrista, "We will get rid of him within three months." "Los Amigos Caudillos" took sides, developed plans to use Gómez against each other. Everyone sought an alliance with Gómez against an enemy. The Nationalists cheered Gómez and tried to win him over. The Liberals organized banquets in his honor and called him the rightful heir to Guzmán Blanco's Gran Partido Liberal.

No one bothered to conspire against him. While aspirants for power wasted their time in futile intrigues, Gómez consolidated his hold on the government. Thanks to the absorption of politicians in their own welfare instead of Venezuela's, the tyranny of Juan Vicente Gómez was born. He would rule absolutely and alone. The caudillos discovered this fact a year after he seized power. One morning, he called in his secretary, Dr. Leopoldo Baptista, who had helped Gómez depose Castro. "Doctor," Juan Vicente said, "ask all the ministers to resign. Those oxen are very tired." Baptista thought the Dictator couldn't get along without him so he decided to use the occasion in order to test his strength. "I'd like a rest, too, General—that is, if you have no objection." Baptista expected Gómez to protest. Instead, the General asked, "And whom would you suggest I name in your place?" To protect himself Baptista decided to mention the name of an ignorant Gómez friend who couldn't possibly serve since he knew nothing about politics. "General, unless you can suggest someone better, I think the man should be Don Antonio Pimentel." All Gómez answered was, "I'll name him tomorrow." He needed the advice of no one, and he wanted everybody to know it.

The true nature of the Gómez regime was clearly revealed with the disposal of this first cabinet in 1909. Into the offices of the caudillos and oligarchs went the staunchest supporters of Juan Vicente Gómez, the illiterate Andinos who had followed him out of Táchira, men like his brother, Juancho, who had always been loyal. For chief counselor, Gómez picked an ill-bred man from the interior named Dr. Ezequiel Vivas, whose main virtue was fanatical devotion to Gómez. He helped the Dictator develop a national policy. The national policy, of course, mirrored the character of Gómez. It was avaricious, cruel, backward, and absolute.

Some caudillos did not take their demotion lying down. They were to plague Gómez with rebellion and conspiracy until the 1930's. The most prominent of them, Román Delgado Chalbaud, a former Castro supporter who switched to Gómez in 1908, had always been anxious to wield supreme authority in Venezuela. His post under Juan Vicente as president of a government shipping company rankled him, and he soon gathered together a knot of supporters to overthrow the government. In May 1913, word of this plot leaked out prematurely. Delgado Chalbaud, fearful that Gómez might have learned about it before he and his friends were ready to act, went to the presidential palace one morning, determined to kill the Dictator if he seemed to have suspicions. At Miraflores, Gómez received him with the usual affability. Convinced that the tyrant had discovered nothing, Delgado Chalbaud left the palace. He was arrested a few minutes later and taken to La Rotunda, the sinister political prison, where he remained for fourteen years.

This same Delgado Chalbaud went to Europe when he was released and as eager for power as ever, launched an invasion in 1929. He wasn't the only one. There were invasions from Colombia and from the sea throughout the Gómez period. One general, Arévalo Cedeño, raided Venezuela seven times. None of these maneuvers could succeed. Gómez reigned during modern times. Soon his army was using machine guns and airplanes. The days when a man could successfully wage a revolution by leading a few hundred badly-armed bandits over the hills had passed. From now on, revolutions would erupt within the army itself. They would be short and relatively bloodless—really coups d'état. The era of the caudillo was over. After Gómez, power in Venezuela would belong to officers of a professional army.

Juan Vicente Gómez could even turn revolutions to his own account. The first Gómez congress in 1909 had carelessly passed a constitution which expressly prohibited the re-election of a chief executive. In 1913, the last year of Gómez' first term, anti-government forces quickly pounced on this provision and began political activity. In the pages of a Caracas newspaper Arévalo González, a dedicated journalist, who went to jail fourteen times under Gómez and eventually died there, proposed the candidacy of Félix Montes, a university professor. Gómez resolved this awkward situation by having lieutenants fake a pro-Castro invasion. Then he declared a state of emergency, imprisoned Arévalo González, and to make the "invasion" appear more convincing, led the army against the "rebels," leaving the presidency to Gil Fortoul, well-known intellectual. The constitution was amended and two years later the Dictator was elected to office for a seven-year term, covering the period 1915–22. For six of these years Gómez preferred to remain "President-Elect" and Commander of the Army while a figurehead, Victorino Márquez Bustillos, occupied Miraflores as Provisional President.

During the first decade of the Gómez regime, a formidable corps of hangers-on gathered around the tyrant. Some of these men were the old oligarchs who in secondary roles had been feeding at the patronage trough since Guzmán Blanco. Then, of course, there were the relatives and friends from the Andes. Caudillos who were content to play second fiddle also swelled the throng and held important posts throughout the Gómez period. The most peculiar group in the Gómez circle, however, were the nation's intellectuals—men like José Gil Fortoul, González Guinán, Pedro Emilio Coll, Samuel Dario Maldonado, Diego Carbonell; historians, writers, scholars, and professors. Many of them had been attracted to Gómez by his opposition to Castro and stayed with him in the mistaken belief that they could influence him and moderate his excesses. Instead they served as scribes, writing speeches, and documents, or decorated insignificant offices with their "illustrious" names.

The government clique formed a royal court. Gómez was king. To Maracay, where he had his "palace," went the intellectuals, the generals, the relatives, and the oligarchs to curry favor with the lord. Gómez received government ministers on Saturdays and gave them weekly instructions. The "Provisional President" used to make the ninety-mile trip for his orders just like any other lackey. At court, these people intrigued against each other and those whose jobs forced them to live in the interior maintained lobbies at Maracay for their own protection. Throughout the Gómez regime Maracay was for most intents and purposes the capital of the country.

For these people Gómez evinced amused contempt. He called them *"buscadores de puestos"*—office seekers. Never did he impute anything but base and mercenary motives to anyone, especially his admirers. When his secretary announced a visitor, Gómez used to say impatiently, "Ask him what he wants." It didn't matter who the man was. If the secretary protested that the visitor was rich and important and only wanted to say hello, Gómez would persist, "No, he's after something. Go ask him what he wants!"

Gómez liked to ridicule the favor seekers as well. Once he was walking on his lands at Maracay with a long train of generals in attendance when he glanced at the darkening sky and said, "Look at the moon. Now, that's a sight to open one's mouth about." He immediately sat down on the ground and stared at the moon with his mouth wide open. The generals promptly followed suit. As the entourage sat gaping at the sky, Gómez asked an intellectual who was present if people lived on the moon. When the man explained that scientists did not believe so, Gómez answered, "There aren't any men there? Well, it's a good thing. Because if there were and they could see this far, what would they think of all these people sitting around with their mouths open?"

Only one thing about his subordinates mattered to Gómez. They had to serve him unconditionally. If they did, they were rewarded, regardless of their past political vacillations. Once an official who had written a pamphlet attacking Gómez before he joined the administration found that an enemy had put a copy of the damaging brochure on Gómez' desk. As the official quaked in anticipation of a prompt sentence to jail, Gómez picked up the pamphlet and said, "Don't worry. You wrote this when you were my enemy, but now you're my friend. It isn't important."

Gómez trusted few men, if any. A pint-sized Colombian Indian named Eloy Tarazona slept at his door and was perhaps his closest confidant. An unofficial bodyguard, he followed the Dictator everywhere—a silent, mysterious dwarf. The court at Maracay had a jester as well. He was a picturesque priest, Carlos Borges, a confirmed alcoholic in ecclesiastical disgrace. The third figure of the triumvirate which was closest to the Dictator was Antonio Pimentel, a lascivious little man who by prior efforts and through his connection with Gómez came to be the second richest man in the country.

There were, of course, others near Gómez—his brothers, his sons, his secretaries. It is doubtful whether any of them exercised a real influence. Gómez only followed their suggestions when they seemed compatible with his interests. In this way one secretary, Dr. Francisco Baptista Galindo, was able to moderate the policies of the regime. On one occasion he persuaded Gómez to release all the political prisoners, close the jails, and allow ten thousand exiles to return home. Naturally, this policy lasted only until the next revolution developed.

Throughout most of the Gómez period the jails were full. Spies circulated in every social circle to see that the populace spoke well of the Dictator in private as well as in public. Even Venezuelans who traveled abroad were not safe from this mental censorship. Gómez maintained an international espionage network to ferret out his enemies. An indiscreet remark, a casual joke, could land a critic in one of the Gómez jails—La Rotunda in Caracas, La Libertadora in Puerto Cabello, or San Carlos in Maracaibo. In these ancient Spanish prisons thousands of Venezuelans languished, existing on thin soup and bananas, lying in their own filth with irons weighing as much as eighty pounds encasing their legs. One priest received this treatment for having preached a sermon on the sin of extramarital cohabitation, a topic Gómez construed to be a reflection on himself. Another priest was poisoned in jail because he denounced the tyrant to the Pope as being unworthy of receiving a religious decoration.

It was for cruelty that the regime achieved major infamy. Methods of persecution and punishment exceeded any of the horrors applied in Venezuela's bloody history. Men suspected of complicity in an army plot were hung by their testicles in 1919. Young students caught distributing anti-Gómez pamphlets were delivered to the tender mercies of assassins like Eustoquio Gómez. Many of them died from neglect or torture wounds. Families learned about the prison deaths when the government told them the number of the plot in the cemetery where the relative had been buried.

Juan Vicente wasn't a sadist or a Hitler-style fanatic, but he was dispassionately cruel in the interests of self-preservation. He sent men to jail, he said, "to teach them to be useful." For Gómez, suspicion of disobedience was enough to warrant incarceration. The pleas of his own relatives on behalf of prisoners left him cold. When people tried to intercede for innocent men jailed by mistake, Gómez scoffed at arguments that the prisoner was harmless. "Now that he has been in prison," the Dictator would say, "he is my enemy." Only if Gómez deemed his regime sufficiently secure would dungeon doors swing open. He saved "indulgences" for public holidays like July 5, Venezuelan Independence Day, or December 19, the anniversary of his seizure of power. On these days, political prisoners who had learned "to be useful" were released.

Stern punishment of opponents raised no moral issue for Juan Vicente. He recognized only practical motives. That a man might fight for an abstraction like freedom seemed absolutely inconceivable to him. Of revolutionaries he used to say, "They want what I have." In some cases, unfortunately, he was right. Román Delgado Chalbaud seemed motivated by personal ambition rather than patriotic idealism. A younger insurgent, Rafael Simón Urbina, became something of a national hero by battling Gómez in the late twenties and early thirties. Yet, in 1950, this man helped murder the President of Venezuela's Military Junta, presumably to further his own political career. An illuminating footnote to Venezuelan politics is the fact that the assassinated Junta president was Carlos Delgado Chalbaud, Román's son.

The Gómez government squelched all forms of expression—press, speech, elections, petition, assembly. On one occasion Gómez prohibited the circulation of anti-Communist literature by Caracas priests. His reason? "I don't care if they speak bad about Communism. It's that I don't want them to speak about Communism at all. Enemies are like the dead. You shouldn't talk about them."

Censorship, of course, had its corollary in extravagant praise. Newspapers heaped absurd compliments upon his grizzly head,

comparing him with the Liberator. He was called Benemérito—
the well-deserving.

To Gómez, the peasant, government was not an end in itself.
He worshiped money. Political power helped him make it. He had
the soul of a robber baron. He constructed a vast economic empire. Haciendas were bought with public funds; factories equipped
the same way. Never did he distinguish between his personal income and the national treasury; government money paid for his
houses, businesses, hotels, and trips. His interests reached everywhere. Sugar mills, cattle ranches, a textile factory, a creamery.
Taking advantage of absolute political power, he destroyed his
business enemies as he liquidated political enemies. Ranchers
who refused to sell their cattle at the price he offered were threatened with imprisonment on trumped-up charges. Gómez businesses were exempt from customs duties on imported machinery
and raw materials. They could undersell and wreck competing
firms. The aim of all this financial piracy, of course, was to make
everything he operated a monopoly. In this way, he became the
only authorized meat wholesaler in Caracas. Naturally, he charged
the Venezuelan people what he chose.

Juan Vicente's flair for practical economics had a salutary effect
on the state of the national treasury. He scrupulously paid all foreign and internal debts. He kept Venezuela's currency hard. When
he died in 1935, the country had a surplus of nearly one hundred
million bolivars. This was a considerable accomplishment in view
of the fact that he and his family spent the twenty-seven years of
his reign robbing the nation blind.

Gómez was no miser. He shared good things with his supporters,
one of the reasons why he stayed in power so long. To obscure
lieutenants, he awarded posts as civil magistrates; to favorites,
generals, and close relatives, he proffered appointments as state
governors and customs collectors. All positions carried with them
the tacit right to pilfer funds from the public pocket. Graft was
collected in every conceivable way. Army commanders absorbed
the salaries of "imaginary" soldiers. Civil officials owned stock in
contracting companies which won public works contracts. Kick-
backs, taxes, bonuses, and direct raids on the Treasury added to
the staggering total the Gómecistas stole.

Juan Vicente presided over this army of organized bandits with
disarming simplicity. He looked sleepy most of the time. Only
when he was angry did animal rage shake his complacency. Then
he acted swiftly and brutally, subsiding immediately into drowsy
impassivity. He liked to visit his lands, making inspection trips,
talking to the peasants, spicing his speech with homey aphorisms
and allusions to nature. Grandchildren were dawdled on his knee.
He gave them delightful little presents and kissed them on the
cheek. He took them for rides on his yacht and entertained them
at beach parties. His families were housed in luxurious mansions.
He himself lived alone. Mistresses were sent for when he wanted
them and dispatched when he was through. He wasted none of
his energy on love, nor did he allow his family ties to distract
him from the business of governing Venezuela in his own way.
Everything he had, every friend, every relative, every ability,
every talent, was forfeited to his insatiable lust for wealth and
power.

Juan Vicente Gómez ran Venezuela as if it were one big hacienda. He knew how to command. He knew what he wanted done.
He chose the best foremen he could find and let them attend to
the details. Government was a mystery he didn't try to compre-
hend. Sometimes he couldn't remember which man he had assigned to which job. They tell a story to illustrate this point,
about Pedro Arcaya, Gómez ambassador to the United States, a
noisy supporter who wrote a fulsome book in English defending
the regime of his patron. While vacationing in Venezuela, Arcaya
went to pay his respects to Gómez. The visit excited the Maracay
courtiers vastly since Arcaya had been rumored to be the man
Gómez would choose as next Provisional President. This rumor
collapsed, however, as the ambassador was ushered in to see the
dictator. "Dr. Arcaya! How are you?" Gómez said. "How are
things going in the customs house?" The Dictator had confused
his envoy with another Arcaya, the ambassador's brother, who
was the head of customs in Puerto Cabello.

The refinements of international politics also escaped him. His
philosophy about relations with other countries was character-
istically elementary. "Let each one command in his own country."
To the arguments of the Papal Nuncio, who wanted Venezuela to

ratify a Vatican agreement, Gómez answered, "I think it's better if the Pope rules over there and I rule here."

He admired strong men like Teddy Roosevelt and Kaiser Wilhelm. Through newsreels he learned what little he knew about the world. He used to see each one several times; his friend, Antonio Pimentel, read the captions for him and pointed out important world figures.

During World War I, he kept Venezuela steadfastly neutral. In 1916, when both the French and German ambassadors were employing every stratagem to make him declare Venezuela a co-belligerent on their respective sides, Gómez eluded the question by a device as clever as any their trained minds might have invented. He granted the ambassadors an audience, a favor each had been seeking for some time. Violating a cardinal diplomatic rule, he told them to come at the same hour. Upon arriving in Maracay they were ushered into the same waiting room. To their extreme discomfort, they sat on opposite sides of the room avoiding each other's gaze until the signaled hour for the interview had long passed. Then Gómez appeared and received them together. "Forgive me, gentlemen, for being late," he said. "But you see I was in the chapel praying that Venezuela may never get involved in a terrible war like the one your two countries are fighting."

Gómez had more to do with foreigners than any prior president. Shortly before World War I, Venezuela ceased to be just another country in Latin America. It caught the acquisitive eyes of American, Dutch, and British capitalists. Between 1910 and 1930, foreign geologists ascertained that Venezuela owned one of the world's richest oil reservoirs. Recognizing that his country lacked the resources to develop this industry and enthralled by the prospects of fat oil royalties, Gómez enticed foreign interests with attractive concession terms. The development of the oil industry was immensely important to the stability of the Gómez dictatorship. Prosperity is a government's surest defense.

For decades men had known Venezuela contained oil. In the nineteenth century, a crude extraction plant produced kerosene in Táchira state. Lake Maracaibo was famous for its oil seepages. Not until 1914, however, did foreign companies discover that oil existed in sufficient quantities to make exploitation profitable. In that year, the Caribbean Petroleum Company, later absorbed by Shell, began pumping oil from the first commercial well in the Lake Maracaibo area.

Those early years of oil development in Venezuela were reminiscent of the Spanish conquest. Geologists ranged the jungles of Venezuela, battling insects, vermin, and reptiles, enduring the tortures of tropical swamps in a search for signs of the black fluid. They even had to fight the Indians. Motilones protected their forest preserves with long bows and six-foot arrows. An occasional oil searcher was killed, others were wounded. Yet they pushed through green labyrinths and across the scorched plains. El Dorado had become El Petróleo.

The Maracaibo area felt the full impact of the oil invasion first. Around the shore of the lake company after company tapped fabulous jets of viscous treasure. With each new find, the city of Maracaibo burgeoned.

Before the oil age, Maracaibo was a pestilential village of fifteen thousand, mainly remarkable as a climatic and scenic approximation of hell. Its environs were swampland. Plagues of insects speckled its colonial buildings. Sewage ran in the streets. Stimulated by the oil development around the lake, buildings shot up to house the flood of oil workers, native and foreign, attracted to the region. Industries to serve them fed the local economy. Roads began to appear on the lip of the lake, connecting the oil camps with the city. It was a boom of staggering proportions and it hasn't stopped yet. Maracaibo became the second largest city in Venezuela.

The first companies in Venezuela were British for the most part. American firms, well occupied with the richer supplies of North America, did not enter the field until the 1920's. The Standard Oil Company of New Jersey (now Creole) began operations in 1921.

Production soared from 318,000 barrels annually in 1918 to one million in 1921, 4 millions in 1923, 63 millions in 1927, 100 million in 1928, and 180 million in 1936. (In 1952 production had risen to nearly 2 million barrels *a day*.) All of the big companies arrived to try their luck. Besides Shell and Standard of New Jersey, the roster of foreign firms included such goliaths as Gulf, Socony, and Texas, plus a host of minor outfits. The extent of the oil fields spread too. Wells were drilled in Estado Falcón and in eastern Venezuela. In the early 1930's the Mene Grande Oil Company (Gulf), using new instruments like the seismograph, the torsion balance, and the magnetometer which permitted profitable exploration even where oil seepages were not evident, began a search for oil in Anzoátegui, a state in the llanos of eastern Venezuela. The first of several fields in this area, which now rivals the Lake Maracaibo area in importance, was discovered in 1937.

Gómez gave foreign investors the complete co-operation of his government. Customs exemptions were granted for the importation of oil machinery. During the first years of oil exploitation when the extent of the preserve was still unknown, the government contented itself with an annual tax of between 1 and 2 bolivars per hectare on the land conceded to companies or individuals. In 1920, however, Congress passed a law with provisions for exploration, land and excise taxes, plus a royalty, in cash or kind, of 15 per cent. Later laws reduced the royalty to 10 per cent as an inducement to increased exploitation of Venezuelan oil.

Compared to the 50 per cent cut Venezuela receives from petroleum production today, Gómez' laws were mild. The Dictator may have had sense enough to realize that he had to curb his greed if he expected to attract foreign capital. The initial years of oil development are expensive. Companies must invest millions in exploration and installations before they get a gallon of oil to sell. Naturally, they will not spend such sums unless they can expect to make an extremely high profit initially.

Gómez profited from the oil bonanza in all kinds of ways. First there were the taxes and royalties which the oil companies had to pay. These amounted to 612,000,000 bolivars in the years between 1919 and 1936. In addition, the new industry and its revenues stimulated exports and imports, on which Venezuela traditionally charged high duties. The national income, as a consequence, doubled in the first decade after 1919. Obviously Gómez did not make off with all the treasure. It was, however, available for his use and he and his family helped themselves. For instance, they purchased land from peasants who did not suspect the value of their property and then sold it for handsome profits to the oil companies.

The oil industry complicated Venezuelan life and the problems of government to an extreme degree. Until the 1920's Venezuela was a semirural country whose economy depended upon the exportation of coffee, cacao, and cattle and the importation of manufactured goods. Her people were predominantly farmers; business and industry occupied an insignificant percentage of the population. The social structure of the country was still divided into two economic classes—the very rich and the very poor: no middle class worthy of the name existed. Upon this retarded, almost medieval way of life, burst the full impact of the twentieth century, suddenly and with shattering force.

Peons left their fields and gravitated toward the oil centers, lured by salaries they considered fabulous. For the first time in its history Venezuela began to have a working class as well as a peasant class. The flood of oil royalties into the National Treasury produced an inflation which together with the shift of the working force from rural areas to the cities disrupted the nation's economy.

Venezuela could no longer supply her own wants. Oil dollars were sent abroad to buy many of the things her people ate and wore. The country strained under one of the world's highest cost-of-living indexes. The hordes who migrated to the cities in search of fat wages found that their money disappeared faster than ever. Acute housing shortages developed. In Caracas, migrants took to the hills and ravines around the city and built rude shacks of old lumber, rocks, and packing cases. The modern age—the era of the urban dweller, the factory, the creed of efficiency, speed, and the machine—had agitated Venezuela with all of its bewildering complexities.

In the face of this cultural and economic shock, Juan Vicente Gómez did nothing. He continued to rule like a tribal patriarch. The nation now had plenty of money to fight disease and ignorance. Yet the funds went to build hotels no one but Juan Vicente and his courtiers have ever really used. As the nation seethed under the stimulus of creative changes, Gómez and his supporters stultified this potential by primitive policies and selfish opportunism. Thus Venezuela lost twenty years of promise.

There were some things, however, which even Gómez could not stop. In the nation's schools and colleges, a generation of men and women who had grown up under his aegis were sorely troubled by the disparity between the words of Bolívar which they were taught and the actions of Gómez which they witnessed. They read books about utopias of which Venezuela under Gómez was an absolute antithesis. News of labor agitation in England and the Communist experiment in Soviet Russia, liberal notions about economic as well as political democracy caught and held their interest. They talked and argued among themselves. In disgust, they watched their frightened elders bow before the Dictator. They resolved to speak out. In 1928, they did. The result was a revolution motivated by ideals rather than lust for power—the first since the Wars of Liberation.

It began quite innocently. From February 6 to 12 the student body of the Central University in Caracas celebrated "Student Week." On the agenda were the usual university highjinks—the coronation of a queen, speeches, dances, student parades, etc. This exuberant expression of collegiate spirit took a peculiar turn from the first ceremony. On Monday, February 6, the students marched with a floral offering to the National Pantheon where the remains of Simón Bolívar and other important Venezuelans are buried. There a fiery young orator, Jóvito Villalba, opened Student Week with a violent attack on the government. The crowd of students forgot about the festivities and thought instead about their oppressed nation. A chain reaction had been set off.

The government quickly picked up young Jóvito Villalba and two other students for questioning. "What do you mean by saying that the university is the country?" asked the governor of the Federal District. "You know that General Gómez is the country." They were jailed.

In the university, other students began a campaign to secure their release. A university society, the Federación de Estudiantes, dispatched delegations to the governor. On February 22, after all other means had been unsuccessful, the Federación de Estudiantes sent an open telegram to Juan Vicente Gómez. The members challenged the Dictator to jail them, too, so that they might share the fate of their comrades. They announced that students agreeing with this declaration would wear blue caps and "FEV" buttons, the insignia of the organization. That night police arrested more than two hundred blue-capped students and whisked them away to Puerto Cabello.

The jailing of the students became a cause célèbre. People paraded through the streets. Anti-Gómez slogans were chalked on the walls of buildings. The police added to the public fury by killing and wounding some demonstrators who had gathered in the Plaza Bolívar to protest against the government. In the midst of this confusion, a group of young army officers intent upon overthrowing the regime began to plot with university students and other civilians. They revolted on April 7, 1928.

Their valiant attempt to seize the army and turn the country's might against the tyrant was quickly stifled. An armed mob of civilians took Miraflores Palace, but before the withering fire of loyal army units in San Carlos barracks, the revolutionaries fell. Hundreds of students and military men went to prison. Some died there. The rest spent years working on the roads or incarcerated at Puerto Cabello.

Nevertheless this revolution was to have a profound effect on Venezuela. After the Dictator's death in 1935, the students of 1928 became congressmen, political leaders, and government ministers. From the Federación de Estudiantes came such men as Rómulo Betancourt, president of Venezuela from 1945 to 1947 and leader of the now-outlawed political party Acción Democrática; Germán Suárez Flammerich, 1950–52 president of the Junta de Gobierno; Jóvito Villalba, head of the political party Unión Republicana Democrática; Gerardo Sansón, the present Minister of Public Works; and Luis Emilio Gómez Ruiz, the present Foreign Minister.

The revolution of 1928 initiated four years of revolutionary activity against the Gómez tyranny. Early in 1929 Rafael Simón Urbina, whose perverted nature found useful expression in opposition to Gómez, launched an invasion from Curaçao. Urbina and a group of Venezuelan exiles kidnaped the governor of the island to prevent interference by the Dutch authorities. Then they boarded an American merchant vessel and forced the captain at gun point to take them to Estado Falcón, Urbina's home state. As the tiny army marched on Coro, the state capital, government forces destroyed it. A few survivors, Urbina included, escaped.

The same year a more ambitious expedition began in Europe under General Román Delgado Chalbaud. Aboard a chartered German vessel, the *Falke,* three hundred Venezuelan exiles sailed home to battle the Dictator. They landed near Cumaná on August 11 and 12, 1929, but government troops parried this blow with their usual brutal efficiency. The invasion lasted only a few hours. Delgado Chalbaud was killed. Though revolutionary activity occasionally disrupted the peace in the next two years, the Falke Expedition was the last large-scale maneuver against Gómez.

He was old now, nearly seventy-five. He suffered from severe bouts with prostatitis. No longer did he personally lead the army into battle. Gómez rested in Maracay, watching his enterprises prosper.

In 1929, the presidential problem cropped up again. The Dictator had been re-elected president of the republic for a seven-year term in 1922 by his lackeys in Congress. As the period expired, Congress naturally asked the boss to succeed himself again. To everyone's surprise, Gómez refused. In fact he resigned. This illogical move bewildered the venal congressmen, unaccustomed as they were to thinking for themselves. They begged the general to reconsider. Finally, the entire Congress repaired to Maracay in a body. Before the assembled legislators, Juan Vicente Gómez delivered the only speech of his career. In monosyllables, he announced that he wished to devote himself to agriculture. If Congress approved, he said, he would like to remain as commander in chief of the army. He also offered to suggest a possible successor —a man "who agrees with me; in this way, everything will go perfectly well." Congress was, of course, wildly enthusiastic. The members applauded and cheered, and when Gómez proposed the name of Juan Bautista Pérez, a timid reactionary and a Supreme Court judge, they elected him immediately.

Dr. Pérez served as presidential puppet until 1931 when Congress demanded his resignation and the return of Gómez. As if he had never suggested the change in the first place, Juan Vicente graciously accepted. He was president in name as well as in fact until his death.

During these final four years of the tyranny, the system rather than the man governed Venezuela. His machine functioned perfectly. The army, the governors, the lower echelons of the bureaucracy were still loyal. Juan Vicente had to conserve most of his energies for a futile fight with age. His attacks of prostatitis became more frequent. Sometimes he lay unconscious for days. In November 1935, Juan Vicente Gómez left Caracas for the last time. Suffering acutely, he traveled to Maracay where he could be among his friends and favorite haunts.

His condition steadily worsened. When December 17 dawned, Juan Vicente was unconscious. It was the anniversary of Simón Bolívar's death. Early in the afternoon, the old Dictator briefly recovered consciousness. One of his sons was with him in the room. "What day is it?" Gómez asked. "December 17th," the son answered. *"Me esperan,"* (They're waiting for me), he muttered and sank back into a coma.

That night, almost as if he had willed it that way, Juan Vicente Gómez died.

Chapter XV

THE PAUPER MILLIONAIRE

JUAN VICENTE GÓMEZ was dead, but the system which allowed him to sweep to power in Venezuela and control the nation for twenty-seven years lived on.

No tyrant ever ruled a nation by himself. Juan Vicente Gómez had thousands of collaborators, even millions, if one counts all those Venezuelans who while not actively co-operating with the regime did not resist it. There were shopkeepers who hung up his picture, there were policemen who arrested their fellow citizens without wondering why, journalists who knew they were writing lies, soldiers who obeyed every order, and men who paid bribes to get "free" documents.

In 1935, as in 1899 or in 1908, Venezuela was a country which invited a dictator. In 1935, however, there was a significant difference. More people knew that by resisting a government, even by passive means, they could change it. Scarcely had General Eleazar López Contreras assumed control of Venezuela with the support of most Gomecistas than this difference began to assert itself.

General López Contreras had been Minister of War under Gómez. His control of the army made him the dictator's heir. A cadaverous man who looked more like a schoolteacher than a professional soldier, López Contreras was renowned for his loyalty to Gómez and his personal honesty. As a boy of nineteen

246

he had run away from school in the Andes to join Castro and Gómez on their victorious march to Caracas. He became a captain in the Restauración, then a colonel after Castro took Caracas. Considered too young for an important post in the capital, López Contreras was sent to vegetate in the interior. Shunting from one army post to another, he did his job and kept free of political conspiracies. As more ambitious officers became corpses, exiles, or prisoners, Eleazar López Contreras climbed the army ladder. By 1914 he was a general and commander of the forces in Ciudad Bolívar.

Throughout this period López Contreras found little favor with Juan Vicente Gómez, who took the officer's neutrality during "La Conjura" in 1906 for hostility. Actually, the young Andean, uncertain whether Gómez or the oligarchs would win the battle for Castro's support, professed friendship to both sides in the interests of his own political security. This same cautiousness catapulted him to the Gómez inner circle in 1922 after the tyrant discovered that while most of his court had been taking sides in a power battle between Juancho, his brother, and Vicentico, his son, General Eleazer López Contreras had stood aloof. He had been neither a Juanchista nor a Vicentista. He was a Gomecista, a strong one, and the Dictator acted accordingly.

It was the alertness of López Contreras which foiled rebellion on April 7, 1928. As young civilians and army officers marched on San Carlos barracks that morning General López personally directed the volleys government troops fired into their midst. Among the prisoners taken after this insurrection was one of his own sons, a student at the military college. Even this family involvement did not prevent the General from doing his duty. The son went to the same kind of jail and received the same treatment as all the other prisoners.

This was the man who emerged from Gómez' shadow on December 17, 1935. Dubiously distinguished by his lifelong attachment to the dead Dictator, López Contreras must have seemed a guarantee of continued despotism to Gómez-weary Venezuelans. Editors of newspapers, not knowing how he might react, played it safe and wrote mournful editorials bewailing the death of El Benemérito Juan Vicente Gómez. The people, too stunned to move, remained impassive for two more days. Juan Vicente Gómez was hustled off to the cemetery with all the pomp his rank required. Then, as if the sealing of El Benemérito's body in a crypt were a signal, the people of Venezuela awakened from their twenty-seven-year nightmare and began to celebrate. They paraded through Caracas and Maracaibo, cursing Gómez and cheering his death. They sacked houses. They ripped down the tyrant's picture from public places and stomped on it. They did all this at considerable risk. The Gomecistas were still in power. In Caracas and Maracaibo, government troops answered these demonstrations with bullets. Still the people marched through the streets. For the first time in more than a century, their wrath exceeded their fear. Results were instantaneous. López Contreras, the Provisional President, removed the governor of the Federal District who had ordered troops to fire on the crowds. That wasn't all. Astounding everyone, he started to repudiate the regime which had produced him. He opened all the jails and informed the exiles they were welcome once again in Venezuela. The most detested officials of the regime were fired. The Gómez clan was invited to leave the country. Censorship was temporarily abolished.

Everyone had misunderstood López Contreras. His loyalty to Gómez had been a façade for his loyalty to himself. Devotion to Juan Vicente had been an expedient. And so was the measure of freedom he gave to Venezuela in 1935 and 1936. Popular support would help him liquidate other ambitious Gomecistas and would confirm his hold on power.

In late of 1935 and early 1936 Venezuela was in a state of ferment. The exiles poured back from overseas asylums. Some of them were old and only wanted to die in their homeland. But the younger ones, particularly the dedicated students of 1928, worked to realize a frustrated dream. They harangued crowds from street corners, founded newspapers, and talked politics from morning to night.

Venezuela had been a political vacuum for twenty-seven years. All the old parties had perished, victims of Gómez personalism. The only group the Venezuelan people could be sure was not tainted with Gómez was the Federación de Estudiantes, the organization of university students which had inspired resistance to the tyrant in 1928. These students, many of whom had spent four or five years in prison, now spoke for all shades of political thought. In this organization of youthful enthusiasts the people had complete faith.

The Federación de Estudiantes began its political activity by fighting every Gómez influence that was left. As the months brought other problems, the organization supported new issues as well. But its primary function as the prosecutor of dictatorship remained until its untimely death.

Its first big test came in February 1936. The new governor of the Federal District, Félix Galavís, angered by the virulence of articles in newspapers, established a censorship board. The Federación de Estudiantes answered this threat to freedom by declaring a general strike. It took place on February 14.

Thirty thousand Caraqueños demonstrated. Traffic was paralyzed. Shops and offices closed. In the morning, the people gathered around the Plaza Bolívar and listened to the students rant against Gomecistas still in office. Suddenly at 10:30 A.M. soldiers appeared on the balconies of the Casa Amarilla. They raised their rifles and fired into the milling crowd below them in the Plaza. More than two hundred people fell wounded; eight of them died. This was the answer of Félix Galavís, the governor of the Federal District, to criticism of his tactics. Though appointed by López Contreras in December 1935, Galavís was a Gómez man.

The shots inflamed the passion of the crowd. Behind Jóvito Villalba, the student who gave the speech at the Pantheon in 1928 and who now headed the Federación de Estudiantes, the thirty thousand Caraqueños marched on Miraflores, the presidential palace. López Contreras quietly submitted to all their demands. He lifted the press ban, charged Galavís with murder, and removed most of the remaining Gomecistas from office. The people had won a great democratic victory, their first and, to this writing, their last.

General López was stepping carefully along a tightrope. While he consolidated his power, he curried favor with as many factions as possible. He played the Federación de Estudiantes off against Venezuela's conservative elements, who feared the leftist leanings of the students. Thus he talked like a Liberal and acted like a Conservative. One day he received a delegation of students who wished to discuss an imminent reorganization of the cabinet. "Tomorrow," López Contreras told them, "you will have a new Minister of Education. I'm going to give you a surprise; he will be one of your own people, young, and a believer in your ideals. You will be very happy about it." The next day he named an old Conservative. In the early days of his administration, his government enacted one of the world's most liberal labor laws. It provided for minimum wages, employees' right to compensation when fired, the right to organize and strike, and high standards for working conditions. Yet when labor leaders tried to make use of this law, he sometimes called them "agitators" or "communists."

This confused policy yielded results. In April 1936, the old Gómez congress met to choose a new president. Public pressure forced the legislators to promote López Contreras from Provisional President to actual President of Venezuela. From now on Congress responded to a new thumb.

In July 1936, some old whorls and loops appeared on the thumb. Ostensibly to counteract the threat of anarchy, a state to which the first half-year of López Contreras sometimes seemed dangerously close, Congress began discussing a Public Order Law. The Law would allow for the suppression of freedoms under critical circumstances.

As they had in February, liberal elements protested. When López Contreras refused to budge, they declared a general strike. Again everything stopped in Caracas, but only for one day. As the government steadfastly maintained its position, workers found their pay more attractive than their liberties and slowly trooped back to work. López Contreras, now firmly entrenched, won the final, decisive round. After twenty-seven days his policemen arrested the ringleaders and the general strike ended.

The Federación de Estudiantes was no longer the force it had been. Its members, who had been drawn together originally by their mutual hate for Gómez, had gone their separate political ways. Catholic students bolted the organization when the FEV decided to support an education bill which would have secularized religious schools. New parties founded by other students of 1928 began to attract the interest of the politically minded. Communists started the Partido Republicano Progresista. Professional men, bankers, and businessmen favored Unión Nacional Republicana. Rómulo Betancourt founded Organización Venezolana, a leftist party, which would give birth to a more famous entity, Acción Democrática.

Agitation and confusion in Venezuela continued for six months after the general strike. The battle between the government and die-hard leftists sharpened with each passing day. Demonstrations were followed by arrests, fines, and imprisonments. In March 1937, López Contreras exiled twenty-seven young politicos and agitation ceased. All anti-López political parties were suppressed. The government was the only active political force on the scene.

General López Contreras was a strong man. This is not to say that he behaved like Gómez. To the contrary. He was more civilized and progressive than El Benemérito and his regime reflected the difference. The scope and number of public works increased. The government was less dishonest. López consciously tried to prepare Venezuela for eventual democracy. During his five-year tenure there were neither conspiracies nor revolts.

The man López Contreras chose to succeed him in 1941 was General Isaías Medina Angarita, his Minister of War. In April of that year, Congress rubberstamped the selection. The opposition candidate, Rómulo Gallegos, novelist, teacher, and former Minister of Education, won the votes of thirteen congressmen. His candidacy had been proposed by Rómulo Betancourt, whose party had come out of hiding under a new name, Acción Democrática.

Easygoing General Medina was one of the most liberal presidents Venezuela ever had. He allowed opposition parties to function freely, gave women the vote, loaded his cabinet with men of widely divergent views, and established absolute freedom of speech and press. Every political party had its own newspaper. Attacks on the government appeared daily. There were no political prisoners and no exiles. In 1943 when a new congress was elected, the government permitted all parties to campaign and win seats. His administration passed the first social security and income-tax laws and charted an ambitious land reform redistribution program. In 1943, a new law covering the oil industry radically revised all existing contracts with foreign companies and provided for higher royalties and taxes.

World War II gave Venezuela an important lesson in basic economics. During the twenty-five-year history of her petroleum industry, she had allowed oil to run away with the national economy. She used her oil dollars to buy what she lacked in Europe or North America. As Nazi U-boats ranged the Caribbean sinking tankers and other merchant vessels, Venezuela suffered acute shortages even of products like sugar which her soil could produce.

Venezuela finally declared war on the Axis powers in February 1945. The move qualified the country for membership in the United Nations.

The liberal tendencies of General Medina had a limit. As his presidential term began to expire, the multiparty Congress employed its parliamentary liberties to push for constitutional reform. Many of its members wanted the president chosen by popular vote. Medina, afraid he might lose control of his machine, balked. He tried to line up support in Congress for a chosen successor. Meanwhile, López Contreras began electioneering in his own behalf, appealing to rightist elements who opposed the liberalism of the Medina regime.

López Contreras had grown disgusted with his man Medina soon after he had him elected president. To the former strong man, Medina seemed alarmingly progressive. In addition, Medina had violated a policy López Contreras held dear. From the day Castro came down from the hills, men from Táchira had controlled Venezuela. Their sons, brothers, cousins, and friends ascended to principal political and army posts. When one Tachirense died or retired, another Tachirense took his place. In fifty years, this procedure became a code. Only because Medina had been born to the purple had López Contreras considered him for president in the first place. Yet, Táchira-born Medina, once in office, surrounded himself with intellectuals from Caracas. The boys from the home state seethed. López Contreras now spoke for them.

Liberty of expression during the pre-election period was absolute. The fight raged in Congress, in the newspapers, and on the streets. Thus the summer of 1945 passed with agitation increasing daily. Medina's men, the Lopecistas and the supporters of popular elections contributed to the noise. Each faction had its eye on April 1946, the month when a new president was to be chosen. In October 1945, all their calculations went up in smoke.

The battle of presidential succession had divided the men who governed the nation. It was the first time this had happened in Venezuela since 1899. As argument weakened the administration, the inevitable happened. Revolution broke out on October 18, 1945. Young officers at barracks in Maracay and Caracas disavowed their commanders and battled for control of the nation's military installations.

The eruption took the divided government by complete surprise. Medina thought López Contreras was responsible. López Contreras suspected the blow was a Medina maneuver to excuse a declaration of martial law and the postponement of elections. By the time they discovered the truth, it was too late. They were both in prison preparatory to long exiles in the United States. There were new faces in Miraflores.

The young officers (none had a rank higher than major) who staged the successful coup had made their preparations as the government debated the election question. They had planned to stage a palace coup in November. But Medina, who had learned something about the plot, forced their hand. On October 18, he arrested one of the ringleaders, Marcos Pérez Jiménez. The rest of the conspirators revolted that afternoon.

Before this threat, Medina crumbled, despite the fact that the bulk of the army and the police force of Caracas remained loyal. With consummate nerve, the little band of junior officers had occupied Miraflores and all communications centers in Caracas, giving the impression that they controlled the entire country. On October 19, at a Caracas barracks, Medina surrendered to Major Marcos Pérez Jiménez, his prisoner of the day before. Bitter fighting with the Caracas police force continued for two more days, but by this time the police were the outs. Their resistance was futile.

Like all revolutionaries in Venezuela, these young officers had surged to power waving an idealistic slogan. Over portable transmitters, and later over the nation's radio stations, they told the Venezuelan people that they were overthrowing the government to institute universal suffrage. They denounced any ambition to rule themselves. They would turn the government over to civilians, they said. To everybody's surprise that is exactly what they did. On the night of October 19, Rómulo Betancourt, leader of Acción Democrática and a strong supporter of popular elections, spoke by radio to the Venezuelan people from Miraflores. He, not one of the military men, was provisional president of the country.

With the Revolution of 1945, the students of 1928, or at least some of them, finally reached their goal. The last connection with the now-moldering tyrant was severed.

Acción Democrática was a party whose political address was left of the British Laborites and right of the Communists. During the Medina regime it had enjoyed complete liberty to organize and campaign. Nevertheless in 1945 it had no more than twenty thousand members. With three seats in Medina's congress, party leaders had considered supporting the government's candidate for president, a man named Diógenes Escalante, a respected liberal with a mind of his own. When Escalante fell critically ill and Medina proposed the candidacy of Angel Biaggini, one of his more colorless ministers, it began to look as if Medina were planning to rule Venezuela for five more years with Biaggini as a front. Acción Democrática, which had not criticized Escalante, vociferously attacked Biaggini. Their dissatisfaction with the government attracted the ambitious young army officers and an alliance was formed. In October, the victorious revolutionaries honored their agreement by calling Acción Democrática to form a new government.

At first this government called itself the Junta Revolucionaria. Besides Betancourt, there were six other members: four civilians, Luis B. Prieto, Gonzalo Barrios, Raúl Leoni, and Dr. Edmundo Fernández; and two military officers, Captain Mario Vargas and Major Carlos Delgado Chalbaud.

Their ideas seemed genuinely revolutionary. They promised universal suffrage, direct election of the president, and a new constitution. They announced the candidacy of Rómulo Gallegos for the presidency. They broke diplomatic relations with Franco Spain and hemisphere dictatorships like the Dominican Republic and Nicaragua. The respect for freedom of expression which existed under Medina was continued, though not to the same extent.

For the first time in several years, the jails held political prisoners. Venezuelan exiles appeared again in Cuba, Mexico, New York, and Paris. AD struck out first against the old regime. Into jail went the supporters of Medina and López Contreras. On November 30, they packed them aboard planes and shipped them off to exile. This was just part of the Venezuelan political game. Said López Contreras from his New York sanctuary, "They ask me to hate Mr. Betancourt, but I can't hate him. And I can't hate him because he added the last touch to my role as a Venezuelan political figure. Without exile or prison, you can't be a real politician in Venezuela."

Against its predecessors Acción Democrática went one step further than any previous administration had cared to go. It began to prosecute men associated with Medina and López Contreras for embezzlement of public funds. During AD's three-year tenure, 168 judgments for embezzlement were passed. Fines as high as twenty million bolivars were assessed by a specially constituted three-man board of inquiry. In some cases, these inquisitors also approved jail sentences. Since AD had booted most of the accused out of the country in 1945 the government collected the fines by confiscating property. It was a highhanded and illegal maneuver. From exile, many of the old regime protested that the so-called tribunals had passed sentence without giving them an opportunity to defend themselves. Landholders throughout Venezuela were terrified by the implications of such a procedure. If the government could confiscate a man's property simply by accusing him of breaking the law, it might choose to expropriate anyone's lands in the same way. Deterred by public protest from distributing the confiscated properties, AD administered them through a public commission. All the holdings were eventually returned to their owners.

The radical thinkers of AD alienated one group after another in their efforts to transform Venezuela overnight. In the same way, however, they won important and vocal allegiance from some of Venezuela's downtrodden.

To bolster the nation's inflation-ridden economy, AD established the Corporación de Fomento, a government investment house, whose function was to stimulate agriculture and industry.

Into fields which did not attract private investors, the government poured funds in an effort to give Venezuela a more balanced economy. They experimented with rice, imported prize cattle, established model farms, and founded small industries. They spent millions in planning for such development projects as the electrification of the Caroní River in Guayana. In effect, the government went into business on a very large scale. Commercial interests began to view AD as a prospective competitor. Though Rómulo Betancourt offered to sell any government enterprise businessmen cared to buy, the talk of socialism did not stop. In the first year of its existence, the Corporación de Fomento had a budget totaling nearly one hundred million dollars. Public fears, however, forced AD to halve the appropriation by the second year.

Under Acción Democrática, Venezuela opened immigration to thousands of Europe's displaced persons and economic refugees. Hungarians, Poles, Germans, Italians, Spaniards, and Portuguese began to trickle into the country from 1946 on, bringing with them skills and business talents sadly needed by an underdeveloped nation. More than 125,000 immigrants have settled in Venezuela since the War. Even this intelligent and long overdue measure lost friends for AD. When uneducated Venezuelans found themselves competing for jobs with well-trained foreigners, resentment was naturally strong.

The good opinion of the lower classes was what AD valued most. The administration actively championed the mass. Workers were encouraged to organize. Labor unions developed everywhere. Printers, oil workers, taxi and bus drivers, textile workers—everybody organized. From a few thousand in 1945, union membership in Venezuela zoomed to 300,000 in 1948.

Acción Democrática endeavored to make the party the spearhead of every union. They aimed to build up a large, disciplined body of supporters who would thwart any attempt to put them out of power. Huge mass meetings attended by as many as 60,000 people were held to familiarize the mass with the government's program. Workers were urged to parade periodically through the streets, advertising their allegiance to AD and its aims.

The oil workers' union, the Confederación de Trabajadores Petroleros, was the largest in the country with nearly 50,000 members—among the most fervent supporters of AD. With good reason. Almost as soon as the union was organized its AD leaders presented the oil companies with a long list of demands. They wanted more schools, more hospitals, more pay, more holidays, more pensions, and more protection. The government was called in to arbitrate and promptly granted the oil workers the majority of their claims. Venezuelan oil workers now have more privileges than their colleagues in the United States.

With supreme good sense the oil companies, realizing that this made for good public relations and that resistance would only foment agitation for nationalization, continued to co-operate closely with the government. When on December 31, 1945, the government imposed a retroactive excess-profits tax raising their share of oil profits to at least 50 per cent, oil companies paid an extra thirty million dollars with scarcely a whimper. The Venezuelan government has received at least 50 per cent of petroleum profits ever since.

The most controversial of AD reforms tried to establish different standards for public and private schools. The move had religious implications since most private schools in Venezuela are Catholic. Protest was immediate and uproarious. Priests painted placards for their students to carry through the streets; the students waved them enthusiastically. Not to be outdone, the government called out its labor cohorts and public school students for counterdemonstrations. Eventually AD had to retreat and the decree was discreetly shelved.

With all these unorthodox measures violently championed and as violently opposed, the AD era was hectic. Enjoying almost complete freedom of press and unhampered by a libel law, the contestants insulted one another with all the delightful nuances of the Spanish language. The incidence of revolts and conspiracies reached an all-time high. Conservatives shook their heads and talked about the good old quiet days of Gómez and López Contreras. The effort to yank Venezuela forward a hundred years in the space of a few months kept the country in a state of constant nervous tension. As a result AD's support among the population began to decline. In the 1946 election, for a constituent assembly to write Venezuela's most liberal constitution, AD polled a million votes of 1,300,000 cast. The next year their presidential candidate, Rómulo Gallegos, won 871,452 votes of 1,100,000. In 1948 in municipal elections AD candidates received 332,833 out of 600,000 votes.

In all these elections, AD polled about 70 per cent of the total vote. The Venezuelan people, AD supporters included, lost interest in the vote and the government too, once the novelty of balloting wore off.

These elections were ostensibly democratic: that is to say, nobody stuffed the ballot boxes, but just the same the result was a foregone conclusion. Even before a vote was cast AD had enrolled half a million registered supporters, enough to insure a landslide.

It was normal that AD's support should decline as the party implemented its program and ideal abstractions became awkward realities. The real danger to their continuation in power came not from the people, but from the military officers with whom they swept into office. Some of the younger officers, notably Mario Vargas and Carlos Delgado Chalbaud, were said to be idealistically in sympathy with Acción Democrática. The majority, however, soon began to wonder why they had risked their lives in 1945 to put a lot of addle-headed lawyers in the country's juiciest posts. They agitated for more power and demanded a bigger say in the government. As AD attempted to build up independent strength among the populace and started to arm and train its most loyal civilian supporters, tension between the army and the government mounted. By summer of 1948, the whole country was aware that the two factions were jockeying for position. Cabinet crises occurred frequently. Finally in mid-November the army presented an ultimatum listing its minimum demands. These, AD refused to accept. They threatened the army with a general strike. Civil war between armed workers and organized army units seemed imminent. Mario Vargas, dying from tuberculosis, quitted a U.S. sanatorium to join Delgado Chalbaud in an eleventh-hour attempt to mediate differences. But when it came to the final showdown, they sided with the military.

The blow came on November 24, 1948. At 10 A.M., a junta of three officers, Delgado Chalbaud, Marcos Pérez Jiménez, and Luis Felipe Llovera Páez, staged a bloodless coup. Before AD knew

what had happened, the army had seized the government and communications centers. It was over in one hour. There was no time
to call a general strike. Venezuela accepted the change with scarcely
a murmur. A valiant experiment had failed.

So Venezuela remained in 1952—an entity somewhat less evolved
politically than it was in 1830 when a group of rich landowners
with the backing of the nation's strongest military figure formed
the first stable Venezuelan government. In these 122 years of un-
contested independence, Venezuela has made notably little progress in the development of her political institutions. One dictatorship has followed another, enriching a few and leaving the mass
of the population in perpetual neglect. Except for theoretical
universal suffrage and the abolition of legalized slavery, the road
to individual liberty seems as long as ever. Venezuela is caught
in a vicious circle. It is retarded because it has dictatorships; it
has dictatorships because it is retarded.

Dictatorship is an expression of Venezuela's political immaturity. This is incontrovertibly true. Totalitarian governments have
developed so often that they cannot be dismissed as accidental.
When Venezuela has toyed with democratic procedures the result
has been revolution. Democracy has failed because only a handful
have ever supported it.

This does not mean that Venezuela will always have dictatorial
governments. Bombarded by twentieth-century theories concerning the rights of the common man, Venezuelan regimes since
Gómez have made public services a prime concern. Hundreds of
well-equipped schools have been built. There is scarcely a town
in Venezuela without some sort of public health facility. Con-
sidering the extent of disease, ignorance, and poverty in Venezuela, the results have been encouraging, even though such conditions are still distressingly prevalent. These efforts will have a
cumulative effect in producing a population which will demand
democratic rights and responsibilities.

This may take a long time. The effect of four hundred years
of misrule cannot be destroyed in a decade. Today's democratic
peoples have struggled for centuries to achieve political freedom.
As far as the United States, Great Britain, and the nations of the
British Commonwealth are concerned, this battle began with the

signing of the Magna Carta in 1215, more than seven hundred years ago. Most of the democratic world derived its tradition from England. Latin America inherited the systems of Spain. The advantage of the one over the other is evident in the difference between the governments of Spain and England today.

The political evolution of Venezuela may be accelerated by the dynamic economic and social changes which have been taking place since 1920. The effect of the oil industry on the nation is profound. It has colored almost every facet of Venezuelan life. Its influence has been both pernicious and healthy.

Oil threatens to do to Venezuela what gold did to Spain in the sixteenth century. Five hundred million dollars in oil profits pour into the national treasury annually, and through public works and other government expenditures, into national circulation. This money supports an inflation which has made everything Venezuela produces more expensive than competing goods made abroad. It is cheaper for Venezuela to buy her rice, her sugar, her furniture, her building materials, and her luxuries in other countries than to make them at home. This has handicapped the growth of native production.

The productive capacity of Venezuela, excluding oil, has remained about the same since 1920. There have been sharp increases in the production of commodities like concrete, beer, cigarettes, and textiles, but these gains have been offset by declines in other fields, notably coffee. As long as oil dollars flood the nation, Venezuelans can purchase what they want abroad. What will happen when oil reserves are exhausted or if petroleum prices drop has Venezuelan economists worried. Diversification of the economy has been an important aim of every government since 1935. Yet in 1952, Venezuela was still cursed by its absolute dependence on the market for an exhaustible resource.

Venezuela is one of the poorest nations in the world, not one of the richest, despite its whopping national income of more than 7 billion bolivars annually and an average individual income of about 1,500 bolivars ($450) per year. This would be a very impressive figure if every man, woman, and child did receive $450 per year. Averages tell us nothing about distribution. How many millionaires and how many paupers does the figure include? **One** look at Caracas—with its streets of gleaming cars and hills of seamy shacks—yields an approximate statistic: Caracas certainly has more Cadillacs and probably more slums than any city of its size in the hemisphere. In 1949, 35 per cent of the Venezuelan working force received nearly 80 per cent of the national income; 65 per cent of the working force struggled to make its 20 per cent match a cost of living which had doubled since 1936. The hard truth is that with Venezuela's unbalanced distribution of her wealth, a disproportionate amount of her national income pays for mansions, luxury furnishings, expensive clothes, imported foods, and flashy automobiles. Since most of these things are brought from the United States or Europe, Venezuela's oil royalties find their way into the pockets of foreign rather than Venezuelan workmen, even though some of them pass through the Venezuelan workman's pocket in transit.

On the other hand, oil royalties have allowed Venezuela to make some important capital investments in her future. Schools, hospitals, public-housing projects, highways, and airfields will enrich Venezuelan life for decades, even though such expenditures contribute to inflation while being built. Government subsidies and high protective tariffs help producers to buck the problem of high costs. The apparent prosperity of Venezuela, plus the tariffs, has also lured foreign capital. For example, Celanese of Venezuela, a subsidiary of the Celanese Corporation of America, has built a factory in Valencia which began to produce cloth for the country's ready-made clothes industry in 1952.

In itself, the oil industry gives direct employment to fifty thousand people. According to the provisions of Venezuelan law, 75 per cent of any firm's employees must be citizens of the country. In the case of the oil industry, however, the percentage of Venezuelan employees to the total working force is 93 per cent. Alerted by the loss of concessions in Mexico and, lately, by the nationalization of Iranian wells, oil companies in Venezuela are voluntarily training their native employees to assume even top-executive positions. The skills Venezuelans have learned through the oil industry have increased the nation's economic potential. Standards and pay are high. The opportunities available in the industry have stimulated many young Venezuelans to qualify themselves for oil-company jobs. In preoil Venezuela, there was little incentive for a man to improve himself. By awarding jobs on the basis of merit instead of pull, the oil industry has rescued thousands of capable Venezuelans from frustration and poverty.

These workers now live in decent houses or apartments instead of huts. They own cars. They send their children to school. In their way of life and their preoccupations, they are developing middle-class standards and ideas. Together with the 125,000 immigrants, most of whom come from the bourgeois and professional classes of Europe, they constitute a new factor in Venezuela's social structure. On the aspirations and industry of a middle class the progressiveness and efficiency of a modern state depend. Bourgeois Venezuelans will set a moral and creative example to the rest of the population that her aristocrats as a class, both before and after independence, conspicuously failed to give.

Yet, the sociological impact of increased industrial activity has had a disastrous effect on Venezuelan family life. Marriage has never been a popular institution in Venezuela. Before 1915, a man and his woman tended to live together and bring up their children jointly whether they had taken the vows or not. On a farm a wife and children are assets. With the high cost of living and the shift to urban areas, however, they turned into liabilities. Love-them-and-leave-them became the Venezuelan sexual code. Unmarried mothers and illegitimate children have a legal right to inherit—if they can prove the relationship, or afford a court case—but they have no right to support. Their immediate welfare still depends on the generosity of the men. In terms of cold statistics, 51.9 per cent of the children born in the country in 1949 were illegitimate; 7 per cent, though illegitimate, were recognized by their fathers, which presumably guaranteed some support; only 41.1 per cent, the products of legal marriages, would know the security of a normal family relationship. What is more, some women—saddled with children they cannot feed—follow the example of the men. According to the Consejo del Niño, a branch of the Venezuelan Department of Justice, there are about ninety thousand abandoned children in the country. That is roughly 2 per cent of Venezuela's total population.

The psychological and sociological implications of this situation are shattering. The family is the very basis of civilization.

With no father and sometimes no mother to support them, these children rarely go to school and go to work before they are trained to do anything. They beg, they shine shoes, they sell lottery tickets and frequently, of course, they drift into crime. This waste and distortion of human material—the most important resource any country can have—constitutes a social enormity of hideous proportions.

Venezuela in 1952 is halfway between a medieval fief and a modern state. Technology has rocketed her into a new century. Like the world itself, she is living in this new century with outmoded political and social institutions. Just as she is ripping down her cities to make streets wide enough for automobiles, she is demolishing an ancient culture to accomodate new economic patterns and class structures. The wreckers have left ugly piles of rubble, to be replaced, they say, by noble creations. Whether the new cities or the new ways will actually be better than the old ones remains to be seen. But Venezuela no more than the world has any choice. She must destroy and rebuild. Fortunately, she seems to have the material to work with.

As the land sweeps south from the Orinoco River to the heights of the Gran Sabana, there are some hills, loaves of rock rising abruptly from the deserted flatlands, as if dropped there by mistake. The Indians used to call one of them god. During thunderstorms, the lightning stabbed at it.

For centuries, adventurers ignored it. They hustled by in search of gold or diamonds or oil. And since the mountain contained none of these, it was left alone. Yet the mountain held magical power, just as the Indians thought. When it was "discovered" in 1947, this hump of land lost in a barren pampa released its power. Suddenly, houses and roads appeared on its skirts. Ninety miles away blossomed a city where none had ever been before. Massive dredges bit into the floor of a river. Rights of way for a railroad and highway were traced across the plain. Three thousand miles away a stretch of farmland became the foundation for one of the world's biggest steel plants. All because of the mountain.

Cerro Bolívar in Estado Bolívar has nearly 500 million tons of ore, 62 per cent of it pure iron. It is one of the richest finds in modern siderological history.

Huge North American combines like Bethlehem Steel and United States Steel, worried by the failing productivity of Minnesota's Mesabi Range, have been scouring foreign jungles, tundras, mountains, and plains for more than twenty years. They tramped through Labrador, Chile, Brazil, and, lured by reasonable concession terms, through Venezuela.

Bethlehem acquired a 50 million ton deposit at El Pao in eastern Estado Bolívar in the early 1930's. After World War II, the Bethlehem Company finished a mining camp at El Pao, a 58-kilometer railroad to the Orinoco, a river loading point, a fleet of shallow-draft ore boats and a port called Puerto de Hierro on the Peninsula of Paria where ore is transferred to ocean-going vessels. Mining operations began in September 1950. The first shipment of Venezuelan ore reached the United States in 1951.

Important though the Bethlehem operation is, the deposit at El Pao was too small to have much effect on Venezuelan economy. Venezuela's iron jackpot was not revealed until the United States Steel Corporation stumbled upon eighteen-hundred-foot Cerro Bolívar in 1947. To get at the mountain, U.S. Steel must open an entire section of the country. They are dredging the Orinoco from its mouth to a point 176 kilometers up river. A city called Puerto Ordaz is being built on the Orinoco to handle the transshipment of iron ore to ocean-going vessels bound for U.S. Steel's new plant in Pennsylvania. Puerto Ordaz and Cerro Bolívar will be connected by a ninety-mile railway and highway. Under the terms of the contract with the government, all improvements in Venezuela will be available to any business. Moreover, the Venezuelan government, with sizable deposits of ore in reserved zones, is currently planning to found a national steel industry.

Venezuela defies prediction. No one knows what other riches lie hidden in her jungles or behind the misty defiles of the Gran Sabana. There are those who say that one day Venezuela will be a country supporting a population of fifty million people. They talk of controlling the capricious Orinoco; of channeling its waters across parched llanos; of crop rows running across the endless plain. Her potential is incalculable.

Her history has just begun.

Last, first. _name book_. Publisher
name ; where published, year.

BIBLIOGRAPHY

Aguirre Elorriaga, Manuel. *La Compañia de Jesús en Venezuela.* Caracas, 1941.

Aldrey, Fausto Teodoro de and Rafael Hernández Gutiérrez, editors. *Rasgos biográficos,* Caracas, 1876.

Arcila Farías, Eduardo. *Economía Colonial de Venezuela.* Fondo de Cultura Económica, Mexico, 1946.

Arciniegas, Germán. *Caribbean, Sea of the New World.* Alfred A. Knopf, New York, 1946.

Arévalo Cedeño, E. *El Libro de mis Luchas.* Caracas, 1936.

Baralt, Rafael M. and Ramón Diaz. *Resumen de la Historia de Venezuela (1797–1830).* Desclée, De Brouwer, Brussels and Paris, 1939.

Besson, Juan. *Historia del Estado Zulia.* Editorial Hermanos Belloso Rossell, Maracaibo, 1943.

Calderón de la Barca, P. *La Vida es Sueño.* Empresa Editora Zig-Zag, Santiago de Chile, 1951.

Depons, François. *Viaje a la Parte Oriental de Tierra Firme.* Caracas, 1930.

Díaz Sánchez, Ramón. *Guzmán, Elipse de una Ambición de Poder.* Editorial Edime, Caracas, 1952.

Diffie, Bailey W. *Latin-American Civilization.* Stackpole Sons, Harrisburg, Pa., 1945.

Frank, Waldo. *Birth of a World.* Houghton Mifflin Company, Boston, 1951.

265

Gil, Pio (Pedro María Morantes). *El Cabito*. Caracas, 1951.

Gil Fortoul, José. *Historia Constitucional de Venezuela*. 3 Vols. Editorial Sur America, Caracas, 1930.

González Guinán, Francisco. *Historia Contemporánea de Venezuela*. 15 Vols. Caracas, 1909.

Gumilla, P. Joseph. *El Orinoco Ilustrado*. Biblioteca Popular de Cultura Colombiana, Editorial ABC, Bogotá, 1944.

Lecuna, Vicente. *Proclamas y Discursos del Libertador*. Caracas, 1939.

Level de Goda, Luis. *Historia Contemporánea de Venezuela (1858–1886)*. 2 Vols. Barcelona, 1893.

Luciani, Jorge. *La Dictadura Perpétua de Gómez y sus Adversarios*. Cooperativa de Artes Gráficas, Caracas, 1936.

Madariaga, Salvador de. *Simón Bolívar*. 2 Vols. Editorial Hermes, Mexico, 1951.

Masur, Gerhard. *Simón Bolívar*. The University of New Mexico Press, Albuquerque, 1948.

Miranda, Francisco de. *Archivo*. Editorial Sur America, Caracas, 1929.

Montaner S., Dr. Manuel. *Geografía Física de Venezuela*. Editorial "Las Novedades," Caracas, 1942.

———. *Geografía Económica de Venezuela*. Editorial Condor, Caracas, 1942.

Morison, Samuel Eliot. *El Almirante de la Mar Océano, Vida de Cristóbal Colón*. Librería Hachette S.A., Buenos Aires.

Oropesa, Juan. *4 Siglos de Historia Venezolana*. Librería y Editorial del Maestro, Caracas, 1947.

Oviedo y Baños, José de. *Historia de la Conquista y Población de la Provincia de Venezuela*. Paul Adams, New York, 1940.

Páez, José Antonio. *Autobiografía*. 2 Vols. H. R. Elliot & Co., New York, 1946.

Pareja, José and Paz Soldán. *Juan Vicente Gómez, Un Fenómeno Telúrico*. Editorial Avila Gráfica, Caracas, 1951.

Parra-Pérez, C. *El Régimen Español en Venezuela*. Javier Morata, Madrid, 1932.

Pereira, Pedro N. *En la Prisión*. Editorial Avila Gráfica, Caracas, 1952.

Pocaterra, José R. *Memorias de un Venezolano de la Decadencia*. 2 Vols. Editorial Elite, Caracas, 1936.

Robertson, William Spence. *The Life of Miranda*. The University of North Carolina Press, Chapel Hill, 1929.

Rojas, Arístides. *Orígenes Venezolanos.* Caracas, 1891.

Rondón Márquez, R. A. *Guzmán Blanco, "El Autócrata Civiliza-dor."* 2 Vols. Caracas, 1944.

Rourke, Thomas. *Gómez, Tyrant of the Andes.* Halcyon House, Garden City, New York, 1936.

Schurz, William L. *Latin America.* E. P. Dutton & Co., New York, 1949.

Soto, César Humberto. *Personajes Célebres de Venezuela.* Bibliografía Cecilo Acosta, Caracas, 1946.

Steward, Julian H., editor. *Handbook of South American Indians,* Vol. 4. U.S. Government Printing Office, Washington, 1948.

Thorning, Joseph F. *Miranda, World Citizen.* University of Florida Press, Gainesville, Florida, 1952.

Uslar Pietri, Arturo. *Sumario de Economía Venezolana.* Ediciones del Centro de Estudiantes de Derecho, 1945.

Waugh, Elizabeth. *Simón Bolívar.* The Macmillan Company, New York, 1947.

Wise, George S. *Caudillo.* Columbia University Press, New York, 1951.

Zweig, Stefan. *Américo Vespucio.* Editorial Claridad, Buenos Aires, 1942.

Anuario Estadístico de Venezuela, 1949. Ministerio de Fomento, Caracas, 1952.

National Petroleum Convention. Ministerio de Minas e Hidrocarburos, Caracas, 1951.

ARTICLES

"López Contreras, Un Estilo Político." *Signo,* Caracas, July 5, 1951.

" 'Juan Vicente Gómez, Un Fenómeno Telúrico.' " *Signo,* Caracas, October 4, 1951.

"Jóvito Villalba." *Signo,* Caracas, March 29, 1952.

"El Petróleo Venezolano." *Signo,* Caracas, September 8, 1951.

"Miguel Otero Silva, Un Hombre del 28." *Signo,* Caracas, April 26, 1952.

Files of the *Caracas Journal,* 1945–1952.

INDEX